A complete guide to the Sabbats, life transitions, and rites of passage

Just as the sun has its seasons, so does each life. Ancient cycles repeat again and again from Spring to Winter: birth, growth, death, and rebirth. When we recognize and celebrate these seasonal and personal landmarks, we remember the past and envision the future.

Dancing with the Sun will help you create your own rituals to explore what each turn of the wheel and life event has to offer. From the solemn rite of a Samhain dumbfeast to the joyful creation of the Green Man and Flower Bride for Ostara, this book offers complete rituals, activities, spells, and guidance for Pagans who want to honor each season and milestone.

Use these rituals as they are or as a starting point for your own unique ceremonies. Either way, *Dancing with the Sun* will help you make each Sabbat and transition a time for spiritual growth and celebration.

About the Author

Yasmine Galenorn (Washington) is a writer, poet, executive editor of *Graphomania E-zine*, and managing editor of *TimeWinder E-zine*. A Priestess of Mielikki and Tapio, Galenorn has been a Witch in the Craft since 1980. She practices both as a solitary and with others, and has led numerous public and private rituals. She holds a degree in Theatrical Management and Creative Writing and has a background in the performing arts. She is happily married and lives with her husband and four wonderful cats.

To Write to the Author

If you wish to contact the author or would like more information about this book, please write to the author in care of Llewellyn Worldwide and we will forward your request. Both the author and the publisher appreciate hearing from you and learning of your enjoyment of this book and how it has helped you. Llewellyn Worldwide cannot guarantee that every letter written to the author can be answered, but all will be forwarded. Please write to:

Yasmine Galenorn
℅ Llewellyn Worldwide
P.O. Box 64383, Dept. 300-X
St. Paul, MN 55164-0383, U.S.A.

Internet: http://www.stormcreations.com
e-mail: yasminegalenorn@hotmail.com

Please enclose a self-addressed, stamped envelope for reply, or $1.00 to cover costs. *Yasmine cannot get back to you if you don't, so always include a SASE!* If outside U.S.A., enclose international postal reply coupon. The author regrets that she cannot answer individual requests for specific magickal help or advice.

DANCING WITH THE SUN

Celebrating the Seasons of Life

Yasmine Galenorn

1999
Llewellyn Publications
St. Paul, Minnesota 55164-0383

FIRST EDITION
First Printing, 1999

Cover design by Anne Marie Garrison
Cover photo of woman dancing by Christopher Grajczk
Book editing and design by Astrid Sandell
Interior illustrations by Anne Marie Garrison

Library of Congress Cataloging-in-Publication Data
Galenorn, Yasmine, 1961–
Dancing with the Sun : celebrating the seasons of life / Yasmine
    Galenorn
        p.   cm.
    Includes bibliographical references (p.   ) and index.
    ISBN 1-56718-300-X (trade paper)
    1. Witchcraft. 2. Feasts and fasts. 3. Neopaganism.
    4. Religious calendars – Neopaganism. I. Title.
    BF1572.F37G35 1999
    291.3'6–dc21   98-56509
                                                                         CIP

Llewellyn Publications
A Division of Llewellyn Worldwide, Ltd.
P.O. Box 64383, Dept. K300-X, St. Paul, MN 55164-0383

Printed in the United States of America

Also by Yasmine Galenorn

Trancing the Witch's Wheel: A Guide to Magickal Meditation

*Embracing the Moon: A Witch's Guide to Ritual Spellcraft
and Shadow Work*

Forthcoming

Tarot Journeys: Adventures in Self Transformation

Dedication

To my sister Claudia
1948–1986

May your path be clear and your heart light
you stood up for me, you believed in me
I love you and I miss you
and I hope that, wherever you are,
you know that I remember the robin's funeral
it was my first introduction to death
to the cycles of life
and the Turning of the Wheel
you eased the path

Contents

Part 6: Rites of Death

Part 7: Rites of Love

Part 8: Celebrations and Traditions

Part 9: Resources

Recipes

Lughnasadh

Mabon

Death

Lupercalia

Weddings

New Year's Celebration

Kalevala Day

Kamehameha Day

Spells and Rituals

Rituals of Childhood

Adult Transitions

Dedication Ceremonies

Death

Rituals of Separation

Handparting

Einherjar

Kitty Birthday

Lupercalia

PREFACE

Holidays come and go and come again. Birthdays slip past. Within our day-to-day lives as we travel through the endless stream of time, ancient cycles repeat themselves. Through recognizing and celebrating these traditions we not only remember the past, but create the future.

As modern Pagans, Witches, and Wiccans we alter many of the ancient festivals to suit our times, our needs, and our world. This is a necessary adjustment. Religion that cannot adapt cannot thrive. So we pick, choose, and embrace those elements that add meaning to our personal lives.

While it is vital to explore the roots of our beliefs, and even more necessary to understand the reasons behind these traditions, it is just as important to avoid tying ourselves to ceremonies that we've outgrown or that have no personal meaning for us.

If I live in the city and have never gardened in my life, a harvest festival will take on a different meaning for me than if I live in the country and raise corn and tomatoes.

Beltane today is not what Beltane was 2,000 years ago.

Our ancestors lived in a rough, difficult world where life was harsh and death a constant reality. They met these challenges with beliefs both as harsh and beautiful as the world surrounding them. By understanding the ancient traditions, we catch a glimpse of our spiritual ancestors and the world in which they lived.

So too, through understanding the tradition behind the holidays, we then can adapt the celebrations and rituals to fit our own lives.

No one today can truly know what the rites of our ancestors were. Our knowledge is limited to scattered bits and pieces that have survived natural disasters, enemy invasions, holy wars, and good old Time itself.

It is up to us to take those snippets of information and rework them so they have meaning today. We adapt, and so our religion lives.

As we explore the past, we also create for the future. We develop new holidays and rituals for our personal traditions and those, in turn, become cyclic.

Life is not static. As a race, as a planet, we must adapt and evolve. While we should not forget the past, we must live in the present, while planning for the future.

Through celebrating the Wheel of the Year, through creating meaningful rituals, we reconnect with the Earth, the Gods and our ancestors and continue the traditions that have sustained us for thousands of years.

Dancing with the Sun: Celebrating the Seasons of Life is intended to guide you in creating your own rituals for the Sabbats and other days which might be meaningful in your spiritual lives.

Each section contains complete rituals which you can use "as is" or adapt; background about the specific holiday in question, suggestions for colors, foods, oils, incenses, and symbols appropriate to the particular holiday, and relevant information that you can incorporate into your own personal celebrations.

Acknowledgments

To all good authors everywhere, for writing the books that allowed me to research my own.

To Samwise Galenorn, husband and lover, friend and cat-father, thanks for the support and encouragement, and for accepting my quirks as just part of the package.

To James Staples, who patiently waded through book and memory whenever I forgot something and called him because I thought he might know the answer (and he usually came up with the information I needed).

To K.G. and Ginger Renslow who offered their land and their magick so I could use our friends as guinea pigs while experimenting with some of the rituals within this book.

To the Hawai'i State Library, for their kind assistance from across the ocean. Aloha and mahalo!

To my Readers, I hope that these books are making your life better in some way and that my experience can help you formulate your own spiritual paths.

To Astrid Sandell and Llewellyn, who have been like a breath of fresh air amongst horror stories of authors and their fire-breathing publishers and editors.

To Mielikki and Tapio, my Lord and Lady, for Your humor, lessons, love, and encouragement.

RITUAL AND THE WHEEL OF THE YEAR

Seasonal Holidays and the Land Around Us

Samhain . . . Yule . . . Imbolc . . . Ostara . . . Beltane . . . Litha . . .
Lughnasadh . . . Mabon . . . for Pagans today, these names conjuring up exotic images of ritual and celebration roll off of the tongue as easily as they did for our ancestors.

Together, the eight Sabbats constitute the cornerstones of the circular calendar we know as the Wheel of the Year.

Most Pagans tend to think of four distinct seasons, each containing two Sabbats, when they think of the Wheel of the Year and for Pagans living in temperate climates this is primarily true, but we have to remember that the seasonal holidays vary depending on where you live.

If you live in Australia it makes no sense to celebrate Litha (Midsummer) in June because at that time Australia lies in the grip of winter.

Hawai'i's seasonal changes are so subtle that cyclic changes are completely different from those of more temperate regions.

So the first thing to understand about the Wheel of the Year is that you should adapt your holidays to match the environment in which you live.

The celebrations in this book are based on the four-season model because I live in the Pacific Northwest, where we experience all four seasons.

1

If you live in a region with few climatic variations, I recommend you look into the indigenous seasonal holidays for your area. Almost every native culture had some form of cyclic nature celebration, and if you do your research you should be able to come up with suitable holidays to create a meaningful Wheel of the Year for your area.

Then use your imagination and creativity to adapt the regional celebrations to the Western-European Pagan tradition. With your holidays in tune to the land around you, you will derive more meaning and connection to the cycles of your year.

The Sabbats and Tradition

There are debates raging over whether the Celts celebrated the equinoxes and solstices. There are differing views on what each Sabbat represents. Ask twenty Pagans to define the nature of Litha and you'll get twenty answers. We have discovered that the concept of the coven was probably created by the Inquisition in order to implicate more people in the Witch Trials.

Quite frankly, while this is all very fascinating, it doesn't really matter. We cannot turn back time. While it is important to understand the roots of our traditions, we must acknowledge that we can never know for sure just what our ancestors were thinking or doing. We take the remnants of the past and work with them to create a meaningful present.

We must remember that we are celebrating the Wheel of the Year as we see it today. We have reconstructed it from information gleaned from the past.

And so . . .

The Corn God still dies at Lughnasadh because we still harvest the corn for food . . .

We remember our ancestors at Samhain because death is never still and it is vital to remember the past, the good as well as the bad . . .

By the same token, though I am pledged to Finnish deities, I don't live in Finland, nor am I of Finnish blood and I'm not going to wear seven scarves on my head to keep my power from leaking out! (An old Finnish tradition among female shamans). Nor are my ritual clothes blue and red, traditional Finnish colors. But I will celebrate Kalevala Day (a relatively new tradition).

Which of our rites and rituals actually date back to the days when Pagans held sway over the planet? It is difficult to say. Our concepts and our essential connection with the land, of course. Some of our terminology, definitely. But our religion, though grounded in the past, is based in the present.

It evolves as we evolve, and so we can be sure it will thrive.

Rites of Birth, Death, and Love

The Wheel of the Year comprises not only the seasonal and environmental changes that surround us, but also encompasses those personal celebrations and losses that affect our daily lives.

Sometimes we may want to celebrate a holiday that holds no religious significance in our lives, but is still an important event or milestone.

These traditions are as vital to our emotional health as the other holidays.

We may find that some days we were celebrating have a history that makes them anathema to us, and we then choose to find alternatives for those days.

The birth or adoption of a child, the death of a parent, the pledging of a Priestess to her Goddess, the dedication of oneself to a particular tradition or path, the wedding of friends, the arrival of a new kitten in the house—these events cry out for a celebration or ritual to note their occurrence or their memory.

Through the creation of rituals for these special occasions, and by celebrating them yearly, we establish personalized traditions for our families that add heart, meaning, and soul to our lives.

Personalized Tradition for Solitary and Group Use

Each person seeking to formulate a path for themselves needs to remember that the key to successfully turning the Wheel (i.e., celebrating each Sabbat in turn) is found by discovering the connection between the holiday and one's self.

In our personal devotions my husband and I celebrate, first and foremost, the four astronomical/seasonal holidays—Yule, Ostara, Litha, and Mabon. The other Sabbats (Samhain, Imbolc, Beltane, and Lughnasadh) we acknowledge as distinct but minor holidays, marking the change-over from one season to another.

Since I am a Priestess of Mielikki and Tapio (Finnish Forest Deities) every year we celebrate Mielikki's Day (September 23), Tapio's Day (June 18), and Kalevala Day (a celebration of Finnish Folk Tradition held on February 28).

Two of our friends, Norse Pagans, celebrate the Feast of the Fallen Warriors (November 11) every year—a Norse festival for those slain in battle (the righteous pursuit of their beliefs).

If I were a Priestess of Demeter, I would celebrate the Thesmorphoria—a five day celebration dedicated to Demeter that occurs during October.

As you develop your spiritual path, each year you hone and refine your observances, cutting closer and closer to the core. Remember what works and build on those moments. Throw out what doesn't. The whole concept of personalized ritual and celebration rests squarely on being true to your spiritual path, and if a celebration doesn't feel right, then it won't bring meaning into your life.

If you celebrate with others, your group must find an acceptable compromise of energies and intents or the rituals are going to be lackluster and leave you feeling empty. If your friends and you are on similar wave-lengths, there is usually no problem.

However, when you hold a public ritual (where you have no control over who attends), there tends to be a noticeable lack of unity. This is not to say that the ritual won't be fun and sometimes I've been pleasantly surprised, but for stronger, more magickal rituals, I opt for private gatherings.

Children and Ritual

My husband and I have made the choice to abstain from parent-hood, so we tend to celebrate with others who have also chosen a childfree path, or with those whose children are already grown.

Likewise, pagans with children tend to celebrate together.

It took a while for me to accept this, but I have come to see it as a natural division and I believe it's going to grow as more couples and women choose to forego parenting. It is my hope that this dividing line doesn't become a point of contention amongst the Pagan factions—we are divided enough as it is and need to respect one another's life-choices. There is room in the Pagan community for all lifestyles to find their particular niche.

But the fact remains that children change the energy of ritual. It can't be helped. So when you plan your celebrations, you must decide which ones are appropriate for children and which ones aren't. Some magical workings are too intense for young children to sit through or understand; others are fun and very child-friendly. The natural noisiness of children can be disruptive in an intensely focused ritual.

Parents need to accept this. If your friends decide to have a rit-ual and they declare it childfree, please respect that they probably have their reasons and that it's not a judgment on your children. In fact, they may be protecting your children from energies better left to adults.

(In my opinion, for example, taking a child into a Kali Ritual would not only be foolhardy but potentially psychic child-abuse).

On the same hand, those who are childfree must accept that par-ents are likely to want to include their children in ritual and if they decline your invitation, it is not because they don't like you. They simply choose to celebrate in a different manner.

Another concern when it comes to minors and ritual is that many law enforcement and social agencies still view Witchcraft and Paganism as evil and there have been all too many recorded instances of Pagans being fined and/or arrested because they included minors in their religious practices. While it's not so bad in my area, there are still places in the United States where freedom of religion is a real concern, where the Constitution and our basic rights are barely given lip-service.

Think long and hard before allowing young children and teenagers (who are not your own) into your ritual celebrations. Is there a chance their parents are going to be angry and set the law on you? Are the children ready for this kind of an experience?

Maturity comes to some at age twenty, to some at fifty, and to some at thirteen.

Use your common sense—if a fifteen-year-old wants to celebrate Beltane with your group, perhaps you might choose to help this young person develop a solitary ritual and then point him or her in the direction of a few good books on the subject. At the age of eighteen, he or she can enter into the Craft and no one can accuse you of corrupting a minor.

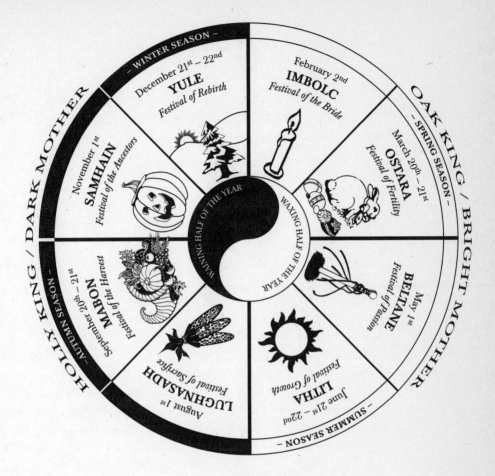

The Wheel of the Year

Part 1

winter

Samhain • Yule

SAMHAIN

The Festival of the Ancestors

Pumpkins, crisp leaves tinged with rust and bronze, a lace-work of frost kissing red-cheeked apples, ghostly mist rising in the shadowed night . . . it is October 31, the eve of Samhain, Festival of the Dead, and we are preparing to mourn and remember our ancestors.

Samhain (pronounced Sow-en) is the primary Celtic festival, celebrated on November 1. It focuses on our links to our spiritual and physical ancestors. The honoring of ancestors is a concept celebrated world-round under a number of different names.

During Samhain, the veils between the world of spirit and the world of mortals are at their thinnest. This is the time of year when the dead roam the earth.

Samhain is considered the third—or meat—harvest (Lughnasadh being the first—or grain—harvest, and Mabon being the second—or fruits—harvest).

In our household, we celebrate Samhain beginning on October 30, and we celebrate for a full three days. Since we consider October 30 to be the end of Autumn, that morning we take down the Autumn altar and purify and cleanse the altar table.

We take the last of the brandy from the Autumn altar and offer it as a libation to the Turning of the Wheel at the tree stump in our backyard that currently serves as our offering shrine.

Then, in the evening, we set up the Samhain altar.

Our basic altars are perpetual; we use them year-in and year-out, adding seasonal accents as desired. For Samhain, we use an altar cloth printed with autumn leaves and cover that with sheer black chiffon. On top of the altar, we place a beautiful pumpkin candle that we never light and two skulls made of wax—one white, one black. A black hand-carved slate knife goes on the altar as well.

We add pictures of the dead we wish to remember, a decanter of port wine, and a new black candle in a brass holder. We also drape silk garlands of autumn leaves around the altar.

Our ephemeral decorations, changing every year, include Jack O'Lanterns, miniature pumpkins, apples, crisp autumn leaves, and so forth.

We then bless and consecrate the altar and open a gate through which the dead are welcome to enter during the three-day interlude.

At midnight on October 31, we hold our ritual. We traditionally prefer the Dumbfeast, a silent ritual honoring the ancestors, but in the past I have also led Underworld rituals and had good results.

On November 1, we hold an evening dinner for friends and watch *The Halloween Tree* and *Something Wicked This Way Comes*, two wonderful movies that always put me in mind of Samhain.

The Colors of Samhain

Thanks to Halloween (a sad, modern-day remnant of Samhain), orange and black—pumpkins and the color of twilight—are two of the primary color associations for this time of the year. But think also of the rusts, bronzes, reds, and yellows of autumn leaves, the brown of the barren Earth, and the grey-green of dying moss.

Incenses, Herbs, and Woods

Gum mastic, copal, and myrrh incenses produce an Other-worldly sensation when burnt in your ritual space. Heather and clove also add to the general ambiance.

Your herbs for this Sabbat should include wormwood and mug-wort (wash your scrying mirror or crystal ball with an infusion made of these herbs). When mixed with chamomile, valerian can produce a drowsy, trance-like state. Rosemary is used for remembrance, so it is perfect for Samhain.

The crackle of bonfire flames—think carefully about what wood you choose for your Samhain fire, be it in the fireplace, the wood stove, the bonfire, or simply a stick of incense. Hazel is commonly associated with Samhain, as are hemlock and apple wood. Inscribe runes associated with divination on the pieces of wood before you place them in the fire and then watch the flames for symbols and omens.

Contacting the Dead

Most Pagans and Witches that I know consider contacting the dead a risky proposal, at best. We do so only when absolutely necessary. Samhain is one of the few exceptions to this rule, but even at this time, we do not hold séances or call up spirits who don't want to be disturbed.

Contacting the dead can be disruptive to your psyche. Death is a transition, signaling movement from one realm to another, and it's not a good idea to encourage spirits to hang around our realm for too long.

While some spirits involve themselves in our world as guides and mentors, others remain connected in more negative ways—through an unawareness of their condition (some don't really understand that they're dead), through fear or an unwillingness to release physical existence.

Spirits need to be free to move on and we can best help them by leaving them alone or, if we are experienced in the Craft, by guiding them out of the limbo between life and death.

During Samhain, we invite those whom we wish to remember to be part of our celebrations if they choose to join us, but we never coerce.

Divination

The three days surrounding Samhain are the most potent times of the year for divination and scrying. The veil between worlds is thinnest then, and we can easily see into the realms of spirit and faerie.

I do not recommend using an Ouija board. I've seen too many people open the door to entities they couldn't get rid of without professional psychic help. But there are many other forms of divination, and you should include at least one of these during your celebration of the holiday.

Tarot cards, Celtic ogham runes, the Norse runes, crystal balls, magic mirrors—these are all good ways to contact the other side without leaving yourself fair game to wandering spirits. To use the crystal ball or magic mirror, light two candles, one on each side of your divination tool and turn off any electric lights. If you like, burn incense to heighten the mood.

You might want music in the background—choose music without lyrics if you do, so that no suggestions enter your mind. Drumming tapes are a good choice, or flute music.

Sit in a comfortable chair and take three deep breaths.

Say:

> **You who have lived before,**
> **And those yet still to come**
> **Visions in my mirror now form,**
> **Let my will be done.**

Look into the mirror, at a point an inch or so above your eyes. Let your mind drift as you watch the glass. Note any images or impressions you might see. Sometimes these impressions may be more mental than physical. Allow about fifteen to twenty minutes per session, and when you are done, clean your mirror and store it in a safe space.

Making a Magic Mirror

Magic mirrors are traditionally black and there is good reason for this. It allows us to focus less on our own reflections and more on the images that form against the black background.

To make your own magic mirror, you will need the following supplies:

> a piece of glass (rectangular, oval, or round)
>   at least 9 inches in diameter
> a sturdy piece of cardboard
> scissors
> black paint (glossy)
> glue
> a sturdy length of black ribbon, at least 1 inch wide
> gold and silver fabric paints

Place the glass on the cardboard and trace around the edges. Cut the template out with a pair of heavy scissors, then paint both sides with black paint and let dry. Apply a second coat of black paint and let dry again. Now, glue the mirror onto the cardboard, spreading the glue ½ inch in from all the edges.

Let the mirror dry overnight.

Fold the ribbon around the edges of the mirror so that it overlaps the glass by ½ inch and glue down. Let dry.

Now use the gold and silver fabric paints to draw runes and designs on the ribbon. Make a simple stand for your mirror and consecrate it and you're done.

When you need to clean your magic mirror, use a very light wash of mugwort and vinegar water and dry it immediately with a soft cloth or paper towel.

Cauldron Magic

Another popular association with Samhain is the magic cauldron. In addition to symbolizing the womb of the Goddess, the cauldron is the Celtic symbol for rebirth. As the season of Samhain concerns the transition from life into death (and from there, into life again), the cauldron and Samhain just seem to go together.

If you don't work with the Faerie, a huge black cast iron cauldron is wonderful to have for your rituals and spellwork. If, like me, you work with the Faerie on a regular basis, you'll want your cauldron to be of brass, silver, or copper.

You can fill the cauldron with salt or sand and create a gigantic incense burner or fill it with New Moon Water (see Appendix One, page 277) to use it for scrying. You can pile it full of apples for holiday decoration. The cauldron also makes a wonderful vessel for mulled wine!

Food for the Dead

On Samhain, it is customary to fix a plate for those you are remembering, filled with their favorite foods. Spare no expense here—if Uncle Joe loved chocolate creams, don't buy him a candy bar, buy him chocolate creams. Of course, your bank account has something to say about this, but if you can afford to splurge, have respect and do so!

The food is usually left out overnight so that the dead might eat of the essence, then it is given back to the Earth for Nature to take care of.

My sister Claudia died in 1986. Every year her plate on the altar contains German pickles and onions, two of her favorite foods. I fill another plate with kitty kibbles for the cats I have known, loved, and lost. Still another plate holds a Baby Ruth bar and a Pepsi, for my husband's father who left us in 1993. I also add favorites of my late roommate, my grandmother, and other deceased relatives.

Totem Animal Work

In my book *Trancing the Witch's Wheel* you'll find a wonderful totem animal meditation that I created specifically for Samhain. For me, the season of Samhain is one of the best during which to work with your animal totems because all of the spiritual realms are so close to our own and shape-shifting energy seems to go hand-in-hand with the transformations taking place this time of year.

Before Samhain, I like to carve my totem onto a pumpkin. I consider it a "working" meditation.

Since my primary totem animal is the black panther, I choose music that I feel embodies the panther spirit and listen to it as I work.

I assemble pictures of panthers around the table where I'm going to work. If I can find a good documentary about the jungle, I make use of my VCR and play that while I'm working, with the sound muted.

One year, my black cat Meerclar volunteered for modeling duty. She sat next to the pumpkin the entire time I was carving.

When I'm ready to begin, I cast a circle, invoke the spirit of the panther, and begin carving the pumpkin into a panther-faced Jack O'Lantern. Not just any panther, but one that matches my connection with the totem spirit.

I do not speak during this carving, unless I'm speaking directly to my totem-spirit, and I focus on the task until I'm done. It's amazing how connected this makes me feel to my panther totem. I also notice that my cats tend to congregate around me when I'm carving the pumpkin. If my totem was a wolf spirit and I shared my life with dogs, I'm sure the same thing would happen.

Drumming

One of the simplest and most enjoyable ways to celebrate the season is to gather together a number of friends. Ask each to bring drums, tambourines, bells or rainsticks, then light a giant bonfire (check your local fire stations for burn bans or laws against bonfires) and spend an evening drumming and dancing around the fire.

Before you begin, go around the circle, and ask each person to invoke the spirits of ancestors they wish to remember. Then let the spirits move your hands. Continue long past midnight and let the thunder of the drums open the veil between the worlds.

Samhain Dumbfeast Ritual

The Dumbfeast consists of a a silent meditation and an offering of food to the ancestors to show them we remember and honor them. You should invite no more than thirteen people or else the energy will become scattered. Before everyone arrives, you should prepare two altars.

The central altar will have your Samhain arrangements on it, as well as a crystal bowl filled with ice cubes, and a brass candle holder with a black candle snugly tucked in it. The altar also must have a bell, and during the dumbfeast the Priestess should sit with a clock in view.

The Altar for the Dead should have pictures of the departed and an orange candle. This is where you will place all the food each person brings in memory of their departed ones (see "Food for the Dead," page 16). Make sure there is plenty of room on this altar—each year our Dumbfeast celebration seems to get more and more elaborate, until it looks like the dead are eating better than we are!

Everyone should arrive at around ten-thirty, each bringing their pictures and food for the Altar for the Dead, food for your Midnight Supper, and a white votive candle in a glass holder.

When everyone has gathered and is settled in, it is time to cast the circle. Light the orange candle on the Altar for the Dead and turn off all electric lights. For clarity's sake, I am presenting the ritual as led by a Priestess (PST) and a Priest (PT). When we actually hold this ceremony, I lead it along with another female friend. Gender makes no difference.

The Priestess should cast the triple-circle three times in silence while the others hold hands and focus on creating sacred space.

PST: *(Holding up the ice.)* **I bless and consecrate this ice in the name of the Lady of the Dead.**

PT: *(Holding up the black candle.)* **I bless and consecrate this candle in the name of the Lord of the Dead.**

He now places the candle and its holder into the center of the bowl of ice, and the Priestess places the bowl back on the altar. The Priest lights the candle.

PST: *(Facing north.)* **I call to thee, element of Ice, you spirit of the cold and frozen wastes. You hold us hostage during winter, threatening us with barren land and ice-drenched trees. You who are the chill touch of endless night and the glistening shimmer of the aurora borealis, come to us this Samhain, join our circle and our rites.**

PT: *(Facing south.)* **I call to thee, element of Fire, you spirit of the crackling flame. You tempt us in with promise of warmth, yet burn our skin should we step too close. You who are the sparks rising to heaven from the bonfire and the glowing embers of the hearth, come to us this Samhain, join our circle and our rites.**

PST: *(Facing north.)* **I call to thee, Lady of Death, Lady of the Ice, Dark Mother of the Cavern. Come to this space, You who tear us from our families before we can say goodbye. Crone, Thread-Cutter, Hag of Fate and Fury, stare down on our rites with Your glassy eyes and accept our tribute as we honor Your realm, for Yours are the last lips we shall kiss, and Yours is the breast to whom we return in sleep. Dark Mother, Lady of Death, welcome and Blésséd be!**

PT: *(Facing south.)* **Lord of the Flame, I call to thee! Lord of Fire and Death, hear my cry. Come to us this night, you who thunder across plain and prairie, choosing those whose lives to end. Harvester, Reaper of the Dead, if 'tis not our time to die, then burn us not but touch ever gently in Your passing and know that we remember. Lord of Flame, welcome and Blésséd be!**

PST: *(Turn to the east and draw an invoking pentacle—see Appendix One, page 278—in the air.)* **I open a gateway for the dead, for those of positive intent. If you choose to visit us during this Samhain night, then be welcome and enter our circle for a brief time.** *(Everyone sits and gets comfortable. Starting with the Priestess and proceeding deosil, each member of the circle should name the dead being remembered along with a brief statement of what each person meant in their lives. This is not a time for long descriptions. After naming their ancestors, each person should light their votive off the black candle and set it on the main altar.)*

PST: *(Holding up the bell.)* **We have called the role of the dead. Now we remember.**

She rings the bell. For the next twenty minutes, no one speaks. Each person should meditate in their own manner on those who have passed on and listen for any messages that might come through at this time. This can be a very emotional meditation and I recommend having tissues and glasses of water nearby, in case anyone starts crying or needs a drink. When twenty minutes are up, the Priestess rings the bell again.

PST: **We have opened our hearts and remembered those no longer with us. May they speed safely on their way, may their journeys be easy and painless. Blesséd be.**

PT: **The dead have feasted with us, and now we offer up the remains of their meal to Nature.**

Each person should carry their plates and votive candles outside, through the eastern quarter of the circle, to a pre-chosen spot. Scrape all the food off the plates onto the ground and then, setting aside the plates, everyone circle around the food, holding their votive candles.

PST: **Lady of the Earth, take this food back into your soil, use it to nourish yourself so that life might spring once more from your body. Blesséd be.**

All: **Blesséd be.**

Everyone return inside, through the eastern quarter of the circle, and reform the circle.

PST: **So we have mourned and remembered this Samhain Eve. Now let the dead be on their way as we continue on with our lives, making the most of our days for they surely are numbered.**

PT: *(Facing south.)* **Lord of the Flames, thank you for joining our rites. May you safely return to your realm and leave us in peace! Blesséd be.**

PST: *(Facing north.)* **Lady of the Ice, thank you for joining our rites. May you safely return to your realm and leave us in peace! Blesséd be.**

PST:　*(Facing east.)* **May the gate between worlds be closed once again for another year and may the dead go from this place in peace and knowing that we remember them.**

Draw devoking pentacle (See Appendix One, page 278.).

PT:　*(Takes broom, sweeps circle widdershins.)* **This circle is open but unbroken.**

All:　**Merry Meet, Merry Part, and Merry Meet Again!**

Everyone clears the space and then proceeds to feast on the midnight supper.

An interesting note to this ritual—a few years ago during the silent meditation, I looked up at the doorway where we open the gate for the dead. I saw a young man, about 23 or 24 years of age walk through. He wore mechanic's coveralls and held a motorcycle helmet. He looked at me and I heard him say (in my mind), "Will you remember me? Nobody remembers me."

After we opened the circle, we talked about what we had experienced. I mentioned him, wondering if anyone else knew anything about him, because I didn't. It turned out that one of my friends used to date a young man about that age who loved to work on cars, and he had died in a motorcycle accident! The next year she included him in her remembrances.

The year before that incident, a tiny kitten spirit wandered through the gate and curled up in my lap while we were meditating. It was obvious that she'd gotten lost and died and that she didn't understand what had happened.

She sat on my lap—I could actually feel her there—the whole meditation and then the Lady came through and gently took her away. I still cry when I think about it. For some reason, that little lost kitten is the most poignant memory I have of all the Dumbfeasts we've done.

Food and Recipes

Roasted Red Potatoes with Basil

    1½ pounds small red potatoes
    ¼   cup basil
    1   tablespoon crushed black peppercorns
    ½   cup dark olive oil

Preheat oven to 350 degrees. Thoroughly scrub potatoes and cut the very ends off of each. Cut a thin (⅛ inch) ribbon of skin off the center of each potato.

Mix basil and pepper and spread in shallow dish.

Dry potatoes thoroughly, then dip them in olive oil and roll in basil and pepper.

Arrange in covered glass casserole and roast for about 45 minutes. Serves 6.

Ham en Croûet

    1   teaspoon salt   ¼   cup water
    2   cups all purpose flour   ¼   cup port wine
    1   cup butter or margarine   1   (3-pound) ham

Preheat oven to 350 degrees. Mix salt and flour. Cut butter into flour until it resembles pea-like crumbles. Slowly add water, 1 tablespoon at a time, while kneading the dough with your hands. Roll into ball, cover, and chill for 2 hours.

Using a syringe, inject the wine into the ham until it is all gone. Cut a few slits on the ham on all sides.

Roll out the pastry dough to ¼ inch thick. Set the ham in the center and bring the pastry up to thoroughly encase the meat. Pinch ends of pastry together, and cut off any excess.

Set the ham in a oiled baking dish so that the seam of the pastry faces the bottom. The weight of the ham will keep it from pulling apart. Use the pastry scraps to cut out interesting patterns and arrange on top of the ham.

Bake for 2 hours. Break off the crust and discard.

Slice ham and serve with gravy.

Serves 8.

Rosemary Biscuits

2 cups all purpose flour
2 tablespoons baking powder
½ teaspoons salt

2 teaspoons chopped rosemary
½ cup butter
1 cup milk

Preheat oven to 400 degrees. Mix flour, baking powder, salt, and rosemary. Cut butter into flour mixture until it resembles pea-like crumbles. Make a well in the center of the flour mixture and pour in ⅔ cup milk. Start kneading in the bowl and if you need to, add the rest of the milk.

Turn dough onto floured board and knead ten times. Roll out, using a rolling pin, and cut into round shapes.

Bake for 12-15 minutes, until browned on top. Serve with butter and honey.

Makes 12 biscuits.

YULE

The Festival of Rebirth

Fresh snow kissing the ground, the smell of bayberry and cinnamon drifting through the kitchen, mistletoe peeking over your shoulder, gold and silver ornaments nestle in their boxes ready to bedeck the Yule tree, holly berries cluster amongst dark glossy leaves . . . it is December, Yule Eve, and we gather to rejoice as the Sun King is born again.

Yule is the celebration of Midwinter. The Winter Solstice is the longest night of the year, when the Sun King is reborn to light the world and free it from the chilling grip of winter. Held in late December, it is an astronomical event so the actual date can vary from year-to-year, but the holiday usually falls on December 21 or 22. Check your almanac and account for differences in time zones. It may fall on December 21 on the west coast, but December 22 on the east coast.

Yule is traditionally a time of togetherness, of parties and festivities. In our not-so-distant past, before supermarkets and snowplows existed, villages and towns were often cut off from one another by snow and ice. Entire families might go through the harshest part of winter without seeing another soul. If the harvest wasn't managed properly or if the crops had been scarce that year, people died from starvation.

Yule became the hope to which people clung, hope for the return of warm weather and planting seasons. In the far north, the sun actually disappeared—the longest night was truly the longest night, with the sun barely peeking above the horizon. It is no wonder that in agrarian societies where everything depended on the success of the crops, the return of the sun each year was cause for celebration. The Gods had been kind—the source of life was re-emerging from darkness.

With the Sun King reborn, the days lengthened, and the season of growth once more overtook the land.

The Sun (or Oak) King reclaimed His place as ruler over the Waxing part of the year, while the Holly King gave way, retreating until Midsummer.

Preparing for the Yule Season

There are many traditions and rituals for Yule, but the one my husband and I prefer incorporates both the rebirth of the Sun and the Holly King/Oak King mythos.

For us, the Yule season begins on the evening of November 2 (what we consider the beginning of the Winter Season) and lasts through the entire month of December. Our preparation happens in stages.

On the evening of November 2, we put away our Samhain altar and purify the altar table. The next morning, we set up the Yule altar and offer the last of the Samhain port at our offering shrine.

The Yule altar cloth is printed with stags, rabbits, and other animals amidst a field of green leaves and holly berries on a black background. Over this, we drape a black net cloth with gold sparkles.

We use plastic gold beads to encircle our altar table (it's round), pinning them on with gold safety pins. Altar dressings include a wooden reindeer from Finland, a perpetual Yule Log with metallic gold candles, holly leaves, a Yule wand, a decanter of cordial, and gold garland. Seasonal additions include a pretty jar of candy canes, bowls of nuts, candy, apples, and pears.

We then bless and consecrate the altar.

Since I have painted seasonal pictures of Mielikki and Tapio, Their Winter pictures go up at this time. I've also put together a framed collage for each season, and change from Autumn to Yule at this point (I've created a purely winter collage—with no hint of Yule in its snowy background—which we hang on January 1—see New Year's Celebration).

The next step in the Yule season comes the weekend after Thanksgiving. That weekend is devoted to stringing cranberries, putting up the Yule tree (we've chosen an artificial tree to save the real ones—there are some pretty trees on the market now and we feel that the energy put into it year after year only accumulates and makes the holiday stronger), decorating the tree and the house. We hang lights, garland, anything and everything.

I want the house to sparkle when we're done.

After the decorations are up, we cast a circle around the house using the Yule Wand and light the candles. Then we invoke the elements, Mielikki and Tapio (since They are the household God and Goddess), the Holly King, and the Pregnant Goddess. We also invoke the spirit of Yule—comfort, joy, compassion, and sharing with our friends.

After this, we ask that our lives and the lives of our friends be blessed and sustained during the approaching winter and after that, we curl up and watch the movies *Holiday Inn* and *A Christmas Story.*

A note about Christmas shows and movies: No, my husband and I do not celebrate Christmas. As Pagans, we consider it a Christian holiday and choose to focus on Yule (which, after all, holds the origin of most Christmas traditions). However, some of the shows at this time of year are wonderful; they embrace the spirit of compassion, joy, and fun that Yule encourages.

If I had to miss watching *Rudolph the Red-Nosed Reindeer*, *A Christmas Carol* (with Alistair Sims) and *Holiday Inn* each year, the Yule season just wouldn't be the same. That's why I have videotaped copies of them.

So yes, we watch Christmas movies and just work around the Christian concepts, but no . . . we don't celebrate Christmas, and by December 22 (depending on which day Yule happens to fall) we've had our fill of the season . . . which is just the way I plan it.

I designate December 1 to send out Yule cards. I look for cards that specifically avoid saying "Merry Christmas" (I go for ones that say "Happy Holidays" or "Have A Joyous Season") and have found some beautiful styles over the year that focus on the natural world. I splurge here, I've always loved sending cards and this is one area where I allow myself to go crazy—I send Yule cards to anyone and everyone I know!

We like to include our friends in our celebrations so each year, about two weeks before Yule, we hold an open house/tea party/et cetera, and invite more people than our duplex can possibly hold and hope that they don't all come at once. We play soft music (Mannheim Steamroller's holiday music is perfect) and serve tons of food. Every year I make more Wassail than the year before, and it disappears just as fast.

Yasmine's Yule Wassail

1 gallon burgundy wine	A muslin bag containing:
2 bottles port wine	15 whole cloves
a fifth brandy	½ teaspoon grated
¾ cup white sugar	ginger
2 oranges, well washed	2 inches candied ginger
1 lemon, well washed	3 cinnamon sticks
2 granny smith apples	

In a large enamel or stainless steel pan (a large stock pot that can hold at least 2½ gallons is ideal), mix all of the wine and brandy. Stir in sugar until dissolved. Thinly slice the oranges and lemons and remove the seeds. Core, peel, and chop the apples, then add all the fruit to the wine mixture. Tie the muslin bag closed with clean string and drop into the pan. Heat over low heat for 2–3 hours (a crock pot is wonderful for this). Do NOT boil. Remove spices and pour into a pre-warmed crystal punch bowl. Serve hot.

Serves 20–25.

Gifts

Yule gifts probably originated as gifts of food, a welcome treat during the cold months of potential starvation. In a world where the supermarket and the mall are a five-minute drive away from most Americans' reach, we have become a nation of consumers. Most of the average retail store's profits are made during the month of December.

I know this isn't right, and yet . . . I admit that I love the presents and packages and brightly colored paper and all . . . and so I do my best to find the line between overspending and penny-pinching.

We have so many friends and I wish I could fulfill all of their dreams, but sometimes we're even lucky to buy gifts for one another. So I've started buying gifts throughout the year, which helps ease the strain on December's budget.

I've also discovered several beautiful and magickal gifts to make at home. If you're artistic, find smooth river rocks and paint them with runes for good fortune. Then charge them in circle and give them as charms to your friends.

Or you can buy 6-inch disks of wood from the craft shop and use a wood-burner to create Pennsylvania Dutch hex symbols. There are several books with information about the hex symbols, what they represent, and how they're made.

You can give gifts of baby-sitting and house-sitting, or back rubs and scalp massages.

One year, when we were very poor, I made up twenty dozen gingersnaps and ten dozen chocolate-peanut butter chip cookies and wrapped them in foil with ribbon. Then my husband and I made gallons of candied corn (using pink and green colorings in the syrups) and our friends got sweet treats that year.

Do not be embarrassed if your gifts come from your heart and hands rather than from the store. With the insistence on buy! buy! buy! that our media pounds into us each December, it's hard to feel okay about home-crafted gifts, but if your friends love you, they will love what you make for them.

One note: I buy gifts for Yule throughout the year, but I won't allow myself to wrap them until the weekend after Thanksgiving. This way I still have the excitement of wrapping gifts without the headache of holiday shopping.

Yule Eve

Yule Eve is a private time for my husband and me. We eat a cold dinner of deli meats, cheeses, and crackers (which we both love), snacking our way through the evening. Then we open our presents and take pleasure in the wonderful things our friends have chosen to give us.

We never forget our cats—each cat has a stocking and we tuck treats and toys in them. They get their presents first, and then they get to play with the wrapping paper as we open our gifts. Watch the ribbons though—you don't want your pets swallowing them!

Kitty's Yule Stocking

You'll want to make a pattern on a plain piece of paper. Make it wide enough to hold a round can of tuna or cat food (a common gift for four-legged felines) after seam allowances are accounted for.

Fold your fabric with the wrong side facing out and pin the pattern to the material. Cut around the pattern.

Turn the top of each side of the stocking down ½ inch (on the wrong side) and sew to prevent frayed edges. If you want to add lace, pin the lace to the right side of the fabric and then stitch across the top. This will attach it to the stocking.

Pin the right sides of the fabric together and sew your side seams—allow for about a ⅜-inch seam. When you are finished, turn the stocking right side out.

Since we have four cats, I covered pictures of each cat with clear strapping tape to protect them, then cut the pictures out and stapled one to each stocking. That way, each cat has its individual stocking and we know which one belongs to which cat. I used a beautiful cabbage rose material and added white lace (they look very Victorian). We hang up the stockings when we decorate the house.

Other Yule Pet Tips

I have always loved tinsel, but it's dangerous to have around cats, so I've developed a way to get a similar look. Buy strings of plastic beads in metallic gold, silver, or iridescent colors (each bead should be about ½-inch diameter). Cut the long strands into 18-inch lengths. You can drape these over the tree limbs and if a cat pulls one off, it's less likely to swallow the beads than it would the tinsel. I was surprised by how pretty they look.

We've found that having an artificial tree discourages our cats from trying to climb it—no small feat with four felines who think the top of the refrigerator is their home. I suppose that it doesn't have the smell of a tree and so they just sit underneath it, on the presents, and occasionally steal one of the satin ornaments and bat it into a corner.

The Colors of Yule

Of course red and green are traditional colors this time of year, but think about gold (for the Sun King) and silver (for the Holly King). White is always appropriate (for snow) and I like to tuck blue into my color scheme. Not only is it a traditional Finnish color, but it reminds me of ice.

Incenses, Herbs, and Woods

Bayberry, cinnamon, frankincense—what Yule ritual would be complete without at least one of these scents? Also consider spruce and pine; although many people are allergic to pine, so be cautious if you're using it in group ritual—ask first.

Use bay leaves to write wishes on, then throw them in the Yule fire. Make cinnamon buns and the aroma of fresh baked sweets will not only satisfy the heart but invoke the powers of protection and success into your home.

Of course holly is associated with Yule (protection and good fortune), and birch (the Yule log is traditionally made from birch wood). Burn ash at Yule and you'll be invoking prosperity for the coming year.

Creating a Perpetual Yule Log

It is best to make this out of birch, if at all possible. Procure a length of birch log about 18 inches long. Cut the log in half length-ways so the bottom is flat. Sand it down. Measure the top and drill three equally-spaced holes to hold taper candles (about ¾–1 inch each). Sand these as well. You can stain the bottom to protect the Yule log, and I recommend fitting the holes with metal so that the candle flames don't burn into the wood. Decorate with runes, gold paint, holly leaves, or ribbons as you like.

The Sunrise Yule Ritual

We usually end up celebrating the actual sunrise of Yule at home, and get together later with friends. This ritual was created for two people, but could easily be adapted to a larger group. You will want to time this so that the Sun rises during your ritual.

The Priest (PT) and Priestess (PST) (feel free to adapt the parts, they are not gender specific) should wake before sunrise and take ritual baths before beginning.

Cast your circle and invoke the elements in the manner in which you are most comfortable.

PST: **Great Goddess, Mother of the Eternal Return, we call you forth. Come into our circle, large in belly, deep in your labor pains. Enter our sacred space as you prepare to give birth to your son once again.**

Light a red candle for the Goddess.

PT: **Holly King, Lord of the Ice and Waning Year, we call you forth. Come into our circle, even as your power begins to wane. Enter our sacred space and prepare to do battle with the Sun as is the nature of your cycle.**

Light a green candle for the Holly King.

PST: **The Lady's pains rock the world as She wrests Her child from Her womb! We sing to help Her ease the ache.**

Both Priest and Priestess begin to chant. Allow plenty of time for the power to rise.

All: *(Chant.)* **We all come from the Sun God**
       As today He is reborn
       With sparks . . . of flame
       Rising from His golden brow.

When the power is ready to peak, the Priestess should grab a sun-face off the altar and hold it up towards the window. As the chant ends, she calls in a loud voice.

PST: **And so the Lord of the Sun is reborn from the womb of the Goddess!**

The Priest lights a golden candle for the young Sun Lord.

PT: **As the light returns, it pierces the heart of the Holly King. The King is dead! Long live the King!**

The Priestess blows out the green candle for the Holly King.

PST: **So we turn the Wheel and the Waxing Year is upon us.**

Both Priest and Priestess should take a few minutes to contemplate the loss of the Holly King and the rebirth of the Oak/Sun King.

PT: **We welcome the young Lord back to this world and bid Him grow in power and strength. So Your season of exile is ended and You return to our midst once more.**

PST: **We embrace the Lady who has given birth to the life of the world since time beginning. Lady, give us the strength to embrace our own changes and transformations and help us find our paths through the coming season.**

All: **Blesséd be!**

Devoke the elements and open the circle.

Golden Yule Dinner and Gathering

We have our dinner in the early afternoon on Yule, and we like to have our traditional Golden Yule Dinner in honor of the reborn Sun King.

In the evening, we encourage friends to come over and we sing songs, tell stories (relating to the season), read poetry and have an exchange of home-crafted gifts. Everyone brings one prettily wrapped present, gender neutral, and puts it in a large basket.

It's great if you can get one of the gentlemen to slip off and dress up as the Holly King, and when the evening starts to wear away, he can exit through the back door with the basket of gifts and come knocking at the front as the Holly King.

Let him in, gift him with wassail and cake and sweets, and then let the Holly King pass around the basket and each person takes one gift (not the one they brought). It's a warm and wonderful way to end the Yule season.

In the tradition of lifting tunes and music from other classical songs, which have no copyright, and because some of the melodies are wonderful, I present to you alternative lyrics for three classical songs.

Yule Songs

Gods Rest Ye Merry Gentlefolk
(to the tune of God Rest Ye Merry Gentlemen*)*

> Gods rest ye merry gentlefolk
> Let nothing you dismay
> Once more the Oak King rises
> He is born on Yuletide day
> To bring the sun back to the Earth
> And drive the snows away
> Oh, tidings of comfort and joy
> Comfort and joy
> Oh, tidings of comfort and joy.

The Goddess writhes with labor pains
Her spasms shake the Earth
The Wheel turns, the cycle moves
As She prepares for birth
The final push, the world cheers.
We celebrate with mirth
Oh, tidings of comfort and joy
Comfort and joy
Oh, tidings of comfort and joy.

The Holly King, He stands His watch
His sword raised to the sky
His reign has reached its end again
Once more His time to die
The light pierces the Eastern dawn
Hear the young Lord's cry
Oh, tidings of comfort and joy
Comfort and joy
Oh, tidings of comfort and joy.

The King is dead, Long live the King
The Waning Year has passed
Light returns, the Sun is born
We shall the snows outlast
The Waxing Year has come again
The days of fear are past
Oh, tidings of comfort and joy
Comfort and joy
Oh, tidings of comfort and joy.

Silent Night
(to the tune of Silent Night)

Silent night, snow-kissed night
All is calm, all is bright
The wolf howls from the mountains once more
The ocean crashed on windswept shores
The Wild Wood rests in peace
The Wild Wood rests in peace.

Silent night, ice shining bright
Gird your doors, shut them tight
Gather 'round to sing the old songs
Keep watch o'er the hearthfire all night long
We await the Oak King's birth
We await the Oak King's birth.

Silent night, hearken the light
The Oak King is born, the Holly King dies.
The Wheel turns, the cycle moves on
The Waxing Year rises, the Waning Year's gone
The Goddess watches over the Earth
The Goddess watches over the Earth.

Holly Boughs and Mistletoe

(to the tune of Greensleeves)

Yuletide Day is here at last
The Wheel turns through winter snows
We gather 'round to sing and laugh
Outside the cold wind shrieks and blows.

Holly boughs and mistletoe
Bedeck the house and Merry Meet
Gather 'round the Wassail bowl
Partake of loved ones' company.

Stave off the chill, sit by our fire
Cloak yourself in tales of old
Sing the songs of Gods and men
Of Faerie Queens and heroes bold.

Holly boughs and mistletoe
Bedeck the house and Merry Meet
Gather 'round the Wassail bowl
Partake of loved ones' company.

The darkest night has come and gone
The Sun is born, we will survive
The young Lord suckles his Lady's breast
Bless this house that we, too, may thrive.

Holly boughs and mistletoe
Bedeck the house and Merry Meet
Gather 'round the Wassail bowl
Partake of loved ones' company.

Food and Recipes

Menu

Turkey Mimosa with Orange Sauce
Mushroom-Onion Stuffing
Mashed Potatoes
Glazed Carrots
Peach Cobbler

Turkey Mimosa with Orange Sauce

1   (15-18) pound turkey, thawed
2   cups pink champagne
1   cup pulp-free orange juice
4   cloves garlic, peeled and thinly sliced
1   cup butter, softened
2   tablespoons oregano
2   tablespoons parsley
2   tablespoons basil
2   tablespoons tarragon
1   tablespoon sage
1   tablespoon finely crushed black peppercorn
2   tablespoons garlic powder
½   teaspoon salt
3   cups turkey stock

Preheat oven to 425 degrees. Gently, using your fingertips, loosen the skin away from the meat of the turkey. Do not tear or remove skin.

Using a syringe, inject the turkey all over both top and bottom with champagne and orange juice. The turkey will look rather strange when you do this but don't worry.

Use a paring knife to make tiny slits in the turkey, through the skin, all over top and bottom (especially between drumsticks and sides) and place a slice of garlic into each slit.

Blend the butter with the herbs. Carefully lift the skin and, using your hands, rub the butter mixture between the skin and meat of the turkey. Do this all over the turkey.

Rub the inside of the turkey with the garlic powder and salt. Stuff loosely and truss.

Place in roasting pan and add turkey stock. Roast uncovered for ten minutes at 425 degrees.

Turn the heat down to 325 degrees and cover the turkey with aluminum foil or the roasting pan cover. Remove from oven every 20 minutes and baste with pan drippings. Roast until meat thermometer reads at least 180 degrees (This should take about 3 to 4 hours, depending on size of bird). Remove the bird from the oven.

Let the turkey set for 10 minutes before carving.

If you want to roast a larger or smaller bird, adjust the amount of ingredients proportionally.

Serves 12.

Orange Sauce

½ cup butter	1 cup port wine
½ cup flour	2 cups chicken stock
4 cups orange juice	1 teaspoon tarragon

Melt butter in skillet. Whisk in flour until roux is a golden paste. Cook over low heat for 5 minutes, stirring constantly to prevent scorching. Slowly whisk in juice, wine, and stock. Add tarragon and bring to a low boil, whisking constantly. Lower heat and simmer sauce for 10 minutes.

Mushroom Onion Stuffing

2 loaves stale french bread	1 tablespoon oregano
2 cups cooked rice	1 tablespoon sage
½ cup cooked wild rice	1 tablespoon parsley
1 pound mushrooms, chopped	1 tablespoon thyme
1 large onion, chopped	2 tablespoons dry chicken bouillon
1 cup minced celery	3 eggs
1 tablespoon basil	3 cups chicken stock

Cut french bread into 1-inch cubes. Mix bread, rices, mush-rooms, onion, celery, herbs, and bouillon in large bowl. Beat eggs and pour into bread mixture. Begin adding chicken stock, ½ cup at a time, and stir with your hand. When the mixture is bonded (when you can pack a handful into a ball and it holds its shape), stuff bird. Any extra can be baked in a covered casserole during the last 45 minutes of roasting the turkey.

Part 2

spring

Imbolc • Ostara

Imbolc

The Festival of the Bride

Sleet beats against the windows, snow still encrusts the ground, you turn up the heat another notch and curl up with a book and a hot cup of ginger tea as you wonder if Spring will ever return . . . it is February 1, the day before Imbolc, the Festival of Brighid.

Brighid (pronounced *Breed*) is the Celtic Goddess of fire, poetry, healing, and craftsmen. She is considered a Triple Goddess, as are so many of the Celtic goddesses, and Her festival coincides with lambing season. Imbolc (from the word *imbolg*) literally means "in milk," referring to the ewes' coming into milk for their lambs.

Imbolc, officially celebrated February 1 and 2, is the season of purification and cleansing. It is time to clear your house for the approaching Spring, for the new growth engendering in your life now.

In magickal terms, the Goddess awaits Her husband and on the night of February 1, He comes to Her in Her bed. Traditionally, a basket-bed is fashioned for Brighid, who is represented by a corn dolly. During the night, a phallic wand or phallic shaped loaf of bread is placed in the basket with the doll to represent the coming of the God.

We consider Imbolc to be the end of the Winter season. The altar stands white and pure, changed over on New Year's Day (see "New Year's Celebration," page 241). On the morning of February 1, we add a bouquet of red carnations, a pitcher of cream, and

43

Brighid's Bed to the milk white cloth and rose quartz sphere that decorate the altar. Then we prepare the phallic bread for the ritual that night.

Making Brighid's Bed

The concept of Brighid's bed surrounds the conjoining of the God and Goddess and is a fertility ritual that hearkens the nearing of Spring. The phallic bread symbolizes the God, the corn dolly the Goddess.

For the Corn Dolly

Choose several long, smooth corn husks and stack evenly in a thick pile. From the top, bend the pile of husks one-third over and fasten securely with twine or floral tape. (Figure 1)

Now take some shorter husks and twist together. Then tie onto doll about one-third down from the top to form arms. (Figure 2)

Half-way down the length of the husks, begin tying or taping additional husks to form the "skirt" of the doll. (Figure 3)

Once you have the fullness you want, then drape a square of white lace around the "skirt" and tie on. Cut a triangle of white lace

Figure 1

Figure 2

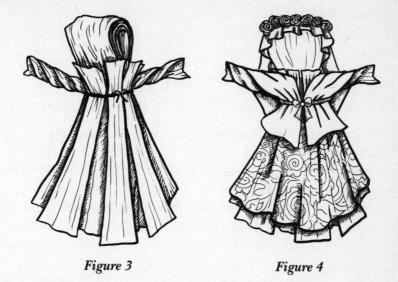

Figure 3   *Figure 4*

and drape around the doll's arms as you would a shawl. Tie at the
waist with red ribbon. Drape a veil of lace over head of doll and
carefully sew onto top of husks. Use red ribbon roses to make a
wreath for head of doll. (Figure 4)

To Assemble Brighid's Bed

To make Brighid's Bed you'll need:
>   a woven basket about 18 inches long
>   dried corn husks or raffia grass
>   (corn stalks are traditional)
>   white lace
>   red ribbon
>   tiny red ribbon roses
>   white cotton twine
>   floral tape
>   white thread
>   white netting
>   sewing needles

Fill the basket with raffia or strips of corn husks. Cover with a
layer of white netting. Gently lay Brighid into basket, leaving room
for the Phallic Bread (recipe, page 46) which is added during ritual.

Imbolc Phallic Bread

2	tablespoons active dry yeast	¼	cup oil
6	tablespoons sugar	½	teaspoon salt
2	cups warm water	1	cup corn meal
2	eggs	5-6	cups flour
		3	tablespoons cinnamon

Stir yeast and sugar together. Add ½ cup warm water and stir. Let stand for 5 minutes.

Beat eggs and add to yeast mixture along with oil. Add remaining 1½ cups warm water. Beat.

Stir in salt and corn meal. Beat. Begin adding flour, 1 cup at a time, until the dough is stiff and begins to pull away from side of bowl (you may not need all 5-6 cups).

Turn onto floured board and sprinkle cinnamon on top of bread dough. Knead for 10 minutes. As you knead, think about the fertility of the grain, about the God coming to His Lady's side. Think sexy thoughts!

When the dough is smooth and elastic, place in a buttered bowl and cover. Set in warm spot until the dough doubles in bulk.

Punch down and let rise once more.

Form a portion of the dough into a phallic-shaped loaf (get creative here—don't be shy!). Bake at 350 degrees for about 25-35 minutes until golden brown and toothpick inserted comes out clean. Time will depend on size of loaf. Form the rest of the dough into rolls and bake for 15-20 minutes. Keep these for Imbolc ritual or dinner.

The Colors of Imbolc

The colors traditionally associated with Imbolc are white, red, and black (Triple Goddess colors). Pink and silver make nice accents.

Incenses, Herbs, and Woods

Imbolc is a time of pungent odors. Not only are fiery scents appropriate (after all, Brighid is a Goddess of fire) but the smells we often associate with cleaning supplies and disinfectants seem right at home during this Sabbat.

Dragon's blood, frankincense, and red sandalwood are all appropriate incenses. If you want to focus on Brighid's healing aspects, you might want to use lavender, heather, or lemon.

Birch wood has a strong association with Brighid, as do brambles, blackberries, and willow.

Cleaning: Physical and Psychic

Imbolc signals Spring cleaning time. It is time to clear out the dust that has accumulated since Lughnasadh and prepare our homes for the activity and growth that generally come during the Spring season.

Begin by cleaning your house. Use a vinegar and mugwort wash to clean your windows and mirrors. Sweep down all the cobwebs, turn the mattresses, vacuum your rugs. Dust under the books and clean off your knick-knacks. Wash all the white sheets in hot water and then settle down with a cup of ginger tea and a piece of cinnamon toast to rest.

Next, you should psychically clean house. Light a smudge stick (sage and lavender work best at this time of year) and let the smoke billow through your house. Blow it into every corner, behind the doors, under the furniture. Watch for stray sparks when you do this.

Open the windows and wave the smoke outside, visualize it taking negative energy with it. Now ward your house, casting a circle in every room for protection, safety, and peace. Do not open these circles. Leave them to settle into the walls.

Throw away all prosperity and protection charms that are dusty and old, and create new ones in their place. Dust and polish all wooden hex signs, witch bottles, and other ritual objects. Anoint wooden, bone, and antler ritual gear with the appropriate oils.

This project may take several days, I recommend beginning on February 3 and allowing a week to go through your home. That way you won't feel so swamped.

After you have cleaned house, it's time to clean your aura.

Take a ritual bath. Fill the bathtub with lavender bath salts or bubble bath. Soak for as long as you like. Scrub your toenails, fingernails, behind your ears—every place you can think of.

After your bath, cast a circle in your (now clean) ritual space and light a piece of self-igniting charcoal (the kind meant specifically for incense—don't use charcoal briquettes—you can cause carbon monoxide poisoning that way). Drop a few lavender buds on the charcoal and let the smoke drift past.

Think about the areas of your life you wish were calm, more peaceful. Ask for ideas and help to create that peace.

Next drop a few pieces of frankincense and some dragon's blood on the incense. Again, let the smoke drift around you.

Think about what you want to strengthen in your life. Ask for ideas and help to create that strength.

Decide what you can do to create peace and strength in your life and formulate a plan you can implement without stress. Never take on too much at this time of year, you'll need your strength as spring and summer return.

The Festival of Lights Ritual

Another traditional activity at Imbolc involves filling the house with light. While designed for a group, with some imagination, this ritual can be adapted for solitary use.

Shortly before sunset on February 1 turn off every light in the house. One woman, representing Brighid, should stand outside with a lit candle. Everyone else waits in the dark for her knock.

She knocks three times on the door. Someone should open the door and say:

Brighid has come! Brighid has come! Brighid has come!

At this point, invite Brighid into your home. The woman representing the Goddess should enter and stand by the door with her candle.

A second person steps forward and says to her:

May Brighid give blessing to the house that is here. Brighid the fair and tender! Bless our house, golden-haired maiden. Let health fill our walls, let success fill our careers and let love fill our hearts.

Brighid should begin turning on lights, with everyone from the house following her, until every light is on. She then says to the household:

> **The light has returned and the season of growth draws near. May health fill your walls, may you succeed and prosper, may love encompass your lives. I am Brighid the Fair, Brighid the Wise, Brighid the Fiery Arrow of Power and so I bless your home and your family. Remember me and honor me on this night.**

She should place the candle on the altar and then everyone join hands and sing:

> **Fire, fire growing higher, bring to us what we desire.**
> **Fire, fire glowing bright, welcome Brighid this Imbolc night!**

Repeat the chant until the power peaks and release it, focusing on the return of Spring, the growth you want to accomplish and the projects you want to complete and/or start during this time.

The Pouring of the Cream

As an effective end to ritual, or a simple ritual in itself, the pouring of the cream is the best libation you could give to Brighid.

Around midnight, take the pitcher of cream off the altar, carry it outside, and say:

> **Lady Brighid, we honor you and return to you the cream that is life itself. We ask for Your blessing in the coming season. Blесséd be.**

Pour the cream onto the ground (if there's snow, pour directly onto the snow) and then spend a moment thinking about Imbolc and what it means to you.

Carnations or Roses?

Although it is traditional among Pagans to offer roses to the Goddess when decorating our altars, somehow I like carnations for
Brighid. They're spicy—belonging to the element of Fire—and
they seem so appropriate for this time of year (being January's
flower). So I always recommend red carnations for her altar, in a
crystal vase on a white cloth. The contrast is striking, and if you can
add a piece or two of rose quartz, it's even more beautiful.

Imbolc Ritual of the Bride

This ritual works best in a mixed-gender group. While it is not necessary that the man to woman ratio be equal, neither should it be
drastically unbalanced. When we performed it, we had five men and
six women and it worked well. You will need at least four women
and four men for the ritual, although you can adapt it for less.

The ritual looks long on paper, but if everything is planned out
in advance, it runs quickly and I like it so much that I want to lead
it again someday.

To prepare the ritual space, decorate the altar with Brighid's
Bed, Imbolc Oil (see page 55), a red candle, and red carnations.
Place a large red scarf beneath the altar.

In another room, which has a door that can be closed, set up a
second altar, this one with ivy on it. Place the phallic bread on a
tray and put it on the altar, along with a green candle and a bottle
of Green Man Oil (see page 56).

Each participant should be familiar with the ritual before you
begin. One man should bring a drum and keep it with him.

Part 1: The Entire Group

The group should cast the circle and invoke the elements in the
most comfortable manner.

Then the men should retreat to the room where the phallic
bread waits and close the door. The men and women separately but
simultaneously perform the Parts 2 and 3 of the ritual.

Part 2: The Women

The Priestess steps forward and lights the red candle on the altar.

PST: **Brighid, Lady of the Fiery Arrow, Lady of Healers and Poets and Craftsmen! We call You to our circle tonight that we might celebrate Your festival. The time of lambing is upon us, the days of purification before Spring kisses the Earth are here! Come now, Lady of Light, You who are the Sacred Bride. Come to Your wedding bed and await Your husband.**

Wmn: **Brighid is come! Brighid is come! Brighid is come!**

PST: *(Passes around a chalice of wine.)* **Drink to the Lady's health and fertility!**

Every woman takes a drink and passes it on.

PST: *(Takes Imbolc Oil and anoints the forehead of the woman next to her.)* **I bless you in the name of the Lady Brighid.**

She passes the oil to the woman, who turns to the next woman and does the same . . . the oil is passed until the last woman in line anoints the Priestess.

PST: *(Takes Imbolc Oil and anoints the forehead of the corn dolly representing Brighid.)* **I anoint thee, creature of corn and lace, you who represent the Goddess Brighid. May Her energy fill your body and fill this room.**

Priestess puts oil back on altar and picks up basket.

PST: **We come together as women to share our tales of love and marriage with our Lady.**

One by one, each woman holds Brighid's basket and relates a brief anecdote or bit of wisdom she has culled from her own marriage or partnership, be it in the past or current. The basket is passed until every one has had a turn.

PST: *(Holding the basket.)* **We come together to ask Brighid's blessing in our lives.**

One by one, each woman holds Brighid's basket and asks Brighid to bless a specific part of her life that needs strengthening.

PST: *(Puts basket back on altar.)* **And so Brighid is ready for the Bridegroom. Knock on the door!**

One of the women goes and knocks on the men's door. Then all women stand so their backs face the men when they enter the room. They block the men's view of the altar with the large red scarf. If the men need extra time, the women sit in silent meditation as they wait. Proceed as in Part 4.

Part 3: The Men

The Priest steps forward and lights the green candle on the altar.

PT: **Great Lord of Life, Oak King and Sun Lord! We call You to our circle tonight to celebrate Your union with the Lady Brighid. Your wedding night has arrived! Enter now, Lord of the Green, You who are the Sacred Consort. Your Lady awaits in Her wedding gown.**

Men: **Lord of the Green! Lord of the Green! Lord of the Green! Come!**

PT: *(Passes around a chalice of wine.)* **Drink to the Green Lord's health and virility!**

Every man takes a drink and passes it on.

PT: *(Takes Green Man Oil and anoints the forehead of the man next to him.)* **I bless you in the name of the Green Lord.**

He passes the oil to the man, who turns to the man next to him and does the same. The oil is passed until the last man in line has anointed the Priest.

PT: *(Takes Green Man Oil and anoints the Phallic Bread.)* **I anoint thee, creature of corn and wheat, you who represent the Lord of the Green. May His energy fill your body and fill this room.**

Priest puts oil back on altar and picks up tray.

PT: **We come together as men to share our tales of love and marriage with our Lord.**

One by one, each man holds Phallic Bread—still on the tray—and relates a brief anecdote or bit of wisdom he has culled from his own marriage or partnership, be it in the past or current. The bread is passed until everyone has had a turn.

PT: *(Holding the bread.)* **We come together to ask the Green Lord's blessing in our lives.**

One by one, each man holds the Phallic Bread—still on the tray—and asks the Green Lord to bless a specific part of his life that needs strengthening.

PT: *(Puts bread back on altar.)* **And so the Lord of the Green is ready for the Bride. We await Her summons!**

Men wait until the women knock, then proceed as in Part 4. If they have not yet finished their blessing of the bread, the men should not rush.

Part 4: The Entire Group

The men emerge from their room, one man carrying the tray of bread, and do not speak to or look at the women as they pass. They go outside and shut the door behind them. The women line up in a single row between the altar and the front door.

The men should go about 10–20 yards from the house and then the drummer, at the end of the line, begins a simple drum beat as they march back to the house. The Priest should be in the front of the line.

When they reach the house, the Priest knocks on the door. The Priestess opens the door with her athame pointing at the Priest. Ritual Participants are noted as M (Man) or W (Woman) 1, 2, and 3 for clarity's sake.

PST: **Who knocks at the door of Brighid's wedding chamber?**

PT: **It is the Lord of the Green, come to claim the Lady for His bride!**

PST: **You must answer three challenges in order to pass to Her chamber.**

The Priestess allows the Priest to enter. He steps to one side and man carrying the tray of bread hands it to him. M1 steps forward. The Priestess stands aside, her athame focused on the challengers until they have passed the tests. W1 faces M1.

W1: What are the names of the Lady's royal oxen, Her royal boar and Her royal sheep?

M1: Brighid's royal oxen bear the names Fe and Menn. Her boar is Triath, King of the Boars and Her golden ram is Cirb, King of the Rams.

W1: You have passed the first test. You may enter the chamber of the bride.

W1 escorts M1 to the altar where they stand waiting. W2 steps up to face M2.

W2: Who fathered the Lady Brighid?

M2: The Great Lord Dagda.

W2: And what are Her titles?

M2: Brighid the Fiery Arrow of Power, Brighid the Renown, Brighid, the Blessed Lady of Britain.

W2: You have passed the second test. You may enter the chamber of the bride.

W2 escorts M2 to the altar where they stand waiting. W3 steps up to face M3.

W3: What was the nature of Brighid's sacred Order?

W3: Brighid's Order of Kildare kept the ever-burning sacred fire. Her Priestesses numbered nineteen.

W3: And over what does the Lady Brighid rule?

M3: Fire and poetry, prophecy and healing, craftsmen and witchcraft.

W3: You have passed the third test. You may enter the chamber of the bride.

W3 escorts M3 to the altar where they stand waiting. All other participants gather around the altar at this point.

PT: The Lord of the Green approaches the Lady Brighid!

PST: The Lady Brighid awaits Her husband!

Priest should take bread off tray—carefully so as not to break it. The Priestess makes room in the basket for the bread. As the Priest lowers the bread to nestle next to the corn dolly, all cheer and shout.

All: **The Bridegroom has come! The Lady Brighid kisses Her husband! The Lord of the Green is wed to the Fiery Bride!**
(Participants can join in with other appropriate salutations.)

All join hands around the altar and chant.

All: **Fire, fire burning higher**
Fuel the Lady's warm desire
Green Lord, Green Lord, rise tonight
Passion burn a brilliant light!

Peak the power through the chant and then release. Ground the energy.

PT: **We thank the Green Lord for attending our rites. Go if you must, stay if you will, farewell and Blesséd be.**

PST: **We thank the Lady Brighid for attending our rites. Go if you must, stay if you will, farewell and Blesséd be.**

Devoke the elements and the circle as usual. Eat snacks of milk and cheese, vanilla cookies or cakes.

Imbolc Oil

¼	ounces almond oil	10	drops orange oil
9	drops siberian fir oil	4	drops nutmeg oil
5	drops lavender oil	5	drops carnation oil
5	drops frankincense oil	5	drops primrose oil
5	drops ginger oil		

Blend all oils, add a few orange blossom petals and a chip or two of garnet and ruby. Bless in circle. Use to anoint ritual objects or participants during ritual.

Green Man Oil

¼	ounce almond oil	3	drops vetiver oil
4	drops cedar oil	4	drops citronella oil
4	drops spruce oil	2	drops cinnamon oil
3	drops patchouli oil	2	drops orange oil

Blend all oils and add a few snips of fern leaf and a citrine or topaz chip. Bless in circle and use in this ritual, or for general anointing.

Food and Recipes

Dairy foods play a big part in Imbolc celebrations, as do breads. Rice pudding and other creamy-colored foods are good choices, too.

Sun and Moon Deviled Eggs

10	eggs, hard cooked and cooled	¼	teaspoon salt
½	cup mayonnaise	1	tablespoon basil
¼	cup minced green onions	1	tablespoon tarragon
1	clove slivered garlic	1	tablespoon paprika
2	tablespoon dijon mustard		Paprika for sprinkling

Carefully peel eggs. Slice each egg in half length-ways and scoop egg yolk into bowl. Rest egg whites on tray.

Add the rest of the ingredients to egg yolks and whip with electric mixer until smooth and creamy.

Using a melon-ball scoop, fill egg whites with yolk mixture, mounding as necessary. Sprinkle with paprika and cover loosely with plastic wrap. Chill.

Makes 10 servings.

Creamy Rice Pudding with Raspberry Sauce

5   cups cooked white rice
1   package unsweetened
      gelatin
2½ cups milk
1   cup white sugar

½   teaspoon salt
2   teaspoons vanilla
4   eggs, separated
½   cup golden raisins
      (optional)

Preheat oven to 350 degrees. Run rice through a food processor to grate.

Sprinkle gelatin on cold milk and let stand 5 minutes. Stir to dissolve and then stir in sugar, salt, and vanilla. Pour into stainless steel pan.

Separate eggs. Reserve the whites. Beat egg yolks into the milk mixture and place over medium heat, stirring constantly as mixture begins to thicken.

Add rice to thickened custard mixture and stir.

Beat egg whites until soft peaks form and fold into rice mixture. Add raisins and pour into buttered casserole dish. Cover and bake for 35–45 minutes, until set.

Serves 10.

Raspberry Sauce

¼   cup butter
1   tablespoon cinnamon
1   teaspoon cloves
½   cup orange juice concentrate
2   (10-ounce) packages sweetened frozen raspberries
      (thaw but don't drain)

Melt butter in skillet. Stir in spices and orange juice concentrate. Stir constantly and add raspberries. Cook over medium heat to reduce liquid by one-third.

Chill. Serve over warm rice pudding.

Yogurt Shake

1   cup lemon yogurt
¼   cup pineapple
2   tablespoons orange juice
    concentrate

¼   teaspoon cinnamon
4   ounces milk
½   teaspoon vanilla

Combine all ingredients in blender and whip into a frothy shake.
Makes 1 shake.

OSTARA

The Festival of Fertility

Sky the color of robins' eggs, a clear crisp breeze, branches covered with tight green buds, a sudden rainstorm breaking through the still-cool sun, the first crocus peeking out from under the cedar tree . . . it is the Spring Equinox, Ostara, and life renews itself.

Ostara is the celebration of the Spring (Vernal) Equinox when day and night balance. Astronomically speaking, the sun crosses the celestial equator at this time.

Held in late March, the actual date can vary from year-to-year, as with the Autumnal Equinox and the two Solstices. The Vernal Equinox usually falls on March 20 or 21. Always check your almanac for your time zone.

Called Ostara after the Saxon Goddess Eostre, this is a time of renewal, regeneration and resurrection as the Earth wakes from her long slumber. This is the time of planting, children, and young animals.

It is the fertility of the Earth that we celebrate, and we symbolize this new life springing from sun and soil with eggs, chicks, lambs, and rabbits (all symbols of the Great Mother).

Ostara promises freedom from the dreariness of winter, it heralds the return of hope and dreams.

With the days lengthening, we fill our lungs with fresh air and drink the pungent cleansing teas that clear our bodies from the heavy foods of winter.

On February 3, my husband and I exchange the white altar of late Winter/Imbolc for the green one of Spring. After purifying the altar table, we drape a bright green cloth over it, then cover that with a pale green and white polka dot chiffon scarf.

Our Ostara decorations include a round basket filled with yellow raffia that contains thirteen wooden eggs painted in bright colors, tiny yellow chicks and pastel rabbits, a garland of silk daisies, and a decanter of rosé wine.

We hang up my Spring pictures of Mielikki and Tapio, and the Spring collage.

Seasonal decorations include bowls of malted milk balls, jelly beans, and a bright yellow pillar candle.

We then bless and consecrate the altar. We like to watch the movie *Darby O'Gill and The Little People* after we're finished.

We hold our ritual on the actual Equinox—usually in the afternoon or early evening, depending on what time everyone can make it.

The day after the Equinox, I like to change the altar to a simple green-print scarf with my Kalevala wreath, the pillar candle, and the last of the Spring wine. My Kalevala wreath is decorated with dried grape vines and silk ivy. (For further information on Finnish magickal tradition, see "Kalevala Day" beginning on page 247.) The altar stays that way until April 29, the end of the Spring season and the beginning of the Beltane Interlude.

The Colors of Ostara

All pastels are appropriate for Ostara—especially the greens, yellows, and pinks. I like the jewel-toned variations of these colors, too. White makes a nice accent, but seems too sparse for an altar cloth representing the season of growth and fertility.

Incenses, Herbs, and Woods

Violet, honeysuckle, narcissus, and lemon make good incenses for Ostara—the scents should be clear and light, floral and evocative, but not overwhelming or intoxicating.

Herbs associated with spring include meadowsweet, cleavers, clover, lemon grass, spearmint, and catnip.

If you want to use wood in your spells and rituals, ash has a strong link with the equinox due to its connection with the macrocosm-microcosm concept in the Celtic ogham runes—the balance of light and dark . . . as above, so below.

Ostara's Flowers

What better way to decorate for the spring season than to use the flowers that blossom into life at this time? There are so many, and they're all beautiful.

Daffodils, jonquils, tulips, narcissus, violets and crocus and snowdrops—fill the house with their color after you've finished your spring cleaning.

Charm Bags for Growth and Health

During the spring season, we concentrate on magic for growth and health. Charm bags are easy, quick ways to cast a spell and their powers last, emanating out to change our lives.

Prosperity Charm

For this charm, you will need:

        a green pouch (home-made or store-bought)
9 kernels of dried corn
9 kernels of barley
        a malachite or peridot bead
        a 6-sided die
        a white stone you've collected near an ocean, lake,
          river, or other source of water

a quarter
a dime
a piece of cedar branch
green ribbon

Carve this rune, for prosperity, into your stone:

Cast a circle and invoke the elements. Into a green pouch (either home-made or bought) place the dried corn kernels, the barley kernels, the malachite or peridot bead, the 6-sided die; the painted white stone, the quarter, the dime, and the piece of cedar branch.

Tie the bag with green ribbon, then ask Eostre to bless the charm and chant:

Silver and gold, corn and grain
Let my wealth increase and gain
Gem and coin, stone and tree
Lady Luck be kind to me.

Chant to peak the power, then release, focusing on your prosperity and abundance increasing over the coming season. Store the prosperity charm in your purse or hang near the front door so the fresh air can touch it whenever the door opens.

Creativity Charm

For this charm, you will need:

    a blue bag
    a white feather
    a few sprigs of lavender
    a quartz crystal
6 pieces of dried lemon peel
    a small brass bell
    2-inch length of hazel wood carved with the rune
      for clear thought, shown here
    purple ribbon

Carve this rune, for clear thinking, onto the hazel wood:

Cast a circle and invoke the elements. In the blue bag put the white feather, the springs of lavender, the quartz crystal, the dried lemon peel, the small brass bell and the piece of hazel wood.

Tie the bag with purple ribbon, then ask Eostre to bless the charm and chant:

> **Mind and vision, chant and wit**
> **Ink and voice and talent**
> **Muses of word, picture and song**
> **I rise to meet your challenge.**

Chant to peak the power, then release, focusing on those creative projects you want to complete, see them blossom and grow through the coming season. Store the creativity charm near your desk or your easel.

Health Charm

For this charm, you will need:

       a gold bag
       dragon's blood resin
9   cloves
       a piece of citrine
       a sprig of heather
9   rowan berries
       an oyster shell painted with the rune for strength
       a miniature brass sun face
       a tin of Tiger's Balm
       a red ribbon

Paint this rune, for strength, onto your oyster shell:

Cast a circle and invoke the elements. In the gold bag put the dragon's blood resin, the cloves, the citrine, the heather, the rowan berries, the painted oyster shell, the sun face, and the tin of Tiger's Balm. Tie the bag with red ribbon and then ask Eostre to bless the charm and chant:

> **Strength and health this charm has wrought!**
> **Disease and pain touch me not!**

Chant to peak the power, then release, focusing on your body and spirit growing strong throughout the coming spring. Store the health charm near your bed and hold it for a moment each night before you go to sleep.

Egg Decoration

There are numerous ways in which to decorate eggs for the season. We've come a long way from when we boiled them with food coloring in the water, although that's still a viable alternative.

One of the most intricate forms of egg decoration is called *Pysanky* and is Ukrainian in origin. Pysanky uses a tool called a *kitska,* a pencil-like handle with a tiny metal cup on the end that has a narrow opening, not much bigger than the prong of a thumbtack. Beeswax is put into this cup and then the metal is held over a candle to melt the wax. Designs are drawn onto the egg's surface and when the wax hardens, dye is applied to the rest of the egg. When the wax is melted off, the design is left a different color.

I'm not sure of the entire process, but the examples I've seen are incredibly intricate. An arts and crafts store would have more detailed information, or you can check your local library for reference material.

For a while we used blown-egg shells on our Ostara altar until our cats decided to have a party one night and destroyed every one of the thirteen eggs I'd hand-painted. So we switched to wooden eggs.

You can poke two holes in the egg, one in the top, the other in the bottom, and blow the inside of the egg out. Then carefully rinse the shell with cool water and allow it to dry. Use magic markers, acrylics or watercolors to decorate your eggs. Paint runes and pictures and designs on them, or color them uniformly and have a basket of multi-colored eggs on your altar.

As I said above, we use wooden quail's eggs and this time I decided to go with plain colors. For some reason, this seems prettier on my altar for now, but I may change my mind later on and paint over them—adding designs and runes again.

Seed Spell

For a long-term project you want a spell that will last the length of whatever it is you're trying to do. Depending on your area, choose a packet of vegetable seeds that do well in your climate (we'll use corn in this example).

Cast a circle around the pot or plot where you'll be planting the seeds. If it is near a larger garden, mark the area off with string so you can tell which are your "magickal" stalks of corn and which are the regular ones.

Invoke the elements and then sit, under the sun, holding the corn kernels in your open palm. Charge the kernels while thinking about your project. Think about what you want it to blossom into, think about the work you know it will take. See any potential obstacles evening out and disappearing. Then see yourself harvesting the rewards of your project as you harvest the corn.

Say:

> **Creatures of corn,**
> **Strength be born!**
> **As you grow, so shall** (name of project)
> **As you flourish, so shall** (name of project)
> **As you mature, so shall** (name of project)
> **As I harvest your bounty, so shall I harvest**
> **The rewards of** (name of project).
> **Eostre, Lady of Spring, bless these seeds and all they bring.**
> **So Mote It Be.**

Plant the seeds. You must tend this little garden carefully, for if you neglect it and let the plants die, then the energy and vitality of your project will also wither away. Just so, you must spend the time and energy on your project that it needs. If you do both, you should flourish and prosper.

When you harvest the corn, return the stalks and husks to the Earth.

Wind Spells

Often spring brings with it brisk winds and we can capture the energy of these winds in our magic.

Wind Spell 1: Scatter Spell

This is a good spell to use when you are searching for something but don't know where to find it. It might be love, a new job, a new home, a new sense of physical strength . . . whatever you are looking for, you will want to gather together your spell components in advance.

You will need a handful of herbs and a brisk wind.

- If you want to attract love, use powdered rose and orange petals and wait for a west wind.

- If you want to attract a new job, use dill and basil and wait for an east wind.

- If you want a new home or other material item, use patchouli and ground (uncooked) oats and wait for a north wind.

- If you want revitalized health, use powdered dragon's blood and cinnamon and wait for a south wind.

Have your herbs ready so that when the wind rises, you can grab them and go. Head to the tallest slope in your area and when you reach the top, wait for the gusts to really blow. Clench the herbs in your fists and visualize what it is you want. Raise your arms up to meet the wind and slowly open your hands, letting the gusts catch the herbs and blow them up into the air. Say:

> **Wind of the** (direction)**, hear my cry**
> **Take this charm and make it fly**
> **With your** (direction) **breezes kiss**
> **My life and bring to me my wish!**

Watch the herbs scatter in the wind and know that they are spreading out through the world, searching for what you need or feel you have lost. Stand and commune with the wind for a few minutes before you go home. Take all physical actions necessary to provide the opportunity for the spell to work.

Wind Spell 2: Knotting The Wind

The old Finnish shamans were respected and feared for their abilities to knot up the winds for later use. They caught up the wind in ropes, knotting the gales to sell to sailors. Their abilities were so well-known that certain Norse rulers would not allow Finns to ride in their ships.

We may not be able to knot up the wind as effectively as some of those shamans, but if you want to capture the essence of the wind for use in your spells (especially if you need to shake up your life and get things moving again) then find a piece of rope about three feet long and go out to a windy slope.

Hold the rope taut in the wind and close your eyes. Feel the wind tugging on the rope, feel it blowing against your body. Visualize the strength of the wind flowing into the rope. Spend some time doing this.

Then, still holding the rope overhead, knot at three equal points, saying:

> **One knot, the power of breeze**
> **Gently shakes the maple's leaves.**
>
> **Two knots, the power to sail**
> **Blow crisply now and do not fail.**
>
> **Three knots, the power of storm**
> **What can destroy can also form.**

Hold the rope taut again, still focusing on the power of the wind and say:

> **Power of wind in these knots three**
> **Untie them and your force runs free**
> **Harm me not, wind and breeze**
> **As I will so mote it be!**

Put a tag on the rope that indicates the wind you've knotted up, i.e., "north Summer wind." Keep the rope with your magickal paraphernalia until you have need of the strength of wind. Untie one, two, or three knots depending on how strong a force or spell you need. Use for spells like clearing away old patterns or habits from your life; shooing pests and negative people from your life; or shaking up a stagnant patch in your career or love life.

Green Man and Flower Bride Ostara Ritual

Hold this ritual outdoors if possible. If you cannot hold it outdoors, then choose a house with a large room that can handle a tangle of vegetation on the floor (in other words, somewhere you can make a mess)!

This is a mixed gender ritual, though balance isn't that important in terms of male to female ratio. It works well if one couple who has borne children is present to capture the energy of reproduction.

Each person should bring at least one big bouquet of spring flowers (lots of flowers with good, strong stems on them) and a bundle of cedar, fir, oak, and ivy branches. You will need more of everything than you think you do.

In addition you will need the following supplies:

> ribbons in spring colors
> floral tape
> floral wire
> beads
> feathers
> dental floss
> thread
> sewing needles
> 2 mask forms
> copper wire
> a hand saw
> pruning shears
> scissors
> needle nose pliers
> wire cutters

Each person should bring a small item that they don't mind leaving behind to adorn the Green Man and the Flower Bride.

You will also need one decorated hard-cooked egg—colored red for the Goddess—and a packet of seeds (nasturtium seeds are a good size) that you have poured into a piece of green lace and tied with a green ribbon for the God.

In your ritual space—which should not be the room containing all the flowers, tree branches, ivy, and other foliage—decorate the altar with flowers, ivy, feathers, crystals, colored eggs, candy, and the like.

Part 1: Building the Green Man and Flower Bride

Half of your group will build the Green Man, the other half will build the Flower Bride. Everyone should be encouraged to work on the image they want to, but the group should be evenly divided so if there is anyone without a preference, assign them to the group that needs more people. One or two people can also be "floaters," helping out where needed.

Your goal in this part of the ritual (which will take about two hours) is to build free-standing images of the Green Man and the Flower Bride out of the natural materials you've brought, and to adorn them for ritual.

It's amazing what creations come out of this ritual. This past spring, we were thrilled by the absolute beauty and strength of our images—they were both about three feet tall and free-standing. The Flower-Bride's skirt was composed entirely of daffodils, tulips, daisies, and the other flowers, interwoven through a framework of ivy and cedar. Her mouth was a bright red round flower. The Green Man had a chest of moss and his testicles and phallus were made of modeling clay covered with moss.

Both had faces created on mask forms, and these were of moss and ivy, too.

So here you must be creative—it requires cooperation and laughter. Enjoy this part of the ritual and don't rush it. As you build the forms, talk to them, ask what they want, listen to inner guidance. Share your joy with them—these are images of the Gods you are creating. Don't worry if you've never built anything in your lives—we did not expect our Green Man and Flower Bride to be free-standing and yet they were.

Part 2: The Ritual

Set the Green Man on the left side and the Flower Bride on the right side of the altar. The Seed of the God is placed at the feet of the Green Man and the Sacred Egg is placed in a crystal dish at the feet of the Flower Bride. Cast a circle and invoke the elements as you usually do.

PST: **We invoke thee, Spirit of Spring. You who are the scent of freshly turned soil, you who are the first flowers of the season, we bid you enter our lives. You who are new beginnings, you who embody youth and vitality and innocence, be with us in circle tonight!**

PT: *(Kneels before Green Man.)* **Lord of the Green and Laughing God, we bid You come to our circle tonight. Be with us, Lord of the Dance, Oak King, be in our hearts and fill us with the vitality of youth, with the strength of new growth. Even as sap rises hundreds of feet through the veins of Your trees, so also let rise our joys and enthusiasm and spirits. Welcome to our rites and Blessèd Be.**

All: *(Chant.)* **Green Man, Spring Man, clothed in moss and mist Come await your Flower Bride, with Your gentle kiss.**

Stop the chant just before the power peaks.

PST: *(Kneels before Flower Bride.)* **Blodeuwedd, Flower Bride, Lady of Spring, we bid You come to our circle tonight. Be with us, Faerie Maid and Queen of the Garden, be in our hearts and fill us with the fertility of spring, with the strength of new growth. Even as the world rejoices in Your wakening, also let us rejoice and celebrate our duties as Your stewards. We raise our voices in Your praise. Welcome to our rites and Blessèd be.**

All: *(Chant.)* **Come Lady come to the Green Man's side**
Most beautiful of Flower Brides.

Stop the chant just before the power peaks. The Priest holds up the Seed.

PT: **Bless now the Seed of the God, that it might take hold and**
root and grow in the Lady's soil.

The lace packet of seed is passed around. Each person should take a turn
blessing the seed, which is then placed back at the feet of the Green Man.
The Priestess holds up the Sacred Egg.

PST: **Bless now the Sacred Egg of the Lady, that She might con-**
ceive and bear fruit in the coming season.

The sacred egg is passed around. Each person should take a turn blessing
the egg, then it is placed back at the Flower Bride's feet. If a married couple
who has had children is present, they should perform this next part; if not,
then it falls to the Priest and Priestess. The man and woman stand in the
center of the circle, the man holding the Seed and the woman holding a crys-
tal dish with the Egg in it. The group chants as the man slowly places the
seeds into the dish with the egg and the couple kisses. Then they lay the dish
between the Green Man and Flower Bride.

All: *(Chant.)* **Seed and Egg, Seed and Egg**
Grow strong now as life is made.
Ivy, rose and Grape vine,
Blossom into sweetest wine.

Peak the power through the chant and release it. The Priest and Priestess
return to the center of the circle.

PT: **So the seed is planted and life grows anew in the womb of**
the Goddess.

PST: **So we plant our own seeds this season, nurturing the ten-**
der sprouts that they might grow strong and healthy for the
harvest.

PT: *(Kneels before Green Man.)* **Oak King, Lord of the Green, be in**
our hearts and our hands this coming season. Go if You
must, stay if You will, hail, farewell and Blesséd be.

All:　　**Blessèd be.**

PST:　　*(Kneels before Flower Bride.)* **Flower Bride, Queen of the Garden, be in our hearts and our hands this coming season. Go if You must, stay if You will, hail, farewell and Blessèd Be.**

All:　　**Blessèd be.**

Devoke the elements and open the circle as usual. Follow this ritual with a potluck.

After ritual and potluck are over, the seeds and egg should be planted somewhere—the egg should be buried under the soil before the flower seeds are planted.

The Green Man and Flower Bride can be kept in a dry spot until Midsummer, when they are thrown on the Litha bonfire.

Food and Recipes

Lemon Cookies

1½　cups white sugar	10　drops yellow food coloring
1　cup butter	2　tablespoons dried lemon balm
2　eggs	
2　teaspoons lemon flavoring	2　cups all purpose flour
1　tablespoon grated lemon zest	½　teaspoon salt
	1　teaspoon baking soda

Preheat oven to 350 degrees. Beat sugar and butter until light and creamy. Add eggs, one at a time, beating after each addition. Stir in lemon flavoring, lemon zest, food coloring, and lemon balm.

Sift flour, salt, and baking soda together. Add to butter mixture, blending until thoroughly mixed.

Roll into balls and place on greased cookie sheets.

Bake for 10-12 minutes (watch carefully) until done.

Makes 2 dozen.

Lamb Stew

¼ cup olive oil
1½ pounds cubed lamb
1 cup chopped tomatoes
1 eggplant, peeled
  and cubed
1 cup chopped celery
1 green bell pepper, diced
½ red bell pepper, diced

1 cup chopped leeks
1 tablespoon basil
1 tablespoon tarragon
1 tablespoon parsley
1 tablespoon paprika
1 teaspoon crushed
  black peppercorns
2 cups chicken stock

Preheat oven to 350 degrees. In a heavy skillet, heat olive oil over medium heat. Sauté lamb in oil until brown on all sides. Remove and place in casserole dish along with tomatoes and eggplant.

Add celery, peppers, leeks, and herbs to the remaining oil and sauté for 5 minutes, stirring constantly.

Stir sautéed vegetables into lamb mixture and add chicken stock. Cover tightly and bake for 40 minutes. Serve over rice.

Serves 4.

Part 3

summer

Beltane • Litha

BELTANE

The Festival of Passion

Daisy chains and lilacs, champagne with strawberries and sweet woodruff, sun filtering into a field of young fern and bracken, a doe and her fawns peering out of the woods, a hint of chaos in the air . . . it is April 30, Walpurgis Night (the Night of the Witches), and we joyfully await the mayhem and passion of the coming day.

A celebration of fertility, Beltane is the time of the rut, when the King Stag races through the woods to join in marriage with the Goddess of Sovereignty.

Our ancestors celebrated Beltane through sex, sacrifice, and fire. It was not a ceremony for those weak of heart, for the sacrifice was both human and animal, made as a plea for abundant harvests.

Those sacrificed in the fires were often criminals, although an occasional holy person might be chosen to represent his or her community. It was considered an honor to serve the Gods with one's life. The Lindow Man was one such Druid priest, and the story of his discovery in the bogs is a fascinating glimpse into the ancient practices of this holiday.

Beltane is also a time of Faerie Magic (as is Midsummer) and the Queen of Faeries is represented by the Queen of the May. Along with her consort, she rules over the festivities and serves as representative of the Goddess.

The bonfire is an integral part of Beltane festivities and although you can always celebrate indoors when circumstances dictate, the balefire on the hill is one of the oldest and most potent magickal symbols of the Sabbat.

Beltane is a time of chaos, of the wild energy and passion found in the Greenwood. Be careful when you walk abroad on Beltane night—you never know what you're going to encounter.

My husband and I celebrate Beltane like we do Samhain, as a three-day interlude. We view Beltane as the beginning of the summer season and so on the night of April 29, we take down the simple spring altar that replaced our Ostara decorations and purify the altar table.

On the morning of April 30, we set up the Beltane altar. A cloth printed with grapes and leaves on a black background, a pair of antlers, ivy vines and dusty rose silk flowers, an ivy garland and an antler-handled bone knife, a mauve pillar candle . . . these all decorate our Beltane altar.

Our seasonal additions to the altar include a decanter of burgundy, plates of grapes and strawberries, chocolates (although we have to watch the cats—chocolate is dangerous to feline health and one of our cats is more than fond of the gooey sweet)!

We offer the last of the Spring wine at the offering shrine and I open a gateway for the Faerie (much like at Samhain—for the dead). We invoke Mielikki and Tapio (Mielikki is a Goddess of Faerie as well as of the Hunt, so She seems to like this holiday), and then we invoke Pan and Queen Mab for the Beltane interlude.

Since my husband and I were married on Beltane, this is a very special holiday for us. We usually reserve the evening of April 30—during which we partake of the oldest rite of all between lovers with no one else invited.

In the morning, we wake bright and early and it is time for festivities. The calendar doesn't always allow us the chance to celebrate with friends, but when we do, there is no lack of fun and excitement.

On May 2, we have a Beltane brunch and watch *The Wicker Man* before taking down the altar to prepare for the Summer season.

There are more traditions associated with Beltane than any other holiday except, perhaps, Yule.

The Colors of Beltane

Bright colors abound at this time of year. I especially connect the colors of purple and green with Beltane—the deep plum of grape wine, the peridot and hunter greens of the forest—and the gold of the sun shining through the trees are, to me, natural choices for Beltane.

Incenses, Herbs, and Woods

Incenses used for Beltane should be intoxicating, heady, and erotic. Rose, jasmine, ylang ylang, peach, musk, and vanilla are all appropriate.

If you want to use herbs to make an incense or spell powder or to throw on the fire, woodruff, fern, rose, chamomile, wormwood, and galangal come to mind.

Often you will read about the nine sacred woods used in kindling the balefire. Obviously, the trees should all have strong connections to magick, but substitutions can be made depending on where you live.

Oak would be the first choice, the backbone of the fire, so to speak. To that add eight other types of wood. Any and all of these are acceptable: apple, hawthorn, birch, elder, ash, thorn (blackthorn), grape vine, rowan (also known as mountain ash), holly, willow, cedar, yew, and hemlock.

The Balefire

A large bonfire, known as the balefire (from Bel, the Celtic God of Light) or the need-fire, is one of the oldest traditions on Beltane. Originally used for sacrifices to get the attention of the Gods, we can retain the old symbolism while keeping within modern ethical standards.

When you lay your fire, use nine of the sacred woods. Try to use as little lighter fluid, et cetera, as you can to retain the integrity of the magic.

Make a big batch of incense to go in the fire—chamomile and wormwood, rose petals and jasmine flowers, galangal and dragon's blood. Wrap in a white linen cloth and tie with purple and green cords. When the balefire is roaring, toss the bundle into the fire and watch the herbs spark as the flames release their magic.

If you happen to own cattle or other livestock, build two fires and drive your cattle between them on Walpurgis Night. This helps protect them from disease and theft for the coming year.

Make a wicker man earlier in the month and when the flames are highest, toss him into the fire to represent all that you wish to purge from your life.

When only the embers are left, shed any clothing that might drape low enough to catch the flames and take turns jumping the balefire—make a wish and then run and leap over the embers. If you and your partner want a child, focus on fertility and jump hand-in-hand, then withdraw to a bower to begin work on the project!

Celebrating Fertility in the Modern Age

On Beltane night it was traditional for young men and women to slip away into the woods and have sex. Any children conceived at this time were known as merry-begets, and were considered children of the Gods.

In this age of rape, AIDS, and sexually-transmitted diseases, we must be careful. Remember: just because someone is Pagan doesn't mean they're a nice person. There are psychos in all religions and ours is no exception. And just because someone is Pagan doesn't exclude them from carrying something you don't want to catch.

I was at a Pagan gathering a few years ago where a man would not leave me alone. He followed me around, tried to touch me when I didn't want his attention, kept saying he felt karmically linked to me and wouldn't accept the fact that I was married, monogamous, and not interested—until a friend and I confronted him. Sadly, that ended my naïveté about the safety of Pagan festivals, and now when I go to public festivals I'm always on guard.

Unplanned pregnancy is another very real, very endemic problem in the Pagan community as well as America in general. For the sake of the women who end up raising those children alone, for the sake of the Earth, who can't support many more people, we must be responsible and use birth control every time we have sex, unless we have planned out a pregnancy. We don't have time to undo the damage already inflicted because of overpopulation, but we can slow down the rate. Celebrating the fertility of the Earth doesn't mean we all need to bear children—there are many species whose babies are just as cute as our own and they are losing the battle against extinction.

If we just remember a few simple rules, then we can enjoy the sensuality of the season. Remember:

Condoms, Mutual Consent, Awareness

Bowers of Love and Lust

It's fun to create bowers for outdoor Beltane celebrations. If you have a large private area in which to celebrate, take small tents or tarps and discreetly place them in the woods. Decorate with flowers and ribbons, and place a bowl of different colored and textured condoms in the tent next to a small plastic sack for the used love tokens. Add vases of flowers, wreaths, and the like. Mark the bowers and have a sign for when they're being used.

Remember, it's nobody's business who uses the bower except those directly involved. On the same note, if you run off to the bower with someone other than your regular partner, it's only respectful to have your partner's permission first—use your common sense, and then have fun!

Daisy Chains and Flower Wreaths

Daisy chains and flower wreaths are fun to make and require little else save long-stemmed flowers, floral tape, and scissors. It's especially fun to gather a group of girls and women and sit on a hill in the sun while fashioning the headdresses.

If you want to make weaving the chain easier, bring floral wire and measure a piece that will fit securely around your head. Twist the ends together.

Begin with a base of daisies or carnations—they have long stems and hold up well. Twist the stem around the floral wire and tape so that the flower is firmly in place. Add the next flower, close behind the first, and continue until your basic wreath is made.

Then add other touches—different flowers, ivy vines, you can weave in ribbons and bows. Use your imagination. Wear the wreaths all day, and after your ritual, toss them into the balefire as an offering to the Goddess.

Beltane Dew Ritual

A very old tradition involves waking up before sunrise on Beltane morning and washing your face in the dew from the grass and flowers. This promises that your beauty will grow strong during the coming year.

We held our wedding in an apple orchard and a group of our friends camped out with us there on Walpurgis Night. At six o'clock on Beltane morning, I led all the women to run naked through the orchard, rolling in the dew, while the men were banished inside the tents. It was cold and raining, but the grass sparkled and our skins turned blushing red from the chill. It was fun and I'm glad we didn't let the opportunity go by.

Beltane Games

It's easy to think of Beltane games for children, but games for adults prove a bit more tricky. For one Beltane ritual, I came up with two games and they resulted in a lot of laughter, a bruised nose, ripped pants, and general mayhem.

Beltane Game 1: No Truth, Just Dare

Depending on how many people you expect at your gathering, cut three times that many slips of paper. On each paper write a suggestive, outrageous, or silly activity. During play, everyone forms a circle. The bowl of slips is passed, each person draws one and acts it out. The bowl goes around three times and at the end, people vote for the best performance and that person wins a small prize.

Examples:

> Kiss the third person on your left with your chin.
> Sing us an original song entitled "Ode To A Duck."
> Dance the fourth person on your right around the circle.
> Give us your impression of a scampering deer.

Beltane Game 2: Catch A Kiss

Men and women divide into separate groups. One by one, each woman tries to make it across a goal line a short distance away. All the men try to be the first to catch a kiss from her before she reaches her goal, but the other women block their way and try to shield her.

Then the tables are turned and the women try to be the first to catch kisses from the men.

This can be a rough game—rougher than football—so I urge you to wear clothing you don't care about and to exercise some caution around the others. It's not meant to be tackle football, though it easily winds up that way, with trying to beat out all your friends for kisses!

The Maypole

Perhaps nothing symbolizes Beltane so much as the Maypole, the origins of which lie in fertility and sex.

The Maypole represents the phallus of the God. The wreath around the top represents the vagina of the Goddess. As the Maypole is danced, the ribbons wind around the pole and the wreath lowers, symbolizing the Divine Marriage, the sexual union of God and Goddess.

To make your Maypole, find a very tall, slender tree. It must be straight and it should be at least twelve feet tall and eight to ten inches in diameter. Oak is ideal for the maypole, but use what is available to you. The men should cut down the tree and de-limb it. Always ask permission, and always leave something in return when you do this. You are taking a life, the tree feels pain and suffers even as it falls. So leave an offering of flowers, food and wine for the spirit of the tree and for the Goddess who nurtured it to life.

You need to decide how many people are going to be able to dance your tree. The taller the tree, the more dancers. At our wedding, we had two Maypoles, each with ribbons for twelve dancers. The number of ribbons (and dancers) should be even for best results.

Cut the top of the tree flat and then divide the number of ribbons you plan to have by two. Make that number of cross-cuts evenly on the top of the tree, approximately 3 inches deep.

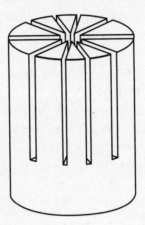

Prepare the top of your Maypole

For each ribbon, you will need at least seven yards (make it eight for extra slack) of 1-inch thick ribbons. (A fair estimate is two feet of ribbon for every foot of height of your pole. But it is advisable to always supply more ribbon than you think you'll need.) You can choose a variety of colors or you can coordinate them (for example, half the ribbons purple, half green). Tie a triple knot (so the knot is thick) six inches down from the top of each ribbon.

Slide the ribbons into the cross-cuts on the top of the tree. Do both sides of each cross-cut before moving onto the next one. The knots will keep the ribbons from sliding out of the cuts.

**Thread the ribbons through the
slits at the top of the pole**

**Knot the ribbons so
that they won't slip**

While the men prepare the Maypole, the women dig the hole, focusing on the womb of the Goddess, the passion that throbs under the soil.

The men lift the Maypole into the hole and everyone cheers as the women fill in the dirt and pack it down.

The women should have already prepared the flower wreath that will sit atop the ribbons.

When it is time for the dance and the ribbons are outstretched and the dancers are ready, one person will scurry up a tall ladder and place the wreath over the pole to rest on the taut ribbons. The opening of the wreath should not be more than twelve inches wider than the tree, so that it rides the ribbons down as the dance progresses.

Dancing the Maypole

Whether you incorporate it as part of your ritual or as a fun activity during the day, dancing the Maypole is easier than it looks. It just involves a simple set of starting instructions. It helps if you have two colors of ribbons and if those ribbons alternate.

Let's say your ribbons are purple and green.

When all dancers are in place, everyone holding a purple ribbon takes one step away from the Maypole and turns clockwise a quarter-rotation. They will be holding their ribbons in their right hands, which will be closest to the pole.

Everyone with green ribbons stays in place, holding their ribbons with their left hands.

As the dance starts, the dancers holding purple ribbons will weave under the first green ribbon held by the dancer they are facing, then over the next green ribbon. The purple ribbon holders will move clockwise, the green ribbon holders move counter-clockwise. Continue this movement until the pole has been wrapped with the ribbons. The dance stops when the weaving stops because everyone is flat against the pole. Tie off the ribbons and let the wreath finish dropping to the ground. Celebrate.

"Oak and Ash and Thorn"

Perhaps one of the best known songs sung at Pagan festivals and Beltane gatherings is a variation of Robert Burn's *Oak and Ash and Thorn*. The well-known verse goes:

> Oh, do not tell the priest of our Art
> For he would call it a sin
> But we shall be out in the woods all night
> A-conjuring summer in!
> And we bring you news by word of mouth
> For women, cattle and corn
> Now is the Sun come up from the South
> With Oak and Ash and Thorn.

What better song to sing when we go A-Maying than this beautiful melody from by-gone days?

The Beltane Ritual

This ritual is for a larger group (at least eight participants). The Maypole should be up and ready to dance. The bonfire should be laid and ready to torch. A second, smaller fire needs to be burning off to one side at the beginning of the ritual. The May Wine should already be made and ready to drink. (In other words, advance preparation is the key here).

Decorate the altar with flowers, grapes, strawberries, chocolate, ivy, and antlers. In addition, add a small bowl filled with the exact number of beans as there are women of the Maiden (past puberty) and Mother age groups in the ritual. All of these beans except one should be white, the other red.

You will also need a plate with the same number of cookies on it as there are men of the Phallic Lord (past puberty) and Green Lord age groups in the ritual. One of the cookies will contain a whole almond (add to dough before you bake).

All the women should help make a special wreath or veil for the Queen of the May and all the men should help make an antlered (if possible) or ivy headdress for the Consort.

Everyone should bring a small gift or token to adorn the May Queen (like a simple necklace or crystal), and a small gift or token to adorn her Consort. Each person should also have a cluster of grasses and weeds tied together that represents all they wish to purge from their lives from Beltane until Samhain (each cluster should have a long string attached to it), their ritual costumes, flower wreaths for the women, and ivy wreaths for the men.

The ritual should begin in the late afternoon.

Everyone gathers and the women and men separate and go off to dress and ornament themselves.

When everyone is ready, gather in the main ritual area and cast a circle. Invoke the directions as usual.

PST: **Queen Mab, Lady of Faerie, come to our ritual. You who are the sparkle of light on twilight's eve, You who are the flicker of green fire in the forest! Dance into our midst, Faerie Queen, and join our Beltane rites. Revel with us, bring passion to our lips and joy to our hearts! Queen Mab, welcome, and Blesséd be!**

PT: **Pan, Lord of the Wilding Night, come to our ritual. You who are passion's Lord and panic's Master! You who dance through the fields under the moonlight! Sweep down into**

our celebration and revel with us, bring the dance to our feet and joy to our hearts! Pan, welcome and Blesséd be!

PST: 'Tis Beltane and once again time to shed the cares of the past. We choose now the burry-man, to carry off our worries and fears and cares. The burry-man is a Fool, who shall also be King. Who shall be the burry-man?

All: Who shall be the burry-man?!

All the men form a line, with the Priest at the end. The Priestess lifts up the plate of cookies.

PST: The Gods choose!

Pass out cookies. Each man who is of age, ending with the Priest, takes one cookie and holds onto it.

PST: Who has the talisman?

The men bite into their cookies. The man who discovers the almond in his cookie lifts his hand in the air.

Man: I have the talisman!

PST: The burry-man! We have the burry-man!

All: The burry-man! We have the burry-man!

Everyone brings out their bundle of weeds and grasses and ties it onto the man—either onto his legs or arms or side or through a belt loop. No one should knot their bundle too tightly. When everyone is done, the burry-man steps away from the group.

PST: Drive the burry-man out of the village!

Everyone drives him over to the second fire and then chases him around it three times.

All: The burry-man! Begone, take our cares and woes away! Begone you worry-burry man! Drive our cares out of the village! *(They continue, shouting similar statements.)*

When the burry-man has run around the fire three times, he stops and everyone else backs away to the ritual area again.

Bmn: **I cast the woes and cares and worries into the ever-purifying flames! Begone from our lives!** *(He unties all the weeds and throws them into the fire, then shakes off his clothing and returns to the ritual area.)*

PST: **The burry-man has freed us from our cares! The Fool has become King for a Night!**

All: **The Fool is dead, long live the King!** *(etc.)*

PT: **Now to the Queen of the May! Who shall be the Queen of the May?** *(Holds up dish of beans.)*

All: **Who shall be the Queen of the May?**

PT: **The Gods decide!**

All the women who are of age line up and close their eyes. The Priest goes from woman to woman with the dish of beans, ending with the Priestess. Each woman takes one bean in her hand, but does not yet look at it.

PT: **Who has the talisman?**

The women look at their beans. The woman with the red bean is the May Queen.

Wom: **I have the talisman!**

PT: **The May Queen! We have the Queen of the May!**

All: **The May Queen! We have the Queen of the May!**

The May Queen and the Burry-man/Consort step into the center of the circle. Everyone brings out their gifts and tokens and adorns them. The Priest picks up the May Queen wreath.

PT: *(Kneels at May Queen's feet.)* **Lady, you are the Queen of the May. Your every wish is our command. You rule over our celebration this night.** *(He stands and crowns her with the wreath.)* **All hail the Queen of the May!**

All: **Hail the Queen of the May!**

PST: *(Picks up Consort's headdress.)* **Fool no longer, you are the Consort of the Lady this night. Every soul serves the Queen of the May and she alone serves you.** *(She stands and crowns him with the headdress.)* **All hail the Sacred Consort!**

All: **Hail the Sacred Consort!**

QM: **To the Maypole!**

The Queen of the May and the Consort lead everyone in dancing the Maypole. After the dance, light the bonfire, toss in the herbs, bring out the wine, drum, dance and celebrate. During the evening, everyone—including the Consort—serves the May Queen, but she alone waits on the Consort. When the party is ready to fold, everyone regroups near the altar.

PST: **And so Beltane is over for another year.** *(She turns to the Consort.)* **Fool for a Day, King for a Night, now you return to your daily life!** *(He kneels and she removes the headdress.)*

PT: *(Turns to the May Queen.)* **Queen of the May no more shall you be, from your sacred office I set you free!** *(She kneels and he removes the wreath.)*

PST: **Queen Mab, Lady of Faerie! Thank you for attending our rites. Go if You must, stay if You will. Hail, farewell and Blesséd be!**

PT: **Pan of Field and Forest! Thank you for attending our rites. Go if You must, stay if You will. Hail, farewell and Blesséd be!**

Devoke elements and open the circle. The May Queen and the Consort keep their headdresses and their gifts as reminders of this night.

When the ritual ends, make sure the fires are thoroughly out, leave no mess in the wild space to abuse the Lady, then tumble home and dream of the Gods.

Food and Recipes

May Wine

1	cup sweet woodruff	1	cup sugar
2	bottles rosé wine	½	cup white rum
4	dozen rose petal ice cubes	2	bottles champagne
1	quart strawberries	1	bottle white wine
1	quart chopped peaches	1	liter lemon-lime soda

Two weeks before serving: clean woodruff and pack into one bottle of wine. Cork and let sit.

The day before serving: Make four-dozen ice cubes by placing rose petals in the compartments before adding water. Freeze until solid.

Hull and wash strawberries. Slice. Mix peaches and strawberries. Add sugar and rum. Marinate overnight.

An hour before serving: Strain woodruff out of wine and discard leaves. Mix champagne, all remaining wine, 7-Up, and fruit in a large silver bowl. Stir.

Add ice cubes fifteen minutes before serving.

Serves about 20.

Lemon Poundcake

1	cup butter	1	tablespoon grated lemon zest
1½	cups sugar		
3	eggs	2½	cups flour
½	cup milk	2	teaspoons baking powder
2	tablespoons lemon flavoring	½	teaspoon salt
5	drops yellow food coloring	½	teaspoon nutmeg

Preheat oven to 325 degrees. Cream butter and sugar. Add eggs one at a time, beating after every addition. Beat in milk, lemon flavoring, food coloring, and lemon zest.

Sift flour, baking powder, salt, and nutmeg.

Slowly add flour mixture to butter mixture.

Beat for 2 minutes on medium speed.

Pour into greased loaf pan and bake for 50–60 minutes, until toothpick inserted in center comes out clean. Cool.

Slice into thin slices.

Serves 12.

Raspberry Glaze

2   tablespoons butter
1   tablespoon orange juice
    concentrate
2   teaspoons lemon juice
½   cup water

½   cup sugar
½   teaspoon nutmeg
2   cups raspberries,
    lightly crushed

Melt butter in heavy skillet over medium heat. Add orange juice concentrate, lemon juice, water, and sugar. Stir until sugar dissolves. Add nutmeg and raspberries. Cook over low heat until slightly thickened. Chill. Pour over slices of lemon poundcake.

LITHA

The Festival of Growth

Summer nights so warm you can sleep under the stars, heady-scented roses shimmering in the moonlight, the sparkling water of a forest pond beckons, cool gauze dresses and sunglasses, ice cream melting under the noonday sun . . . today is Midsummer's Eve, the day before Litha, and the season of growth is upon us.

Litha is the season of expansion, when the crops burgeon forth. We forget winter's cares and spend our days basking under the brilliant light. The Summer Solstice brings us the longest day of the year—the zenith of the Sun King, and also His death as the Holly King dethrones him and takes reign over the now waning year. From now until Yule, the light will fade into darkness.

This is the time of lovers and gardeners. The rutting fervor of Beltane has deepened into the passionate eroticism that grows when partners become familiar with one another's rhythms and moods. It is the love between those committed by heart as well as body, it is also the love of parents for their children (be they two or four-legged). Nature is at her most fecund and everywhere we look ripeness spills out from field and forest.

Litha is the height of the Divine Marriage, then the Oak King falls, His vigor and prime giving way to the sagacity of the Holly King even as the Goddess prepares Herself for harvest and Cronehood.

The actual date varies from year-to-year, as with the Winter Solstice and the two equinoxes. Litha usually falls on June 20 or 21. Once again, check your almanac for the actual date in your time zone.

We also celebrate Midsummer's Eve, the day when the Faerie Realm is most strongly connected to our own world. Though all Sabbats (especially Beltane and Ostara) have some connection with the Faerie Realm, on Midsummer's Eve the denizens of Faerie enter our own, ruling the night before the Solstice.

The realm of Faerie is a realm of power and inspiring strength. All too often the inhabitants are infantalized, dis-empowered by those who would represent them with gentle, Victorian images of child-like beings. History, legend, and the reality of those who work with that realm prove the Faerie quite different.

While there are helpful and ambitious faeries who may fit the Victorian image, the majority of Faerie Folk are wild, chaotic beings, ranging from mischievous to terrifying, from awe-inspiring in their beauty to hideous.

Faeries don't play by human rules; they don't live by our ethics. We only have to look at the history of the Kelpie, the Black Annis, and Jenny Greenteeth to know that.

These are beings of the elements, with a connection to the natural world so strong that we cannot even begin to fathom it. Earth, air, fire, and water—all have their Faerie Folk. We give them names, but they were there long before humans walked on the planet.

So on Midsummer's Eve we honor the Faerie Realm and then, on the morning of the Solstice, we rejoice in the season of abundance even as we mourn the passing of the Oak King.

On May 2, as the Beltane interlude ends, my husband and I take down the Beltane altar and purify and cleanse the altar table. We put up the summer pictures of Mielikki and Tapio and the summer collage.

Our summer altar cloth is covered with sunflowers. Over this we drape a large square of gold lace. Decorations include a sphere of orange calcite to represent the sun, an antler-handled bronze sickle, antlers, an ivy garland made of silk, a green pillar candle, a crystal bowl of Full Moon Water (see Appendix One, page 277) tinted with turquoise food coloring to represent a wishing well, and a decanter of mead.

We bless and consecrate the altar. To finish our celebration of the change-over of seasons, we like to watch *The Secret Garden* and *The Secret of Roan Inish*.

The Colors of Litha

Gold and green are two of the most prevalent colors this time of year. Not only do they represent the sun and the verdant forest, but they represent the colors of Faerie Fire Magic. Other color accents include sea green and red (especially when red roses are added to the altar).

Incenses, Herbs, and Woods

Incense should be full and robust—rose, violet, fir, and cedar are good. Tangerine, frankincense, and frangipani also work.

If you want to work with herbs at this time, St. John's wort is one of the most popular associated with Litha. Also connected with the holiday: basil, parsley, mint, thyme, violet, dragon's blood, fern, vervain, and lavender.

Woods of Midsummer include oak, fir, mistletoe, and holly.

Midsummer's Fires

Instead of nine sacred woods being used, these were kindled of oak and fir. The midsummer fires were used much like the balefires, to hex the cattle for health and safety, to drive away baneful influences and they also represented the power of the sun at its zenith.

The Summer Tree

A curious Litha custom includes cutting down a fir tree and decorating it in ways similar to the Yule Tree. Decorations include ribbons, colored eggs, hoops, bows, garlands of flowers, and bells.

On the night of Litha, the summer tree was thrown into the fire and burned.

If you want to practice this custom without cutting down a tree, gather a few fir branches (or if you own your own home, you can plant a fir tree in your yard and decorate it every summer, cutting one branch to go into the fire instead of burning the whole tree) and weave them into a wreath, decorate the wreath, and then burn it instead of the actual tree.

In retrospect, this custom makes sense when we think of the balance. If we burn a Yule Tree at Midwinter to represent the return of the light, shouldn't we burn one at Midsummer to represent the waning of the light?

Jack-in-the-Green

Sometimes invoked during Beltane, other times at Litha, the spirit of Jack-in-the-Green represents the spirit of the vegetation god.

You can make a full-sized Jack-in-the-Green or a smaller representation and use it for decoration on your altar, then return it to the Earth or burn it at Lughnasadh.

If you opt for a full-sized figure, follow the idea in the chapter on Ostara for making the Green Man (another symbol of the vegetation god, see page 68). Or you can have someone play out the role, as was commonly done throughout Britain during the mummer's dances.

If you have someone enact the role of Jack-in-the-Green, create a wicker or grape vine frame that can rest on his (it should be a man) shoulders, leaving a wide enough hole at the top for his head to easily slide through after the addition of the foliage. Then weave a light layer of branches and ivy through the framework in a cone-shaped manner. You can then make a mask out of moss and a crown of ivy to cover the man's face.

Have him wear this during the Litha celebration and then keep the framework in a dry place and burn it at Lughnasadh.

To make a miniature Jack-in-the-Green, make a simple framework of thin branches and fill with cedar, ivy, oak, and other foliage. Set on your altar and then keep dry until Lughnasadh.

If you can't have a Lughnasadh fire, simply disassemble the figures and return the foliage to the Earth at that time.

Bees, Honey, and Mead

June is the month of the Mead Moon. What better drink with which to celebrate the intoxication of faerie and forest than the nectar of bees?

Honey has a long history of sacred correlations and is connected to many goddesses. The bee is sacred not only to the Great Mother, but to Mielikki, Cybele, Hannahannas, Freya, and a number of flower-goddesses.

A number of marriages and pairings took place shortly after Beltane, and the couples were given mead to drink for one month after the wedding to insure fertility. The month during which they drank this was known as the honey moon, (i.e., Mead Moon) and this is where we get our modern concept of the honeymoon.

Mead is the mixture of honey, yeast, and water. *Maser* is mead with the addition of fruit. *Metheglin* is mead with the addition of spices and/or herbs. If mead has both spices and fruit added to it, the result is still called metheglin.

There are a number of books written about brewing mead, should you decide to try your hand at it. I have not dabbled in it as of yet, but I did enlist a friend who makes the most incredible mead to help me when my Lady Mielikki voiced (during meditation) a desire for a brew dedicated to Her specific design. The result, a metheglin with raspberry, lemon, cinnamon, and galangal, is the most gently intoxicating taste of autumn (Mielikki's season) we've ever encountered!

A Honey Spell for Beauty

Summer is a time of beauty, and honey is a food connected with beauty, both inner and outer. This is a simple spell to perform on Midsummer's Eve and you can enchant enough honey to last through the year until the next summer! You can double or triple the ingredients depending on how much you think you'll be using.

On the Full Moon before Midsummer's Eve, gather the following ingredients:

1   pound honey
1   sliced vanilla bean
1   tablespoon grated orange zest
1   inch sliced ginger root
1   teaspoon cinnamon

In heavy pan, stir together all ingredients. Stir over medium-low heat for twenty minutes. Strain into pretty jar with a tight lid. Store until Midsummer's Eve.

Near dusk on Midsummer's Eve, take your honey, a fifth of apple brandy, a hand mirror and your hairbrush outside (if it's raining, you can perform this at your Litha altar).

Set up the mirror on a tree stump or rock so you can see yourself in it. Place the honey jar, the apple brandy and the brush on the rock with the mirror.

Cast a circle and invoke the elements. Say:

> **Queen Mab, Queen of Faerie, Your blessing I ask**
> **Reflect Your beauty in my looking glass.**

Look into the mirror and see your unique beauty. Say:

> **Like honey my words will both charm and enchant**
> **Stirring memories of wine and the labyrinth dance.**

Eat one teaspoon of the honey and hear the sweet sounds of your voice. Say:

> **Like brandy my presence bewitches and glows**
> **With elegance, strength and the power of poise.**

Drink one teaspoon of the brandy and feel your carriage shift, your posture straighten and your demeanor take on an other-worldly refinement. Say:

> **Be it shorter or longer, I find in my hair**
> **The power of beauty, my looks they are fair.**

Take up brush and brush hair, feeling the strength of your beauty ripple from your inner core to radiate through your body and in your face.

Meditate on your individual and unique beauty, comparing yourself to no one, and then close the spell saying:

> **Queen Mab, Queen of Faerie, bless my mirror and my brush,**
> **To my lips bring bright crimson, to my cheeks, a fair blush,**
> **To the honey bring charm and the power of song,**
> **To the brandy bring strength for the winter so long,**
> **To my heart bring both courage and the power to see**
> **The beauty and glamour belonging only to me.**
> **Blesséd be.**

Devoke the elements and open the circle. Take the honey and brandy and keep them on your personal altar or on your vanity table with your brush and mirror. Each evening before bed, eat one spoonful of the honey, and drink one spoonful of the brandy.

The Flowers of Midsummer

Flowers abound at this time of year and there are many ways we can tap into their energies and powers besides just using them to ornament our houses.

Marigolds are a natural pest-control for the garden, driving away several types of insects. Plant them around the borders of your vegetable garden and watch the plants thrive. Violets can be candied and used to decorate wedding cakes. Nasturtiums are both spicy and colorful additions to salads. Nothing cools at the end of a hot summer day like iced mint tea or a mint julep . . . and why not add a spring of lavender to your drink? It's both pretty and flavorful.

Make sure that when you use a flower for consumption that it's both edible (there are poisonous flowers like foxglove and the buttercup) and free from pesticides. Always wash them before eating or using in a recipe.

Rose Petal Chamomile Jelly

4 cups tightly packed rose petals
2 tablespoons chamomile
3½ cups boiling water
1 package dry fruit pectin
4 cups sugar

Clean rose petals. Blend with chamomile in a large enamel or stainless steel bowl. Pour boiling water over petals, making sure they are saturated, and cover bowl. Let stand for one hour. Strain, squeezing petals to get all of the liquid out of them. Discard petals and strain liquid again.

In large enamel pot, stir pectin into rose water. Bring to a boil. Add sugar all at once. Bring mixture to a rolling boil, stirring constantly. Boil for one minute exactly.

Remove from heat. Skim foam from top (good to eat, just put in a little saucer). Pour jelly into clean, hot jars and seal with paraffin or according to canning instructions.

Makes about 5 cups.

The color of the jelly will depend on the color of the roses—the whiter the rose, the paler the jelly. Deep red roses make a dusky rose jelly. Rose petal jelly is a treat and the flavor reminds me of a very delicate strawberry.

Protection Charms

Midsummer is a good time to fashion protection charms for your house and car. Simple charms can be made by harvesting a small sprig of rowan tree or mistletoe and tying a red ribbon around the branch. Charge by visualizing protective energy and focusing it into the wood (both contain protective energy), then hang the charm in your doorway or over a window. Ask the Goddess to bless and protect your house.

Picnics and Hoe-Downs

What better way to celebrate Midsummer than with a Pagan-oriented barbecue and picnic? Picnics can be romantic getaways for two (with a wicker basket, china and crystal, cold roast duck, grapes, and tarragon biscuits) or they can be family affairs (fried chicken, watermelon, and chocolate cake), or more extensive parties with barbecued ribs and chickens, corn on the cob, fruit salad, cakes, and cookies.

For a change put together a clam-bake on the beach or a Hawaiian luau (please look into the traditional styles of this, the tourist-hotel versions can be an insult to the native culture).

After everyone is satiated, light the fire, bring out the drums and music-makers, and put on those dancing shoes!

The Litha Oak King/Holly King Ritual

This ritual, taking place at sunrise on the Summer Solstice, requires some advance planning and practice, but is a striking ritual to perform.

One man will represent the Holly King and one man the Oak King. If they are married, their wives will represent the Oak and Holly wives, if not, then choose other women from your group for these parts.

One woman will represent the Goddess Arianrhod. The Priestess leads the ritual.

The rest of the participants join in when they are called to do so.

Lay a bonfire ready for the torch.

A little before sunrise, the Oak and Holly Wives go through the woods or around the ritual space, one with a small gong, the other with a drum, and call everyone to the ritual.

The Oak Wife should be dressed in full summer regalia, with a wreath of red roses around her head. The Holly wife should wear a traditional winter dress and a wreath of white roses. The Priestess wears black with gold accents and a simple gold head circlet.

As everyone files into the circle, the Priestess hands them a small oak branch tied with a red ribbon.

The circle is triple cast by the Oak Wife, the Holly Wife, and the Priestess.

OW: **I cast this circle in the name of the Oak King, Lord of the Summer, may His fiery breath surround and protect us.**

HW: **I cast this circle in the name of the Holly King, Lord of the Winter, may His icy breath surround and protect us.**

PST: **I cast this circle in the name of Arianrhod, Goddess of the Silver Wheel, may She balance all elements and bind the light and the dark.**

When the circle is cast, the Oak and Holly Wives move to the side and the Priestess stands in the center of the circle.

PST: **We gather to witness the zenith of the Oak King even as He relinquishes His throne and gives way to the Waning Year. We celebrate His life and His death, and call upon the Goddess Arianrhod to balance the brilliance and the shadow.**

OW: *(Turns to the south.)* **I call you, element of Fire, you who are the Summer Sun and the mighty Oak! I call you, element of vitality and growth. Power of life, light, abundance and action, come to our circle and join our rites! Blesséd be.**

HW: *(Turns to the north.)* **I call you, element of Ice, you who are the Winter Moon and the stalwart Holly! I call you, element of restraint and barren lands. Power of death, shadow, sagacity and thought, come to our circle and join our rites! Blesséd be.**

PST: *(Turns to the east.)* **I call you, element of Balance, you who are the Silver Wheel upon which turns the cycle of the Year! On but four days do you touch the world, two days of balance and two days when the elements wage war for that balance. On this, Midsummer, when Light spreads across the land, when Shadow rises to do battle in their age-old conflict, come to our circle and join our rites. Blesséd be.**

After a moment of silence, the Oak Wife raises her hands to the south.

OW: **Oak King, Lord of the Greenwood, come to this circle to meet Your challenge, You who shine Your light throughout our lands and bring life to the Lady's forests and fields! Come, my husband of Summer, be with us now.**

The Oak King enters the circle from the south. He wears a crown of Oak and Ivy, and his clothing is green and gold. He carries a staff adorned with gold accents. He enters the circle and stands by the Oak Wife. The Holly Wife raises her hands to the north.

HW: **Holly King, Lord of the Winterwood, come to this circle to give Your challenge, You who glaze the lands with ice as the Lady's forests and fields slumber under Your kiss. Come, my husband of Winter, be with us now.**

The Holly King enters the circle from the North. His clothing is of green and silver. He carries an identical staff to the Oak King, except the accents are silver. He enters the circle and stands by the Holly Wife. The Priestess raises her hands to the east.

PST: **Arianrhod, Goddess of the Silver Wheel, come to this circle to keep the balance, You who dwell in Caer Arianrhod as You watch over the world. Come, Lady of the ever-turning Wheel, be with us now.**

Arianrhod enters the circle from the east. She wears a black dress and is cloaked in a black veil, with accents of silver. The Oak and Holly Wives and the Priestess retreat to the edge of the circle. Arianrhod stands at the eastern quarter, watching.

HK: **I raise my staff in challenge, Lord of the Oak! I claim the right to ascend the throne. Will you meet me in battle?**

OK: **I raise my staff in answer to Your challenge, Lord of the Holly. I fight to keep the throne!**

The Oak King and Holly King engage in a pre-choreographed battle. After a few moments, the Holly King lands the decisive blow and the Oak King drops to the ground. The Holly King picks up the Oak King's crown and hangs it on his belt. He then parades victorious around the circle, bellowing out his triumph.

HK: **I have slain my brother! For six months I will rule over the Waning Year. The Holly is King of the Forest once again!**

Arianrhod kneels by the Oak King and drapes a sheer black veil over his head and shoulders. He stands and she leads him towards the west. Before they leave the circle Arianrhod turns to the Holly King.

AR: **You have won the battle, King of Holly. But remember that you have only gained your kingdom for half-a-year. Your brother will be born again on Midwinter and there he will challenge you and you will lose your crown once more.**

The Oak King turns to the Holly King, still veiled.

OK: **I have relinquished my throne for now; but Yule will come again and there I will challenge you on the field. Until that day I dwell in Caer Arianrhod, the castle of the ever-turning Silver Wheel.**

As Arianrhod leads the Oak King west, out of the circle, the Oak Wife starts to mourn and wail. Everyone joins in.

OW: **The Oak King sleeps in the arms of the Goddess! Mourn my Lord, the King of the Waxing Year!**

As Arianrhod and the Oak King disappear from sight, the Holly Wife begins to cheer for the Holly King. Everyone joins in as he parades around the Circle.

HW: **The Holly King lives again! Hail the Lord of the Waning Year!**

The Oak Wife lights the bonfire.

HK: **Be not saddened, for though my season is barren and some-times harsh, it is a beautiful time. Frost kisses the fields with delicate lace, trees color the forest with their flame-dipped leaves, snowflakes drift down to gently blanket the fields that they might sleep and rest after the season of growth. Icy is my grip, and chill my breath, but we shall also rejoice in our Yule celebrations and I will welcome my brother's rebirth, even as I prepare for battle.**

He holds up the Oak King's crown.

HK: **The King is dead!** *(Throws crown into fire.)*

The Holly Wife presents the Holly King with a crown of holly and He takes it and places it on His head.

OW: **Long live the King!**

A drummer starts a simple, consistent single-beat. The Oak Wife kneels at the Holly King's feet.

OW: **You have vanquished my Lord of the Oak, thus the balance is maintained. I recognize your reign over the Waning Half of the Year. As proof of your power, I cast my token of summer into the fire and accept the coming seasons for what the Goddess means them to be.**

She tosses her oak branch in the bonfire, then the Holly King gives her a holly branch tied with a green ribbon for protection during the coming months. The Holly Wife follows suit, then the Priestess, who leads the rest of the circle in a line. Arianrhod and the Oak King slip in at the end of the line, just before the drummer, and toss their branches in the fire as their turns come. When everyone has tossed their oak in the fire then the Oak King, still veiled, joins the Holly King in the center of the circle, with Arianrhod between them.

PST: **So the balance is struck. Light for dark and dark for light. Fire and ice. Summer into Winter. As it has always been in our lands, it shall always be. The Oak fades as the Holly rises. Midwinter they shall exchange places and the cycle begin anew. So Mote It Be.**

Together, the Oak and Holly Wives sweep the circle open with their brooms, and the Holly King, Oak King, and Arianrhod lead the way out.

After the circle is empty, the Oak and Holly Kings and Wives, Arianrhod and the Priestess should gather and take a few minutes to formally devoke any lingering energies that might tie them to their respective "parts."

Food and Recipes

Herbed Butter for Corn and Biscuits

3   tablespoons olive oil   1   teaspoon basil
1   teaspoon tarragon   1   tablespoon orange zest
1   teaspoon spearmint   1   cup softened butter

Heat olive oil in a small skillet over medium heat. When hot, add herbs and zest. Sauté 5 minutes, stirring constantly. Remove from heat and allow to cool.

Using spatula, incorporate olive oil and herb mixture into butter, stirring to thoroughly blend.

Serve with corn or biscuits.

Snow on the Sun

2   large beefsteak   ½   teaspoon crushed black
    tomatoes   peppercorns
6   teaspoons olive oil   6   slices french bread
½   teaspoon tarragon   6   slices mozzarella
½   teaspoon parsley   Parmesan

Preheat broiler. Remove stem end of tomatoes. Cut into three slices each, saving the very end pieces for another use.

Blend olive oil and herbs. Brush bread slices with mixture.

Place slice of tomato on slice of bread and top with mozzarella.

Broil until mozzarella just starts to brown and bubble.

Serve with parmesan.

Serves 6.

Champagne Sorbet

3 cups lightly crushed raspberries	1 tablespoon lemon juice
2 tablespoons sugar	2 tablespoons orange juice
1½ cups white wine	3 tablespoons Framboise
1½ cup water	2 cups champagne
¾ cup sugar	3 teaspoons orange zest

Rinse raspberries and mix with 2 tablespoons sugar and the white wine. Cover and chill.

Combine water, ¾ cup sugar, and zest over medium-high heat. Bring to a boil and reduce heat to low. Add juices and Framboise. Stir, remove from heat, and chill for three hours.

Add champagne to the sugar mixture. Pour into 8-inch pan. Freeze until slush has formed.

Process in blender until smooth. Pour back into pan and freeze until frozen.

Scoop sorbet into goblets and top with raspberry mixture.

Serves 8.

Part 4

autumn

Lughnasadh • Mabon

LUGHNASADH

The Festival of Sacrifice

The golden glow of late summer sun, the tang of early morning that tells you autumn will soon be here, the scent of dill and mustard seed and pickle brine, the first ears from the corn patch, tomatoes so ripe they burst when you touch them . . . it is August 1, the Festival of Lughnasadh (pronounced Loo'-na-sah).

Lughnasadh is the Celtic festival dedicated to the God Lugh, the Long Handed, who is associated with light and fire. The festival is also considered to be the first harvest, the harvest of the grain, and is linked to the God/Spirit of the Corn, personified by the name John Barleycorn. In Lammas, the Christianized version of Lughnasadh, we see a strong connection to the sacrifice of the corn god, for Lammas means *loaf mass*, what one might consider a requiem for the grain.

Lughnasadh, celebrated on August 1, is the season during which the God of Grain is sacrificed that the harvest might take place and thus the people can live through the coming seasons of autumn and winter. Once again it is a time of cleansing, it is time to clear your house for the approaching Autumn, for the waning of the year.

In magickal terms, the Oak King journeys deep into the underworld where He will rest until Yule. The Holly King increases His grasp over the season as the days grow shorter. As the fruits of the

111

Lady ripen, She becomes the Dark Goddess, the Crone, who sacrifices the God of Corn that the people might live.

We consider Lughnasadh to be the end of summer and the beginning of Autumn.

On July 31, I make a batch of creamed corn bread and bake it in a man-shaped pan, turning it onto a tray when it's done. We decorate the corn man with holly and ivy and give him blackberry eyes and raisin genitals, and that evening we behead him with the antler-handled sickle that sits on the summer altar. We sacrifice his head at the offering shrine, then eat the rest of the corn bread for dinner, along with wine to represent the blood of the God.

We retain the same altar as for Litha, but remove the wishing well bowl and the ivy vine to leave the altar a brilliant gold. We add bright ears of yellow corn and a bowl of dark blackberries (if they aren't yet in season, I buy frozen ones and use those), and I also might add a few peaches or apricots.

We then prepare ourselves for the Lughnasadh ritual the next day.

Creamed Corn Bread

2	cups yellow corn meal	2	eggs
1½	cups all-purpose flour	½	cup milk
½	teaspoon salt	½	cup oil
½	cup sugar	1	cup creamed corn
2	tablespoons baking powder		

Preheat oven to 350 degrees. Stir corn meal, flour, salt, sugar, and baking powder together. Form a well in center. Add eggs, milk, oil, and creamed corn to well. Mix to blend all ingredients but do not over-beat.

Pour into man-shaped pan and bake for 25–30 minutes until golden brown on top.

Serves 8 (after the head is severed in ritual.)

The Colors of Lughnasadh

Colors associated with Lughnasadh range from golds and yellows to black. Although we still see green, for the fields and trees have reached their full spectrum of foliage, the focus is on the yellows and golds of the corn, and the black of the Dark Mother.

Bone and tan (as in antler and bone ritual objects) accent this holiday nicely.

Incenses, Herbs, and Woods

Incenses for Lughnasadh include frankincense, heather, sandalwood, and copal.

A wide variety of herbs are associated with this time of year including sunflowers, rye, oats, corn, yarrow, dill, wheat, acorns (these are poisonous unless properly leached of their toxins), and hazelnuts.

Woods connected with the Sabbat include grape vine, hazel, and oak.

Blackberries

Blackberries are intricately linked with Lughnasadh, as is the berry known as bilberry (a dwarf blueberry). Both ripen at this time of year and both have been important food staples in history. With berries, one could make jam which would keep for long periods, or ferment them into wines.

I have long had a love affair with blackberries. Although I know they can quickly take over a plot of land and have to be pruned, I adore the huge bramble patches. The blackberry is a survivor, the spirit of this plant so hardy that almost nothing can destroy it. In return for the land it claims, the brambles return fruits sweeter than the most tempting chocolates.

One summer, some fourteen years ago, my then-partner and I were extremely poor. We had little to eat, we couldn't find work, and every day was filled with worry and hunger. Then the blackberries began to ripen.

Every day we would go out and pick blackberries.

I would stand in silence in the bramble patch, methodically picking berry after berry under the golden sun. After a few days of this, I began to notice a feeling of welcome from the brambles. I would enter the patch and immediately feel safe and protected, a feeling I didn't experience much in those days.

The droning of bees, the warmth of the sun, the smell of the berries all converged, creating a drowsy, trance-like state to which I willingly submitted. I listened to the whisperings of the plants, I felt the energy of the Bramble Lord, as I began to call him (it was definitely masculine), and I fell in love with the gentle, unshakable strength the blackberry possesses.

The berries kept us eating all summer. We didn't have much else, and we were still hungry, but somehow those buckets of berries sustained us through that rough patch and I have never forgotten the generosity of the plant—I don't know how many times I went out there to strip the vines, but there were always more the next time.

Cheesecake with Blackberry Sauce

2	(8-ounce) packages cream cheese	1	teaspoon vanilla
4	egg yolks	¼	teaspoon salt
1	cup whipping cream	1	graham-cracker crumb crust
½	cup honey		

Preheat oven to 325 degrees. Beat cream cheese, egg yolks, and whipping cream for 5 minutes on medium speed using electric mixer. Beat in honey in thin stream, then vanilla and salt.

Pour into crust and bake for 45 minutes. Remove and let cool. Serves 8.

Blackberry Sauce

3   cups very ripe blackberries
2   cups blackberry tea
3   tablespoons cornstarch
½   cup sugar

Wash and lightly crush blackberries. Drain juice into tea. Mix ½ cup blackberry tea (cold) with cornstarch and stir with a fork until cornstarch is dissolved.

Heat 1½ cups blackberry tea (and juice from berries) over med-low heat. Add sugar and stir to dissolve.

Slowly pour cornstarch mixture into tea and increase heat to medium. Stir constantly with wire whip. As mixture begins to bubble and thicken, add berries and whip to blend.

When mixture is thickened, remove from heat and chill. Spoon over slices of cheesecake.

The Corn Mother

The corn dolly made at Imbolc represents Brighid. At Lughnasadh you might choose to make another. She will represent the Corn Mother, the personification of the Goddess who watches over the harvest to see that it ripens.

If you grow your own corn, it is traditional that the Corn Mother be made from the last stalks to fall.

The Corn Mother should be placed in your barn or your pantry to ensure that your family doesn't go hungry during the coming autumn and winter.

A Garlic Braid

The season of colds and sniffles is a month or two away, but now is the time to hang up charms to ward off their influences (and to eat a healthy diet of fresh foods to ensure you are doing all you can for your health.).

A garlic braid in the kitchen will ward off disease.

An onion placed on the kitchen windowsill attracts illness and disease away from the family—don't eat the onion, but replace it with a new one when it starts withering away.

Don't put the onion in your compost pile, though. Toss it out in the woods away from your home or in a body of running water.

This is also the time to gather and dry herbs for winter. Tie in bundles and hang in a warm, dark place. When dry, strip and store in dark glass jars. Be sure to label your herbs—when they are dried, it's hard to tell the difference between some of the plants.

The Perseids Meteor Shower

During the second week of August each year we witness a beautiful, breath-taking display that embodies the wonder of the universe.

Each year, starting about August 8 and lasting for a week or so (check your almanac each year for exact dates), the Earth passes through the Perseids meteor showers. Every night, from dark until early dawn, meteors race through the sky, dazzling us with the most incredible fireworks display we could hope for.

The number of meteors racing through our atmosphere grows each night as the shower peaks, until they reach a rate of one or two a minute—or more.

Take a blanket and a friend or two outside on one of the peak nights and spend the evening watching the cosmic rain as it showers down its power and strength.

You'll soon find yourself shouting, "There's one!"

"Look at that one!"

My husband and I have fun competing to see who can spot the most meteors—he accuses me of using my magick to entice them into the corner of the sky that I'm watching. I laugh and thank him for having so much trust in the power of my Witchcraft.

While it's traditional to make a wish on every shooting star you see, I think that we have to be careful and not get too greedy during this time—make one or two charms and then when you see a meteor, focus the energy into the charm. That way you can capture the energy of the display without spreading your intent too thin.

Or just enjoy the show. You don't have to cast spells to actively experience magic—the sheer brilliance of the display is enough to set our hearts to fluttering. Anything more is just icing on the cake.

The Corn Sacrifice: Lughnasadh Ritual

A very intense ritual, the Corn Sacrifice focuses on the sacrifice of the John Barleycorn spirit.

For this ritual, everyone needs to bring a big bundle of corn, still in its husks. You will also need lots of ivy, sturdy grape vines, a sword or sickle, twine, a pitcher of burgundy, a small bottle of bourbon, and a hoe or shovel.

A bonfire should be burning at the beginning of the ritual (the ritual takes place outside).

Part 1

Much like the ritual for Ostara, everyone joins in building the Corn God out of corn, ivy, and twine on a grape vine frame. It should be life-sized or larger. While you are building John Barleycorn, focus on the coming harvest, the sacrifice of the grain that people might live through the winter, the sun that—while still golden—is waning in power, and the Dark Goddess who waits for the Spirit of the Corn God.

Part 2

When the Corn God is ready, everyone gathers in a circle near the bonfire. The corn God should rest on a stone or bench in the center. The ritual is led by the women of the group, since the harvest mysteries were most often performed by women.

Cast the circle and invoke the elements as you usually do.

PST: **We are here to mourn the passing of the Corn God and to welcome in Lughnasadh—the harvest of grain. Without the harvest, there would be no food and without food, the people would die.**

With her two Assistants, the Priestess kneels at the feet of the Corn figure.

PST: **Creature of corn thou art, creature of ivy and vine, now transform and become the Spirit of the Corn, the embodiment of the God who willingly goes to sacrifice that His body might sustain His people.**

AT1: **Thou art the King of the Corn!**

AT2: **Thou art the Lord of the Harvest!**

PST: **Thou art John Barleycorn!**

They stand up and the Priestess takes up the pitcher of burgundy.

PST: **Creature of wine thou art, creature of grape and sugar and yeast. Now transform and become the blood of the God that He will spill this day in our midst.**

Assistant takes the wine. Priestess holds up bourbon.

PST: **Creature of alcohol thou art, creature of corn and mash and sugar. Now transform and become the spirit of the corn, the spirit of life.**

Pours bourbon into wine.

PST: **So the blood of the God and the blood of the Corn are bound.**

Women move aside. The Priest holds up the shovel.

PT: **We furrow the Earth, that She might prepare to accept the sacrifice John Barleycorn so willingly makes for His people.**

All the men of the group take a turn digging a furrow about three feet long and six inches deep near the figure of the Corn God. They then step back. The Priestess with her two Assistants step up to the Corn God. The Priestess wields a sharp sickle or sword. One assistant holds the pitcher of wine/bourbon, the other holds a crystal or brass bowl.

PST: **Reverence the God, that He knows our honor and love!**

One by one, each member of the circle comes forward and spends a brief moment giving thanks to the Corn God. When everyone is back in place, the Priestess holds up the sword.

PST: From the Goddess You came and to the Goddess You shall return. Lord of the Corn, we have come for Your body!

As the Priestess beheads the Corn God, Assistant 1 pours the wine/bourbon into the trench. Assistant 2 catches some in the bowl.

PST: Mourn the God of the Harvest, for His blood is spilled upon the Earth and His spirit returns to the Mother!

All: *(Mourn the God with shrieks and wails.)*

PST: Rejoice for the God of the Harvest, He died that we might live! His spirit will infuse us with life!

All: *(Cheer for the God.)*

Priestess and Assistants throw the Corn God into the bonfire.

PST: Fire cleanses and purifies. The Spirit of John Barleycorn is set free.

Assistant 2 holds up the bowl of wine/bourbon. The Priestess dips her hands in the wine and anoints the face of Assistant 1.

PST: Blessed and marked thou art, Child of the Corn. *(She dips her hands in the wine and anoints Assistant 2.)* Blessed and marked thou art, Child of the Corn.

AT1: *(Anoints the Priestess.)* Blessed and marked thou art, Child of the Corn.

Going deosil around circle, the Priestess anoints each person's cheeks with the wine/bourbon mixture. Assistant 2 follows her with the bowl. After anointing each person the Priestess says: "Blessed and marked thou art, Child of the Corn." When she is finished, she and Assistant return to the center of the circle where any remaining wine is poured into the trench.

PST: The Spirit of the Corn is dead. The people shall live. Bless̩ed be John Barleycorn, Lord of the Harvest!

All: Bless̩ed be John Barleycorn, Lord of the Harvest!

The men fill in the trench.

PST: The Wheel turns as we step into the Autumn months. Long grow the nights and short the days. As the darkness reaches out over the land, we secure the abundance of the harvest against the barren months to come. With every meal in this waning season, remember the spirits that gave their lives so we might live, bless, and revere them. Blesséd be.

All: Blesséd be.

Devoke elements and circle as usual.

Food and Recipes

Chef's Salad

1 clove garlic	1 can tuna in oil
1 head leaf lettuce	1 cup cubed cooked
1 head red lettuce	chicken
1 large cucumber,	1 can drained tiny shrimp
peeled and sliced	2 eggs, hard-cooked
2 tomatoes, cored	1 teaspoon tarragon
and cubed	½ teaspoon crushed black
¼ cup sliced radishes	peppercorns
½ cup minced green onion	1 teaspoon basil
1 cup diced celery	1 cup grated cheddar
1 cup shredded carrots	cheese

Cut garlic clove in half and rub salad bowl with both halves. Then mince garlic and add to vegetables and toss. Stir in meats (do not drain tuna), cheese, egg, and herbs.

Serve with variety of dressings.

Serves 8.

Yogurt Herb Dressing

2 cups plain yogurt	½ teaspoon crushed black
¼ cup dill vinegar	peppercorns
1 tablespoon sugar	¼ teaspoon salt
½ teaspoon mustard	½ teaspoon garlic powder
1½ teaspoon dill weed	

Blend all ingredients with wire whip. Serve over salad or as a dip for cold salmon.

Spinach Salad with Mandarin Orange Dressing

1   bunch cleaned, dry spinach
1   large Jonagold apple
¼   cup raisins
1   cup mandarin orange yogurt
¼   cup orange juice

Tear spinach leaves into pieces and arrange on salad plates. Core apple and slice into thin slices. Fan on spinach. Top with a few raisins. Whip yogurt and orange juice together, then pour over salads.
Serves 3.

Baked Salmon

½   cup butter
2   tablespoons dill weed
½   teaspoon crushed black peppercorns
1   (2-3 pound) salmon, cleaned
½   cup orange juice

Preheat oven to 325 degrees. Blend butter, dill, and pepper.

Wash the salmon and dry with paper towels. Thoroughly butter inside of fish. Cut slits on both sides of salmon and press the rest of the butter into slits.

Arrange salmon on a piece of aluminum foil that's at least six inches longer than salmon. Drizzle with orange juice. Tightly wrap the foil so that it completely encases salmon and no steam can escape.

Place on baking sheet and bake 35-45 minutes, checking after 35 minutes. After you unwrap fish to check, re-wrap tightly if it needs additional cooking.
Serves 6.

Mabon

The Festival of the Harvest

The first rainstorms of the season, the scent of wood smoke fills the night air, a sudden gust as a brisk wind hurls leaves off the trees in a maelstrom of color, the last rush to harvest the garden before the frost sets in . . . it is the Autumnal Equinox, Mabon, and the year is winding down.

Mabon is the celebration of the Autumnal Equinox, when day and night are once again in balance. Once more the sun crosses the celestial equator and day and night equal one another.

Celebrated in late September, the actual date varies from year-to-year as with all astronomically-based holidays, but Mabon usually falls on September 21 or 22.

Named after the Welsh God Mabon, the festival is primarily one of harvest and thanksgiving and is a time of rejoicing in the bounty of the season as the Earth prepares to enter her long slumber. This is the time of last-minute details before the winter's siege. It is considered the second harvest, or the harvest of fruits.

At this time, we celebrate the hard work of the growing season and the energy expended throughout the Waxing Year, when we see the results of our labors.

Mabon is a time of rest and relaxation, of good food and quiet introspection on all the blessings in our lives. We remember the warmth of summer as the days grow short and we prepare for the austere seasons ahead. It is a time of reflection, when we slowly let go of the bustle that always attends growth, and turn our attention to quieter pursuits.

With the days becoming shorter, we fill our pantries with food and make our houses secure against the coming chill. We lay in wood and meat and provisions, and we silently eye the calendar, wondering what the season of darkness holds.

My husband and I take down the summer altar on August 2 and we purify the altar table. We offer the last of the Summer mead to the Goddess, then decorate for autumn.

My altar cloth for the fall is a kaleidoscope of bright fruits and vegetables against a black background. Atop the cloth we place a cornucopia woven from grape vines around which I've twined a silk autumn-leaf garland. On top of the cornucopia, peeking out from the leaves, nestles a plastic mushroom patch. Bunches of lifelike plastic grapes and charm boxes spill out of the cornucopia onto the table.

The altar also contains a yellow pillar candle and scattered silk leaves. Ephemeral decorations include apples, gourds, Indian corn, and a decanter of brandy.

We hang up my autumn pictures of Mielikki and Tapio, and the autumn collage I made, and then bless and consecrate the altar and settle back to watch the movies *Dead Poets Society* and *The Four Seasons*, both of which capture the spirit of the season. Another wonderful movie for this time of year is the 1994 remake of *Little Women*.

Charm Boxes

These are simple charms that you can keep year after year for your altar (I put them in the cornucopia), or you can make new ones each year.

You will need tiny boxes (ring box sizes), one for each type of charm you are making. You can make them for the household, or if anyone has a particular wish, make personalized ones.

Prosperity Boxes

You will need:
>   sandalwood or cinnamon incense
>   a box
>   green wrapping paper
>   a quarter and a dime
> 9 kernels of dried corn
> 9 oats
>   a malachite bead
>   a peridot bead
>   Scotch tape
>   a pen with green ink

Light a stick of sandalwood or cinnamon incense. Hold the box over the smoking incense to thoroughly saturate it with the scent.

Hold the money, the corn, oats, and beads in your hands. Charge them with energy, focusing on an increase in wealth and prosperity. Visualize yourself harvesting the rewards toward which you've been working.

Put the ingredients into the box and close the lid. With the pen, draw prosperity runes on the box and then wrap in the green wrapping paper. Hold over the smoking incense again and say:

> **Summer's sun is Autumn's gold**
> **In my life, wealth be foretold**
> **Fortune increase, luck be mine**
> **By harvest dreams and barley wine.**
> **Lady, see my need for more**
> **Send abundance to my door.**

Protection Boxes

You will need:
>   heather, sage, pine, or cedar incense
>   a box
>   white wrapping paper
>   a sprig of rue
>   a holly leaf

a tiger's eye bead
a piece of dragon's blood resin
Scotch tape
a pen with red ink

Light a stick of heather, sage, pine, or cedar incense. Hold the box over the smoking incense to thoroughly saturate it with the scent.

Hold the herbs, bead, and resin in your hands. Charge them with energy, focusing on protection and safety for all who dwell within your household. Visualize a web of protective light encasing your home.

Then put the ingredients into the box and close the lid. With the pen, draw protection runes on the box, and wrap it in the white wrapping paper. Hold over the smoking incense again and say:

Amidst the Autumn's darkest nights
Our home be bound by brilliant light
A web of hope and joy and peace
Be woven now, all danger cease
By watchful eye, by lock and key,
Protect our home, so mote it be.

The Colors of Mabon

The colors of Mabon are vivid and brilliant. Just look at the burst of color that runs through the forests. The autumn leaves are thick with red, bronze, orange, yellow, and rust. The night glows a deep indigo and the stars shine clear through the colder sky. During the day, the sun splashes the Earth with a soft golden wash—a far cry from the brilliance of Litha and Lughnasadh, this gold is still warm, but it is gentle and pale in comparison to the strength of summer. The fields lie fallow—stripped of their foliage—and we now can see the dark soil below.

Incense, Herbs, and Woods

Nutmeg, cloves, spice—these are the scents of Mabon. Sandalwood and myrrh, heather, pine, and cedar also make good choices.

Herbs commonly associated with this Sabbat are mace, cinnamon, cloves, cypress, juniper, oakmoss, marigold, ivy, and sage.

Kindle your fires with pine, apple, and oak, and make your wands and runestaves from hazel at this time of year.

Herbal Vinegars

Harvest season means different things to different people. I write full-time, so I don't usually have the energy or the hours to devote to gardening or extensive homemaking. However, I still like to dabble in some of the arts I learned as I grew up—canning fruits and vegetables and baking bread are two activities that immediately come to mind when I think of September.

I find ways in which to satisfy these urges without expending more time than I can comfortably share. One way is by making herbal vinegars every year for my husband and friends. It is simple, quick, and fun, and the results look beautiful sitting on the kitchen windowsill.

Herbal vinegars can be made out of just about any herb or spice. Here are two recipes that have proved to be favorites among family and friends.

Dill Pepper Vinegar

1   quart white vinegar
2   tablespoons crushed black peppercorns
     Fresh dill stalks

Pour vinegar into large stainless steel or enamel pan. Add peppercorns.

Stuff a quart jar very loosely with clean dill stalks until it is full.

Heat vinegar mixture over low heat for thirty minutes, then pour over the dill. Cork and place in window (south would be best, magickally speaking) for three weeks, shaking daily. Stores well. Use in cooking or on salads.

Lemon Pepper Vinegar

1   quart white vinegar
1   tablespoon crushed black peppercorns
2   tablespoons sugar
1   large lemon

Pour vinegar into large stainless steel or enamel pan. Add peppercorns and sugar.

Scrub and slice lemon (do not peel) and put in clean quart jar.

Heat vinegar and pepper mixture over low heat for 30 minutes, then pour over lemon. Cork and place in window (west would be best, magickally speaking) for three weeks, shaking daily.

Remove lemon slices from jar. Stores well. Use in cooking or on salads.

Rumtopf

Another way to share the harvest bounty is to make Rumtopf for Yule. You will want to start now. Begin with pint jars—as many as you want to give for gifts (or keep for yourself). You can also use quart jars, but this size can get pricey.

To each jar, add a layer of mixed strawberries and blueberries, a tablespoon of sugar and enough dark rum to just cover berries. Cover loosely and store in dark place.

The next week add a layer of peaches, another tablespoon of sugar, and more rum to cover the fruit. Cover loosely and store in dark place.

The third week add a layer of cherries, more sugar and rum, and return to storage.

The fourth week add a layer of pears, sugar and rum, and store as above.

The last week, add a layer of oranges, and sugar, and then fill the remaining space in the jar with dark rum. Store for another month with loose-fitting lids.

Tighten covers and decorate with pretty ribbons. The Rumtopf is ready to give as gifts. Serve over vanilla ice cream or pound cake.

Magical Pomanders

Pomanders have long been used to cover unpleasant odors (before the era of air freshener and Lysol), as well as for magickal and aesthetic purposes.

Pomanders are useful long-term charms for your house. Make a fresh one each autumn to keep love and harmony alive in your home.

You will need:

> one large orange, round with no blemishes
> whole cloves (many)
> red ribbon
> red netting
> ¼ cup ground cinnamon
> ¼ cup ground cloves
> ¼ cup ground ginger
> ¼ cup ground nutmeg
> 2 tablespoons orris root powder

Your thumb will probably hurt for a while after this spell, so have plenty of lotion around!

Cast a circle and invoke the elements.

Invoke the Goddess and/or God you feel most comfortable working with. Say:

Harmony and happiness do not roam
But stay instead within my home

Pour whole cloves in a bowl for easier access. Sit over a table or tray so that no juice falls on your clothing. Begin by pushing the cloves (long end first) into the orange to create the shape of a heart while focusing on love filling your home.

Next use the cloves to create this rune—Wunjo, the rune of joy—within the heart. Focus on happiness filling your home.

ᚹ

Then cover the entire orange with cloves, including inside the heart, placing them as close together as possible. This will take some time and as I said, your thumb will probably hurt for a while afterward. As you are pressing the cloves into the orange, focus on the joy and happiness and serenity you want your home to project.

After you have covered the orange with cloves, hold the orange in both hands and say:

> **Love and joy come to this place**
> **Bring a smile to my face**
> **Tears be gentle, words be kind**
> **Though to faults we are not blind**
> **Peace be with us as we strive**
> **For success, let us thrive**
> **By the power of three times three**
> **As I will, so mote it be!**

Mix the ground herbs and the orris root in a wide bowl and roll the orange in the spices so it is caked with them.

Set in dry place. Every day, roll the orange around in the spices. Within three weeks, it should be dry. Shake off the excess herbs and wrap with a piece of red netting. Tie with a length of red ribbon and hang from the ceiling in your family room, living room, or dining room.

You can give pomanders to friends and family—they make lovely yet magickal gifts.

A Hazel Spell for Concentration

Whether you are in school or working, there are always going to be times when you need extra concentration to learn new skills or new information. This spell can help you focus your thoughts so you will retain more of what you are learning.

You will need:

    a hazel leaf

    a piece of smoked salmon

    two hazel nuts—one shelled, the other whole

    a permanent marker

    a small green pouch

    a clear quartz crystal

    a flat river rock

    yellow thread

This spell needs to be performed near a lake, large pond, or the ocean. Ideally there would be a hazel tree growing over the water, but I think that's asking too much from most areas.

Perform the spell on a windy morning, during the phase of the waxing moon.

Sit or stand next to the water. Cast a small circle around you and your immediate area and invoke the elements as you usually do. Then turn to the west and say:

> **Taliesin, ancient bard with silver tongue, hear my call on the autumn winds and come through time to charm my quest.**

Close your eyes and imagine Taliesin striding through history and time. See Him approach from the west.

Turn to the east and say:

> **Cerridwen, Mother of Taliesin, Goddess of the Cauldron of Wisdom, hear my call on the autumn winds and come through time to charm my quest.**

Close your eyes and imagine Cerridwen flying in on the winds. See Her approach from the east.

Take the hazel leaf and write your name on it with the marker. Write your name on the unshelled nut as well.

Hold both leaf and nut between both hands and focus your energy into them, saying:

> **By nut and leaf of hazel tree**
> **I ask for strength and clarity**
> **To understand all that I see**

> **To remember that which befalls me**
> **To walk the path so truly mine**
> **The Hazel's power I now bind.**

Drop the nut into the pouch. Hold the leaf up in the wind and say:

> **Spirits of Air, Spirits of Wind,**
> **You who rule thought and intention**
> **You who rule intellect and mind**
> **Come to my aid, this spell now bind!**

Using the yellow thread, tie the leaf to the rock. After it is tightly bound, hold it in both hands and turn to the water. Watch the waves or currents as they move. Draw the energy of that movement into your body as you breathe and focus it into the stone and leaf. After a few minutes, say:

> **Spirits of Water, Spirits of the Deep**
> **You, who all things hidden keep,**
> **Salmon who knows the ancient tongue**
> **Dolphin who sings the ancient songs**
> **Whale who keeps the ancient rules**
> **Shark who guards the sacred pools**
> **As I come to you, please come to me**
> **Sharpen my wit and curiosity.**

Throw the rock into the water with as much force as you can. Immediately close your eyes so you won't see where it lands. Now take the quartz crystal and dip it in the water, then hold it between your hands. Focus on the clarity, the crystalline structure of the quartz. Say:

> **Stone of clear intent I ask**
> **Aid me in my mental tasks**
> **Let me see what needs be seen**
> **Make my vision clear and keen.**

Put the quartz in the pouch with the hazel nut and tie the pouch closed. Take out the smoked salmon and shelled hazel nut.

Hold the salmon up to the west and say:

Taliesin, bless this fish that as I eat I gain my wish.

Eat the salmon of knowledge and silently thank the fish for its life. Take out the shelled nut and hold it up to the east and say:

Cerridwen bless this nut that it strengthen my thought.

Eat the hazel of wisdom and silently thank the plant for its energy. When you have finished, sit quietly for a while on the shore and think about what you want to accomplish intellectually over the coming months. Don't limit yourself, but neither should you overextend your abilities. When you feel ready to leave say:

> **Taliesin, Cerridwen, Air and Water,**
> **Thank you for attending my rites.**
> **Go if You must, stay if You will**
> **Hail, farewell and Blesséd be.**

Keep the pouch in a place near your desk or your office when you go home. If you are stuck on a project, take out the crystal and meditate for a few minutes with it to clear your thoughts.

Mabon Harvest Ritual

This is a relatively simple ritual and should be performed before your group feasts on a sumptuous dinner. This is not the time to spare expense and focus on frugality. It is not the time for paper plates and plastic forks. No, bring out the good china and the imported wine. Set out the tablecloths and napkins—it's harvest feast time and a wonderful, luxurious ambiance is called for. After all, the darkness of Samhain and the chill of winter lurk in the shadows.

For this ritual each person needs to bring three cans or packages of non-perishable foods.

Decorate the altar with autumn accents such as colored leaves, Indian corn, gourds, bowls of fruit, and bottles of wine.

Everyone gathers in a circle, their food items at their feet. There should be a large cauldron or decorated box in the center of the circle. The Priest and Priestess officiate. Cast the circle and invoke the elements as usual.

PST: Once again we stand on the balance, as light fades into darkness we rejoice in the bounty of the harvest. The grain is long cut, the fruits are now gathered, and all that remains before winter is the Hunter's Moon.

PT: Mabon arrives and with it we feel the chill of autumn's breath, the touch of her brilliant leaf-covered cloak. Jack-in-the-Green gives way to Jack-Frost and the mornings will soon be covered with His lace-work.

PST: We gather to offer our gratitude to the Gods, our thanks for the blessings They have bestowed upon our lives since last Samhain. We gather to offer our generosity to those in need, for even if we have moments of poverty in our lives, there are always those who have less than we do.

Starting with the Priestess, then the Priest, each person takes a turn placing one food item in the cauldron and then stating something they are thankful for that happened to them since last Samhain—this does not have to be solemn, it should be a joyous, grateful affair. Go around the circle three times until all the food items are in the cauldron or around it.

PST: Now join hands and raise the power that what we give today might grow and multiply ten-fold and ten times that.

Everyone join hands. As the chant progresses, keep the focus on the food in the center, see it grow and attract more food to it—magnetize it with your energy that when it is delivered to the food bank in your area, it will magickally spur others to give until the shelves overflow.

All: *(Chant.)* **By Lady's bread and Corn God's blood**
Let the blessings pour and flood
To those in need, to those in pain
Fill their house with fruits and grain.
(Peak the energy and release.)

PT: By the Blessings of the Lord and Lady, we send this food out to those in need and ask that it be matched one thousand times over, that all who hunger might find peace of mind, honorable work, and a full belly in their home every night.

PST: *(Draw invoking pentacle over cauldron—see Appendix One, page 278.)* **Blessèd be thee, sustenance that life is made of. In the sight of the Lord and the Lady, we send it out with love and care.**

PT: **Even as we are generous to others, we are generous to ourselves. Let the circle be open and let our own feast begin!**

Open circle and start your harvest feast. Later, take the food to a local food bank and give it with a clear and generous heart.

Food and Recipes

Yasmine's Famous Pumpkin Soup

¼ cup olive oil
½ onion, chopped fine
½ teaspoon parsley
½ teaspoon nutmeg
½ teaspoon cinnamon
½ teaspoon cloves
½ teaspoon salt

½ cup chopped Granny Smith apple
2½ cups puréed pumpkin
2½ cups chicken stock
2 tablespoons brown sugar
⅔ cup dry milk powder
Chives

Heat olive oil in heavy skillet. Add onions, herbs, spices, and apple. Sauté over medium heat until onion is translucent. Remove from heat.

Use a wire whisk to whip together the pumpkin, the chicken stock, sugar, and dried milk. Stir in onion mixture. Heat thoroughly but do not boil.

Serve with a sprinkling of chives.

Serves 6.

Yasmine's Even More Famous Clam Chowder

Warning: This is not a low-fat food nor is it meant to be! I developed this recipe for taste and for taste alone!

8	strips lean bacon	1	teaspoon crushed
9	large red potatoes		black pepper
2	tablespoons olive oil	1	teaspoon basil
1	bunch green onions	½	cup chopped celery
½	cup chopped yellow	3	cans clams
	onions	2	cups half-and-half
4	cloves garlic, minced	¼	cup butter
1	teaspoon parsley		Salt to taste
1	teaspoon tarragon		

Fry bacon until crisp. Drain and crumble. Set aside.

Peel potatoes and cut into ¼-inch cubes. Cover with boiling water (just barely cover the tops of the potatoes) and set over medium-high heat.

Add 3 tablespoons bacon drippings to olive oil and heat over medium-high heat. Add chopped green onions, yellow onions, garlic, herbs, and celery. Sauté for 5 minutes. Add clams (do not drain) and sauté another 5 minutes. Add bacon and sauté 5 minutes more. Remove from heat.

When potatoes are soft, pour out all but 3 cups of potato water. Mash potatoes lightly, add potato water and half-and-half. Stir in vegetable mixture and butter. Heat through but do not boil. Salt to taste.

As good as this chowder is when freshly made, it's even better if you let it sit overnight (refrigerate, of course) and re-heat again the second day.

Serves 8.

Pumpkin Brandy Cake

Cake:

1 boxed carrot cake mix	¼ teaspoon ground cloves
⅓ cup oil	¼ teaspoon cinnamon
1¼ cup canned pumpkin (don't drain)	¼ teaspoon nutmeg
	¼ teaspoon ginger
3 large eggs	

Sauce:

1 cup water	¼ cup butter
1 cup white sugar	¼ cup brandy

Topping:

1 cup whipping cream	¼ teaspoon nutmeg
2 tablespoons white sugar	Pinch of salt

Preheat oven to 325 degrees. Combine cake mix, oil, pumpkin, spices, and eggs. Beat for three minutes on medium speed. Mixture will be thick.

Pour into greased and floured 13"x 9" pan.

Bake for 45–55 minutes (keep a close eye on cake after 40 minutes)—until center is still slightly moist but top springs back to touch.

Remove from oven and, using a fork, prick holes all over the top of the cake. Let cool.

In heavy skillet, combine water, sugar, and a pinch of salt. Stir until dissolved. Bring to a boil over medium heat, stirring constantly. Add butter and brandy. Cook until mixture reaches 234 degrees F on a candy thermometer.

Remove from heat and immediately pour over cake. Spread to completely cover surface of cake. Cover with foil and let sit at room temperature for one hour before refrigerating.

In a medium-sized bowl, beat whipping cream, sugar, and nutmeg until it forms stiff peaks. Serve with cake.

Serves 10.

Part 5

rites of birth

Rituals of Childhood •
Adult Transitions • Dedication Ceremonies

Rituals of Childhood

Birth, Adoption, and Youth Transitions

There are many pathways through life and one path includes the addition of children to our families.

A family, by definition, should include people and creatures who love and care for one another.

Families come in all shapes and sizes—single parent (mother or father) with children, a husband and wife who have decided to remain childfree, two-parent households (with parents either male-female or same-sex), extended families, families in which four-legged species act as our children.

In an age when we still struggle for religious tolerance we must search within ourselves and develop support for lifestyle choices that may not be our own—we must not only tolerate these choices but accept them as valid options. If, as Pagans, we do not do this, we become hypocrites and unworthy of our religion.

To Parent or Not to Parent

Women today have the freedom to choose whether or not to engender children. Exercising our option to forego pregnancy does not in any way diminish our femininity, nor does it preclude parenthood. If we want to parent but do not want to experience pregnancy (or—in the case of infertile women—cannot become pregnant) there are so many children out there who need loving homes—millions world-wide waiting for someone to open their hearts.

When we adopt, we are telling that child, "We chose to open our family to you. You are special and we want to take care of you and share our lives with you."

Bearing a child in no way insures that maternal or paternal love will follow. The number of children abused and murdered by their biological parents sadly attests to this. If you want to adopt, don't allow anyone to convince you that a birth-mother's love for her child is always greater than the love an adoptive mother can give. It's a cruel, bitter thing to say and the sooner we end the stigma adoption carries, the better.

If you do choose to get pregnant or adopt, do so with fore-thought. Make sure for your child's sake that you are ready to take on the responsibility of parenthood.

Are you financially prepared to take care of the child? Are you emotionally stable? Can you live with the fact that children eventu-ally leave, that no matter what values and background you instill in your child, they will ultimately make their own choices?

What if your child chooses to become a Christian? What if your child is gay? Can you still love your child if he or she chooses a path in life that doesn't agree with your own?

I am not saying that love should be unconditional. If your child (Goddess forbid) turns out to be a murderer or an abuser, then you shouldn't condone that behavior. As Pagans, we must take responsibility for our actions, and so must our children.

But remember that children are people, not possessions, and they have distinct personalities. It is a sad possibility, but you might actually find that you don't really like your child. It happens. Can you still love him/her if that is the case? Do you have the patience and time needed?

Parenthood is a full-time job and not one that suits everyone. There is no shame in recognizing that you want a different lifestyle than one including children can offer. A husband and wife (with or without pets), a woman and her four cats, a man and his golden retriever . . . all of these pairings still constitute the sense of family.

The choice to remain childfree is not necessarily a selfish choice—if you recognize that you don't have the desire or the patience to fulfill all of a child's needs, then your choice to forego parenting is stating that you care enough about children's welfare to sacrifice that experience rather than chance harming or neglecting a child.

On a personal note, I know I'd resent giving a child the time she or he needs; I don't have a lot of patience and I have a nasty temper when I'm pushed too far. I like spending my days writing and reading and puttering around. I want the freedom that being a mother negates. My husband would probably make a better parent than I in some ways, but he has interests that take up his time and he likes the freedom we have without children.

We still interact with children—we have friends with kids and whenever my biological clock ticks a little too loudly we spend some time with them, talk and play with their children, observe the enormous amount of time and energy that it takes to parent, and realize that we've made the correct choice for our own lives.

It is also important to remember that just because a woman becomes pregnant, it doesn't mean she has to have the child. If your personal ethics do not object, abortion is a safe and legal alternative. Every woman has the right to choose what transpires in her reproductive life. For thousands of years our ancestors used herbs for birth control, and abortion when that birth control failed.

There are more than enough humans on this planet now, more than the Mother can comfortably sustain, and we have to start thinking on a world-wide scale as opposed to gratifying every personal whim. In my opinion, with the birth rate still skyrocketing, no couple has the ethical right to engender more than two children.

A Note on the Term "Childfree"

While some readers may object to this term, I prefer it to the word childless. If we are to empower all lifestyle choices, then we must accept that women who opt not to parent are no less women than those who bear children.

For an infertile woman who wants children, the term childless may be appropriate—she wants children and cannot bear them (although she can adopt).

However, those of us (and our number is growing) who are choosing the alternative have made this choice freely; we consider it not a sacrifice, but a desirable state of existence for ourselves.

I am not implying that everyone should make this choice, but I am standing up for those of us who have—mothering is simply one aspect of womanhood, not a necessary component. There are many other ways to express one's creative urges and still remain feminine.

Rites of Parenthood Ritual

The Rites of Parenthood Ritual that follows (both birth and adoptive versions) are meant for use when you first decide to open your heart and home to a child. The Rites of Parenthood Ritual can be adapted to any parent combination and is not meant to exclude same-sex couples.

Ideally, if a woman decides to parent, she will prepare herself both emotionally and physically for childbirth before conceiving. When the decision to become pregnant is made, the couple (or woman, if she's using artificial insemination) should perform a rite to open their personal space to the spirit of the child that will be their son or daughter.

Cast a circle in the bedroom and invoke your household Gods, or Isis and Osiris (two of the most popular Gods for parenting).

The couple turns to the north, where a plate of salt rests on a pentacle.

Wom: Spirits of Earth, come to me. Strengthen my body as I prepare for conception. Ripen my womb, that my child might find firm support and nourishment in my body.

Man: Spirits of Earth, come to me. Strengthen my seed as I prepare for paternity. Enliven my semen, that any child beget by me grows full with health and vigor.

W/M: Spirits of Earth, bless us with your power.

The couple turns to the east, where a stick of incense smolders.

Wom: Spirits of Air, come to me. Quicken my mind as I prepare for conception. Open my thoughts, that my child might find a mother who is wise and knowing.

Man: Spirits of Air, come to me. Quicken my mind as I prepare for paternity. Open my thoughts, that my child might find a father who is wise and knowing.

W/M: Spirits of Air, bless us with your power.

The couple turns to the south, where a white candle burns.

Wom: Spirits of Fire, come to me. Inspire my actions as I prepare for conception. Kindle my creativity, that my child might find a mother who is artistic and visionary.

Man: Spirits of Fire, come to me. Inspire my actions as I prepare for paternity. Kindle my creativity, that my child might find a father who is artistic and visionary.

W/M: Spirits of Fire, bless us with your power.

The couple turns to the west, where a chalice of spring water sits with a white rose floating in it.

Wom: Spirits of Water, come to me. Soothe my emotions as I prepare for conception. Nurture my patience, that my child might find a mother who is tranquil and just.

Man: Spirits of Water, come to me. Soothe my emotions as I prepare for paternity. Nurture my patience, that my child might find a father who is tranquil and just.

W/M: Spirits of Water, bless us with your power.

Woman and Man should embrace and kiss.

Wom: By Isis and Osiris, I promise to do right by my child. Bless me with fertility.

Man: By Isis and Osiris, I promise to do right by my child. Bless me with fertility.

W/M: Blesséd be.

Devoke elements and open circle.

Variation on Rites of Parenthood for Adoptive Parents

If a woman decides to become an adoptive mother, she should prepare herself both emotionally and physically before the adoption is complete. When the decision to adopt is made, the couple should perform a rite to open their personal space to the child who will be their son or daughter.

The rite is similar to the Rite of Birth given above, with only the Earth invocation changed. The other invocations may stay the same, except substitute the word motherhood for conception and the word fatherhood for paternity.

Cast a circle in the bedroom and invoke your household Gods, or Isis and Osiris.

The couple turns to the north, where a plate of salt rests on a pentacle.

Wom: Spirits of Earth, come to me. Stabilize my home as I prepare for motherhood. Strengthen my body, that my child might find firm support and nourishment in my arms.

Man: Spirits of Earth, come to me. Stabilize my home as I prepare for fatherhood. Strengthen my body, that my child might find health and vigor in my arms.

Proceed, with noted changes, as in Rites of Parenthood Ritual, beginning on page 144.

Child Blessing Ritual

This ritual is designed for when the baby is born or when the adopted child is brought home. It is not meant to be what Wiccans call a Wiccaning—it is not a dedication of the child to the Gods, but instead, the rite asks for protection for the child until the child comes of age and can decide his or her own spiritual path.

If either parent is unwilling to participate, then do not force them to attend. If there is religious discord in the home, you should decide what to do about your son's or daughter's spiritual upbringing before the child arrives and the situation becomes critical.

For this ritual, decide which Gods you are going to appeal to for protection. If you are pledged to certain deities, then you may want to ask Them for Their blessing.

I wrote the blessing invoking Isis and Osiris. If you choose another deity(ies) then adjust the pineapple juice and dates according to foods appropriate to your choice. You will need to have ready:

> a bowl of water
> a pinch of salt
> a sage smudge stick
> a white candle
> a small piece of amethyst or rose quartz
> a small pouch with three sides already sewed
>   (use cream or lavender colored material)
> 2 slips of paper
> a purple-ink pen
> cedar or pine needles
> rosemary sprigs
> rowan or holly leaves
> olive oil
> a bowl of pitted dates
> pineapple juice

Cast a circle and invoke the elements.

Ask the spirit of the Earth to provide your child with security and stability; ask the spirit of the Air to provide your child with quick thought and imagination; ask the spirit of the Fire to provide your child with vitality and the spark of creativity; ask the spirit of the Water to provide your child with wisdom and the ability to feel and understand their emotions.

Using a pushpin thumbtack, carve the full names of the child, the father, and the mother on the candle. Also carve the names of Isis and Osiris. Then carve these runes:

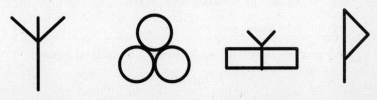

protection   peace   knowledge   joy

love   goddess   god   health

Rub the candle with olive oil and firmly place it in a candle holder.

Both father and mother should each take a slip of paper, draw the above runes on the paper in purple ink, then write out their hopes and blessings for their child. Don't say something like, "I hope you'll be a doctor" but instead, "May your life be filled with love, safety, and joy."

Light the candle. Invoke Isis and Osiris into the circle. Hold the child while you ask Isis and Osiris to watch over your child until he or she has grown to adulthood; ask Them to help you guide your child wisely until your child is ready to make decisions independently; ask for patience, the ability to discipline wisely and with love, and ask for emotional support for yourselves as parents.

Draw a pentacle on the child's head with the olive oil.

Light the sage incense or smudge stick and gently waft a little of the smoke around the child and say:

With fire and air, I purify and protect thee.

Mix the salt into the water and anoint the child's forehead and say:

May your mind be free and quick,
may wisdom lead your actions.

Anoint the child's lips with the water/salt and say:

May you speak the truth of your heart.

Anoint the child's ears and say:

May you hear the truth with clarity and understanding.

Anoint the child's heart and say:

> **May you know you are loved and may love fill your heart.**

Anoint the child's hands and say:

> **May you discover your talents and use them wisely and with joy.**

Anoint the child's feet and say:

> **May you walk the truth of your heart and may the Gods lead you to your own path.**

Into the pouch put the folded wish-papers, the crystal, a lock of both parents' hair, and a lock of the child's hair.

Add cedar, rosemary, and rowan to the bag.

You can also add a pentacle and a figure (like a jewelry pendant) of Isis if you like.

Sew the pouch shut and keep it in a safe place (on your altar or in your jewelry box). If your child has decided to go into the Craft upon reaching eighteen, give him or her the pouch at that time.

Thank Isis and Osiris. Toast them with dates and pineapple juice, and then devoke your circle.

Baby Showers

One thing my friends and I don't understand is the practice of having the baby shower before the baby is born (or before the adopted child arrives). It seems wiser to wait until the child has arrived safely. If something goes wrong, the mother won't have to cope with all the gifts meant for the baby.

It also makes more sense to have a shower after the child arrives and the parents know what they need.

Rites of Passage into Puberty

Passage into young adulthood is a precarious emotional time for most of us—the adolescent years are traumatic, hormonal, and confusing, even at their best.

Our society makes little distinction between the young child and the teenager when it comes to rights and responsibilities. Because of our varying religious and cultural backgrounds, we have no formal passage ceremonies to welcome the child into young adulthood.

Menstruation is treated as if it's something to be ashamed of, and when a boy's voice starts to change and crack and he begins having wet dreams, he's laughed at.

In the Pagan community, however, these transitions are noted and celebrated as natural events. Most Pagan parents and groups prepare special rites of passage for the young adult to mark the transition.

Your family might want to discuss what added privileges and responsibilities go along with the physical and emotional changes that your child is experiencing.

When your daughter starts her period, does she want a ceremony with other women to mark her entrance into the beginnings of womanhood?

Of course, a twelve-year old having her first period isn't going to be as emotionally mature as an adult woman, even though both can conceive. But it is a time of change and she should be given the respect for that change.

In devising transition ceremonies for your children, take into account their emotional growth as well as their physical growth.

Perhaps you will have two separate ceremonies . . . one to mark the physical changes they are going through, the other a series of tasks they must complete to demonstrate their emotional and intellectual grasp of the responsibilities that go along with the rights teenagers so desperately want at this time in their lives.

When they have demonstrated their understanding of what it means to enter adulthood, then they have earned more freedom.

Rites of passage should be tailored to each child's needs, for all children are unique in their growth.

Sample Rites of Passage into Womanhood and Dating

You have a thirteen-year old daughter who has just started to menstruate. She also wants to be a writer. You hold a ceremony with other women to welcome her into her menstrual and potential child-bearing years.

But, now that she's a teenager, your daughter wants the freedom to date and wear cosmetics, and you're not sure if she's ready.

As a gift for her passage into her menstrual years, you decide to allow her to wear the cosmetics (buy her a good book on applying them, too).

However, in order for her to win the right to date, you set up a series of tasks for her to complete. Since she wants to be a writer, you tell her that she must interview eight women over the age of eighteen, and that four of them have to have children.

(You pick the women—make sure each woman has a healthy self-esteem, is mature in her own right, and that those women who are mothers agree to show your daughter the hardships as well as the joys of raising children.)

She's to spend a day with each woman, observing and helping with chores and work. She's to interview the women about sex and children and work and career and self-esteem, and then write a one-page essay on her experiences and what she learned from each woman.

When your daughter completes the interviews and essays, then you allow her to date.

This way, she'll have gotten an overview of what being an adult woman is like, she'll have a better idea of the responsibilities that go along with having children, and she'll see women whose self-esteem is internally based.

Rites of Passage into Adulthood: Letting Go

Just as a child moves into puberty, so he or she moves into full adulthood. A coming-of-age ceremony allows the parent to let go of their child, to set them free, and gives the youth a sense of independence, as well.

This doesn't mean giving up your role as mother or father; it doesn't mean you can't or won't help your child, but the young man or woman who is embarking into the adult world needs to feel that their decisions will be respected. Every one of us makes mistakes and most of us learn from our errors. True, some mistakes are more dangerous than others, but we can't always predict the outcome of our choices.

If you've given your children a firm ethical and emotionally supportive foundation, then let them use their wings.

While graduation is a common ceremony people use to signify their movement into the adult world, I think each family should create their own, personal ceremony to note the transition.

What better time than the day before your child's eighteenth birthday—the year that our society has officially earmarked for most adult responsibilities? This allows the young person to go out and celebrate the birthday with friends, while still participating in a family gathering.

Each family will differ in the manner in which they formally welcome their child into the adult world.

Perhaps it is through the institution of a token rent payment (if the youth is still living at home) in return for a withdrawal of certain rules . . . perhaps some other method. Only you and your son or daughter can figure out what will work best.

Whatever you do, it is important that the parents retain control over their physical house–space. After all, the child will separate and move someday, but the home was originally designed for the husband and wife and remains their home until they decide to sell it.

Perhaps this means no drugs or alcohol on the premises, or perhaps sleep-over dates are taboo, but the newly-emancipated youth should have a definite sense of control over his or her life while respecting the parents' space.

This is a difficult time for many families and the youth's struggle for freedom from the family unit will no doubt continue, rites of passage or not.

But special ceremonies can ease the emotional interplay, becoming life-markers that the child looks forward to throughout childhood.

Unfortunately it seems that young people have too much freedom thrust on them too early, not enough direction or boundaries, and those who would be quality role-models are overshadowed by sports stars (e.g., Mike Tyson, a convicted rapist) and angst-ridden rock stars.

Start when they are young. Introduce children to the adult world in stages and make their transitions special and meaningful. Show them the true role models—the artists and writers, scientists and engineers who are making a positive and powerful impact on this world. Encourage their talents and give them a firm basis for self-esteem. This will enable them to tackle new subjects, to create goals, and to live a spiritual, productive, and meaningful life.

Then let go and watch as they find their unique path through the world. That's all you can do.

Adult Transitions

Change and the Ceremony of Naming

Several years ago, I realized that I had undergone significant changes in my life and that my beliefs and habits had altered in a substantial number of ways.

I began the process of redefining myself and was finding it difficult to winnow out who I had been from who I was becoming. Everyone around me had a particular vision of who I was, and I found it difficult to grow within the confines of each person's limited view of my personal nature. At one time or another, each view had essentially been correct, but I suddenly felt constrained and boxed in by my own and others' definitions of just who Yasmine Galenorn is or was.

We Pagans and Witches have a responsibility to be true to ourselves, to our spiritual paths, and to the world around us. If we show honor and honesty in our actions, we invite honesty and respect into our lives. Honoring ourselves and our truths is the first step to this state of existence.

It is vital to know the difference between what you truly believe and what you think you believe, between what your true nature is and what you think it is.

Only when you have accepted yourself as you truly are can you walk the path of the Gods knowing that you walk with certainty.

When I realized that there were lingering energies I had once touched on that no longer proved part of my nature, when I understood that change was not to be feared but embraced, I began to accept myself for who I was at that moment.

Each day I attempt to reaffirm who I am—in the moment.

When I was seventeen I was a vegetarian. I am not a vegetarian anymore. When I was twenty-two I wanted to live on a farm and be totally self-sufficient. I know now that I wouldn't be happy doing that—I'd rather spend my days writing than farming.

When I was twenty-eight my favorite season was autumn. Now my favorite time of year is summer.

When the change is spiritual it can be disconcerting.

At eighteen, I dedicated myself to the Craft and the Goddess. At age thirty-one, I pledged myself as Priestess of Mielikki and Tapio. In some ways that act narrowed my path—it is much more specific now—but it also freed me to explore the spiritual side of myself that I had denied as I realized that not all women pledged to Huntress Goddesses are tall and thin and young!

When I turned thirty-three, my husband and I went to Hawai'i so I could meet his relatives, and here I encountered the power of Pele. Though I am pledged to Mielikki and Tapio, I also know that lava runs in my blood and I will always honor and respect the Goddess of Volcanoes and long to live in Her land. My spiritual path now includes shamanistic magick as well as Western European traditions and is evolving even now as I begin to study Buddhism, Taoism, and other eastern mindsets.

To come to terms with the changes in energy and direction I was encountering, I turned to my poetry to compose a Ceremony of Naming.

I spent weeks thinking about what attributes I saw in myself. I listened to my inner guidance and jotted down images and notes as they came to me.

I drew on the *Song of Amergin* for inspiration in style as I wrote up my own "song."

When I was ready, I invited a few close friends over for the ritual.

I am including my personal Song of Naming at the end of this chapter to give you ideas for writing your own, but I caution: your song must be entirely true to you—do not use an image or concept because it seems exciting or because it's what you'd like to be— every line must be true to your nature as you are now!

Also, it's not necessary to list your negative traits. I'm highly competitive, I'm temperamental, at times I am abrupt and intimidating, but these are aspects of some of the energies I list in my song and it's not necessary to note them separately. My totems— the black panther, the green boa, and the peacock aren't exactly gentle little bunny rabbits (come to think of it, rabbits can be pretty fierce when cornered).

When you write your own song, remember that every image will have a light and shadow side, and if we embrace one, we embrace the other.

The Ceremony of Naming Ritual

This can be done in a solitary setting or among close friends. If you invite others to join you, caution them that this is your ritual and that while you value their points of view, this is not the place for them to disagree with your opinion of yourself.

The ritual itself is simple.

Dress in clothes that really represent who you feel you are, decorate your altar to your personal tastes, and prepare a meal of your favorite foods. This ceremony is to celebrate your uniqueness and your individuality and if others choose to share this time with you, it should be on your terms.

Cast a circle and invoke the elements in your own manner. Invoke whichever God(s) you choose.

Then stand in the center of the circle with your friends sitting around you and read or sing out your song.

Use a clear voice, do not let your words quaver. Do not doubt your inner guidance. You are proclaiming yourself to the world and to the Gods during this ritual, so do it with belief, with certainty, and with strength.

When you are done, thank the Gods and elements for attending, then devoke the circle and sit down to a feast of your favorite foods!

A Note About Change and Relationships

Unfortunately, when we seek change in our lives, our friends can sometimes become fearful that we will leave them behind and, consciously or subconsciously, they often try to discourage us and shake our confidence.

Change and transformation can be frightening to someone who needs stability and security in life. I know this from experience, but I also realize that to grow and reach our goals, we must allow change to occur.

If we don't stretch and reach and grow, we stagnate.

Sometimes it can help to reassure your friends that you still like them, that you won't forget them, and that if you make these changes you'll be happier and more fulfilled.

Once your friends see that you are content with yourself they'll probably relax. You'll be more fun and interesting to be around, and your example may encourage them to seek change in their own lives if they want it.

Never try to force change on someone. It doesn't work. If a friend's behavior is a problem, tell them. If they won't change, then it's up to you to either leave the relationship or decide to accept the behavior.

Sometimes change involves moving away and that is probably the hardest thing for good friends to face.

There's always the feeling that, "If you really liked me you wouldn't go," but this simply isn't the case.

We have friends who are planning on moving to Vermont in a couple of years, we have other friends who have bought a boat and are planning on sailing off into the South Seas . . . I know I will miss them, but these moves will make them happy.

I also know that if my husband and I ever do get the opportunity to move to Hawai'i, we'll miss our friends, but I'll want them to be excited for us.

The Post Office still delivers letters, there are telephones worldwide, and the Internet has become an inexpensive way to communicate. Moving away doesn't have to mean leaving the friendship forever. Of course it will change—they'll meet new friends and so will you—but it doesn't mean that you can't keep someone in your heart (see "Separation Ritual: Moving Away" on page 188.).

When you are facing a spouse or partner's reaction to changes you're making, the answer is not so easy.

To be fair, you must ask yourself if their fear is legitimate—are you considering leaving a long-term relationship? Are you bored with your partner? Are you thinking of pulling up roots and moving to Mexico?

If the answer is yes, then you must accept that their reactions are appropriate for them and that you are, to some degree, responsible for the way they feel. So be certain that the changes you're considering aren't just spontaneous acts of boredom, but really need to be made, before you disrupt another person's life.

Once you have ascertained that you definitely need to make a change and that it will have a significant impact on someone else, then you must make that change as easy as possible for them.

If you want to leave a long-term relationship ask whether or not they want the living space (apartment or house)—be willing to move since you're the one who wants the change.

You might want to suggest a handparting—a ritual of separation (see Handparting Ritual, page 203) to formalize the transition. This allows both parties to emotionally move away from the relationship.

Do not expect your ex-partner to be supportive and nurturing during your time of transition. It isn't a fair request. They must focus on the changes your decision brought about in their lives. They have the right to be angry and hurt.

Instead, turn to friends for support and don't try to make your friends choose sides in the dissolution. You will retain their goodwill more than if you force the issue.

Yasmine's Song of Becoming

This is my song of naming, which I wrote a few years ago. It has since been altered as I have changed and no doubt in the next few years will transform even more. When it becomes significantly different, I will perform a new Ceremony of Naming Ritual.

The Song of Yasmine

I am Yasmine Feasil Galenorn
I am Priestess of Mielikki
I am Priestess of Tapio
I am devoted admirer of Pele
This is my life
This is my song

I am the Witch who greets the Sun
I am the Witch who basks beneath the Moon
I am the Mistress of Magic
I am the Enchantress of the Silver Forest
I am the sparkle of Faerie Magic
I am the Priestess of the Hunt
I am the Witch of the Wild Wood
I am the Huntress with swift arrows
I am the blade of the Goddess who slices through
    obstacles and opens new gateways.

I am the roar of the ocean
I am the shifting sands on the beach at sunrise
I am the warm rain sparkling in the grass
I am the rustling of trees in the twilight forest
I am the stars wheeling overhead
I am the midnight shadow in the forest
I am the languid currents of tropical grottos
I am the brilliant blue of summer mornings
I am the wild orchid in the palm-shrouded ravine
I stand between the forest and the ocean and raise my
    arms in salute to the vastness of the world.

I am the lover committed by heart
I am the faithful wife of my husband
I am the foster-mother of my cats
I am the woman of strong thighs
I am the rounded belly of abundance
I am the full breast of womanhood
I am the passion of coupling bodies

I am the pulse of the drumbeat
I am the ecstasy of the Dance

I am the Singer of Siren Song
I am the Guardian of Magic
I am the Webweaver of Language
I am the Storycrafter
I tell the tales of Goddesses and women and paint
   pictures of their souls

I am grounded in the body of the Goddess
I soar with the spirit of the Sylphs
I glow with the golden-green fire of Faerie
I dip my toes in the flowing Lava
I bathe in the tears of the Ocean
I balance the elements and weave them together
   to form the web that is my life

I am a seer of fortunes
I am the feral huntress of justice
I am the black panther in the treetops of the jungle
I am the brilliant vision of the peacock feathered fan
I am the healing venom and sensuality of the green boa
I welcome the joy of the hummingbird
I court the strength of the bear
I long for the swiftness of the stag
My taste is that of golden honey and strawberries
My scent that of dark musk, ripe peaches, and autumn spice
My will is my own and My Lady and Lord's and none other

I am daughter of the Green Goddess
I am consort of the Wild God
I am Priestess of Mielikki
I am Priestess of Tapio
This is my life
This is my song

To read my song and listen to its energies is to understand me. Creating your song, making sure every word expresses your personal truths, will allow you to understand yourself.

DEDICATION CEREMONIES

Pledging Yourself to the Gods

Dedicating yourself to the Gods, by my definition, means you dedicate your loyalty, love, and actions to working within the Old Religion without making a definite lifelong commitment. If you later discover this is not your path, then you can gracefully withdraw without betraying trust.

When you add an oath to your dedication, you bind your trust and loyalty to the Gods for a specified or unspecified amount of time and breaking that oath is considered a betrayal.

If you pledge to a God or Goddess (or both), you have bound yourself to a particular path and the God or Goddess to whom you are pledged comes first, above all others, including yourself. Not many Pagans pledge themselves to the Gods in this manner. It is a very serious commitment, usually taken for life and breaking that pledge not only will incur the anger of your God or Goddess, but also shows that you have no integrity and that you have become what is known as a Warlock (an Oath-Breaker).

When people enter the Craft, they are often confused by so many options.

Should they become a Norse Pagan?

Are they a Witch?

Should they look to the Egyptian path?

And what about ceremonial magick and natural magick and shamanism and Dianic Witchcraft and Wicca?

The list goes on and on . . . no wonder new Pagans feel overwhelmed.

When you first enter the Craft, your duty is to yourself. Read and practice—don't do any pledging or dedication no matter what anyone asks of you. You need to know what options are available before you commit to a specific path, and if anyone insists otherwise they don't have your best interests at heart. Unfortunately, our religion does attract those looking for followers.

So read and read widely. Read Starhawk and Laurie Cabot and the Farrars and Buckland and Doreen Valiente and my books. Read Scott Cunningham and the numerous other authors who have attempted to pave the way through the tangle of traditions. Read the book *Drawing Down The Moon* by Margot Adler for a wonderful overview of Neo-Paganism and Witchcraft.

If you have the opportunity to work with a group or coven, be cautious about accepting their tradition as the only viable one—what works for one group doesn't necessarily work for another and you should expose yourself to differing opinions, even if only through books, so you can decide what works best for you.

After you have read several authors, you can start trying different spells and rituals to get an idea of what the Craft feels like. Perhaps you are meant to be a Pagan but not a Witch, like my husband. He celebrates the Sabbats, and he believes in magick, but he doesn't work it unless I need his energy for a household spell.

Perhaps you will be a kitchen Witch, not dedicated to any one particular God or Goddess but aware of them all, committed to natural magick and the celebration of the holidays.

Perhaps you will, like me, turn out to be a Priestess as well as a Witch, bound for life by blood and oath to a specific God and Goddess.

It is difficult to know which way to turn in the beginning, so take your time, study, and learn. Dedicate yourself to the pursuit of knowledge in the Craft, a dedication that does not bind you to the religion should your true path lie elsewhere.

There is no hurry.

Spiritual growth isn't a race to be won, it's a path to be forged out of hundreds of possible combinations. You work one step at a time, testing this and that, discovering what works and what doesn't.

Sometimes you get a jolt—a jump start—and you're thrown into the maelstrom of magick and come out the other side forever changed by your experience. Then you begin again, testing and trying new things from your new vantage point.

Then, perhaps a year later (a year and a day is the typical waiting period, but it might be one day and it might be ten years), you will know if you want to pursue this path. If you do, you perform a dedication ceremony in which you dedicate yourself to the Old Religion. You might dedicate yourself for a year and a day, until the Gods decide otherwise, or for life.

A few years later you might wake up one morning and hear the Lady's voice—only it's a very special Lady, say Isis or Freya or Artemis, and you know who She is by the surety in your heart.

She tells you She's chosen you to be Her Priest or Priestess and you know there's no other path in the world you want to follow so much as the one She's offering. You pledge yourself into Her service for a year perhaps, or for life because your heart and your head and your soul all confirm that this is the destiny you are meant to walk.

You see, we do not choose the Gods—They choose us.

Remember: if you have to ask yourself if dedicating or pledging is the right thing to do, it probably isn't.

Maybe it will be tomorrow, or the next week, or next year . . . but not right now. Don't worry about time—the Gods will be there and the Craft isn't a religion that preaches salvation through fear.

You won't go to hell if you aren't ready to commit.

But if you have no choice, if this is the only path you want to walk, then you are probably making the right decision.

Dedication to Knowledge Ritual

This ritual is designed to be an entry-level ritual into the Craft after you have read several books and practiced casting a circle and invoking the elements. It will not bind you any more than you wish to be bound.

On your altar, set a black candle on the left side, a white candle on the right side and a red candle in the center. Place a bowl of salt in the north, a stick of incense in the east, a piece of citrine or carnelian in the south and a chalice of wine or spring water in the west.

Put your Book of Shadows/Book of Mirrors and/or journal in front of the altar, along with a pen that you really like.

Take a ritual bath, using lavender bath salts or soap. After you finish your bath, you may wish to work skyclad, in ritual attire, or in whatever you choose.

Approach the altar and cast a circle. Invoke the elements. Then say:

> **Great Mother of the Earth and Moon, Horned Hunter of the Forest and Field, I come before you today to dedicate myself to pursue knowledge about the Old Religion.**

Take a pinch of salt and put it on your tongue. Say:

> **By the powers of Earth, I will strive to ground my knowledge in both the magick of the planet and the practicality needed to wield it.**

Wave the incense smoke around you. Say:

> **By the powers of Air, I will strive to gain a clear picture of the different paths before me and I will search my heart for the truth of my own path.**

Pick up the citrine and hold it. Say:

> **By the powers of Fire, I will actively practice what I learn as I strive to understand the nature of this planet and of the Gods.**

Take a sip of the wine or water. Say:

> **By the powers of Water, I will seek the recesses of my soul for the truth of my path as I acquaint myself with my psychic gifts.**

Light the white candle. Say:

> **By Maiden and Young Lord, I am in the youth of my Learning. I ask that You teach me how to enjoy Nature and Her ways.**

Light the red candle. Say:

> **By Lady and Lord, I am in the youth of my Learning. I ask that You teach me how to grow into the fullness of my power and abilities.**

Light the black candle. Say:

> **By Crone and Sage, I am in the youth of my Learning. I ask that You teach me how to use my knowledge and experience with wisdom and compassion.**

Pick up your journal/BOS/BOM and pen. Sit for a while and if anything comes to mind that seems important, write it down. If not, record how you feel about making this dedication. When you are finished, say:

> **Lord and Lady, I dedicate myself to the pursuit of knowledge about the Old Religion and its varied Paths until such day that I know it is not the path for me or until I am ready to take the next step in my commitment. I ask that You be with me and that You guide my journey. Blesséd be.**

Devoke the elements and the circle and continue your quest for knowledge.

Self-Initiation Ritual (without oath)

When you feel ready to formally enter the Craft, when you've done your research and you know that this is the path you want to take and that you'd like to dedicate yourself to the Goddess and/or the God, then you can perform a self-initiation ceremony. The following ritual is designed to give you a starting place from which to create your own. You can use it as is, but I suggest personalizing it to your own needs. It does not contain an oath or a specified time limit other than linking you to the Craft and the Gods, as long as that's meant to be your path.

Perform this ceremony outside if possible. If it is too cold or the weather too inclement, you can set up your altar inside, but try to have a window near so you can at least see the outdoors.

For your altar you will need:

> a bowl of salt in the north to represent Earth
> a feather in the east to represent Air
> a piece of carnelian or citrine in the south to represent Fire
> a chalice of wine or water in the west to represent Water

Place three candles in the center—white, red, and black—to represent the Goddess and God, and another candle in front of them to represent you. Choose your favorite color. If you want incense, frankincense is a good choice for this ceremony.

Cast a circle and invoke the elements. Hold up the bowl of salt to the north and say:

> **By the powers of Earth, I have grounded my path in the religion of the Earth, in the ancient and magickal realms our ancestors still tread. I dedicate my body and works to the Great Mother and Her Horned Consort as long as our paths are to meant to meet and ask Their guidance as I work, play, and interact with the world today.**

Hold the feather up to the east and say:

> **By the powers of Air, I have turned my studies to the religion of the Earth, to the ancient and magickal realms our ancestors still tread. I dedicate my thoughts and intuition to the Great Mother and Her Horned Consort as long as our paths are meant to meet and ask Their guidance as I work, play, and interact with the world today.**

Hold the citrine up to the south and say:

> **By the powers of Fire, I have attuned my energy to the religion of the Earth, to the ancient and magickal realms our ancestors still tread. I dedicate my actions and creativity to the Great Mother and Her Horned Consort as long as our paths are meant to meet and ask Their guidance as I work, play, and interact with the world today.**

Hold the chalice up to the west and say:

> **By the powers of Water, I have found my peace with the religion of the Earth, with the ancient and magickal realms our ancestors still tread. I dedicate my joys, sorrows, and psyche to the Great Mother and Her Horned Consort as long as our paths are meant to meet and ask Their guidance as I work, play, and interact with the world today.**

Light the white candle and say:

> **White unto the Maiden's brow**
> **Her rose a gentle bud for now**
> **The Young Lord He doth run and play**
> **From dawn's first light til end of day.**

Light the red candle and say:

> **Red as blood the Mother's womb**
> **From gentle bud, the rose full-blooms**
> **The Greenwood Stag, he rules the Sun**
> **Until the growing season's done.**

Light the black candle and say:

> **Black as night the Crone's dark kiss**
> **The rose now withered, autumn's abyss**
> **The Holly King holds sway the land**
> **Snowflakes kiss His outstretched hand.**

Light the candle representing you and say:

> **I come before the Gods today**
> **To dedicate myself, my heart**
> **To the Old Religion's ways**
> **Unless our paths diverge and part.**

> **Study now, all that I can**
> **And practice that which I preach**
> **I'll never hurt the sacred land**
> **And promise to learn before I teach.**

> **To the Sabbats I will keep**
> **As moon and sun dance 'round the Earth**
> **I'll harvest all that my actions reap**
> **And celebrate with joy and mirth.**
>
> **Ancient Gods smile down on me**
> **I drink this wine in honor of thee**
> **By the powers of three times three**
> **As I will so mote it be**
> **Blesséd be!**

Drink the wine or water in the chalice.

This is a good time to spend reflecting on your dedication. If you are outside, take a long look around—do you see any animals? Any insects? Do any birds fly overhead?

Rabbits and frogs are strong symbols of the Goddess, so are sea gulls. Crows and ravens are magickal birds . . . hawks are sometimes called the messengers of the Gods. The ladybug and the bee represent the Lady and butterflies are omens of transformation. The stag, fox, and wolf are symbols of the God. Cats are notoriously fond of Witches, and Witches and Pagans are notoriously fond of cats!

Observe the world around you. Let your sight drift beyond the ordinary and later record what you felt and saw in your journal.

Treat yourself to a nice dinner after your dedication and spend the rest of the day in some peaceful, thoughtful activity.

Adding an Oath to Your Dedication

If you want to add an oath to your dedication, or if you later wish to re-dedicate yourself and add an oath when you do, I suggest that you tailor it specifically to your own needs.

Here are a few ideas, but be sure the oath you make is an oath you can keep. You don't want to break your promises to the Goddess—it's not healthy nor is it honorable.

> "I pledge my life and my heart to the Lord and Lady, that I will walk Their path for a year-and-a-day. I pledge by oath that I will not dishonor the name of the Gods. By my word, my name and my soul, so mote it be."

"I pledge my life and my heart to the Lord and Lady, I will walk Their path for as long as the blood flows through my veins. My heart is Their heart, my thoughts are Their thoughts, my hands do Their work, my lips speak in Their behalf. If I break with my oath, may the wrath of the Dark Mother find me. By my word, my name and my soul, so mote it be."

Pledging to a Specific God or Goddess

Pledging to a particular God, Goddess, or pair of Gods is a life-altering, binding compact that should never be made without thought, soul-searching, and inner guidance.

The only way to describe the process is to give you my own example. Everyone's story will be different.

On February 29, 1992, the twelfth anniversary of my entrance into the Craft, I pledged myself as Priestess to Mielikki and Tapio, Finnish forest deities who had been calling me since November of the previous year. I pledged my life, my soul, and my heart to Their service.

Why did I do this?

For many years I had worked with the Goddess Cerridwen, I had dedicated to Her for as long as She wanted me. I fully expected to pledge in Her service. Her energy was always around, watching over me.

Then one day, after a period of very intense magick (during the early summer of 1991), She vanished. It was as if there was a hole in my energy field.

I went into trance and was informed that Cerridwen wasn't the Goddess I was meant to serve and that She had withdrawn so that the Goddess I was meant to serve could make Herself known. I was instructed to throw my moonstone pentacle, which had been dedicated to Cerridwen, into the ocean and let go.

It was a difficult experience. Bereft, I felt as if I had lost someone to death. I was alone and frightened, and it didn't help that my life was in turmoil. What had been a wild, passionate run of magick for eight months suddenly dried up, leaving me nerve-wracked, angry, and confused.

However, I did as I was told. I wasn't stubborn enough to ignore direct orders. I went to Tolmie State Park (a beautiful and enchanting place), tossed my pentacle into the waves and watched as the tide carried it away. It had been the first pentacle I ever owned. When I gave it back to the Earth, it felt as though a part of me went with it.

After a month or so, I began to adjust. It had been a long time since I had experienced the psychic world without feeling like I had a safety net (Cerridwen is a powerful Goddess). At times, however, I felt incredibly lonely.

One night in early November I fell asleep and had a dream. In the dream I remembered my first introduction to the Craft, when I had been out walking in the woods.

In late January 1980, about a month before I met the Goddess and entered the Craft, I had taken a late-night walk with a friend and we saw a unicorn in the woods. My friend was frightened by the experience, but I was entranced and to this day I remember exactly what I saw.

In my dream, I relived the wonder of that night and then heard a voice say, "The Goddess you serve must also be a Goddess of Faerie."

Then I heard the name "Mielikki."

I woke and wrote down the dream. I vaguely remembered the name Mielikki from years ago when I played *Dungeons and Dragons*—She had been listed in one of the books.

So I began my research.

She turned out to be a Goddess of the Hunt, also connected with the Faerie Realm. She rules over the Metsanhaltija, (the Finnish spirits/daughters of the wood) and with Her husband Tapio (also a beloved forest deity from Finnish legend) watches over the realm of Tapiola.

I began to meditate on the pair and sparked an immediate connection.

Though written information on the Finnish mythos is sparse—for theirs was a purely oral tradition marked by bards who would use their songs to spar with one another—I began receiving images of Mielikki, Tapio, and Their realm.

Within a short time, I knew I had found my Goddess. I also knew that if I pledged myself to Her, I would also pledge to Tapio. It was both or neither.

Since I worked with Herne and Pan, turning to Tapio wasn't a problem—He was also a God of the forest and woodland.

By the time my twelfth anniversary in the Craft arrived, I had no choice. I had been called. I could not turn away.

On the evening of my anniversary, I re-dedicated myself to the Craft and to the service of the Lady/Earth Goddess, and I pledged myself to Mielikki and Tapio.

I have never regretted it.

Their methods of teaching range from mildly irritating to downright ridiculous, and They have made me laugh at myself more than any person ever could.

Pledging brought major changes to my life.

My ritual room must be kept very clean because Mielikki is a stickler for order.

I used to invoke the Norse God Loki when I wanted a little chaos in my life. They put an immediate stop to that. Shortly after I pledged myself, They showed up in one of my meditations, insisting that I pledge never again to invoke the Norse trickster. I will never break that promise.

I'm married to a man much like Tapio in temperament. I met him a week or so after I cast a love spell given to me by Mielikki in a dream. We moved in together on October 12, 1992—the first night we realized we were mutually attracted. We got engaged on December 8, and were married on Beltane, 1993. It's an incredible relationship.

I gave away every cast iron pot and pan in the house because, as a Goddess of Fey, Mielikki detests cast iron.

I've developed a love affair for bears, bees, and reindeer (Her animals) and also collect images of wolves, salmon, and hawks (related to Tapio), though I never used to.

There have been so many changes that I wouldn't know how to list them all.

I've learned not to resist what They guide me to do. There's always a reason even if at first I don't understand.

So, pledging to a specific deity is a life altering experience.

The only reason to make such a drastic commitment is that you can't NOT do it—if the call comes you will know. It it doesn't, or if you're not sure, then perhaps you weren't meant to be bound in this way during this lifetime.

A Pledging Ritual

Because of the vast differences in the Gods and Goddesses and Their ways, I'm going to reprint the text of my pledging ritual to Mielikki and Tapio to give you an idea of what I did. You must create your own ritual, based on the desires and needs of you and your particular deity.

For this ritual, my friends and fellow Witches James and Daniela acted as Priest and Priestess, drawing Mielikki and Tapio down into one another.

I realize now it would have been better to let the Lord and Lady of Tapiola say whatever They wanted to say, but at the time I had composed a ceremony and the Gods graciously used what I had written.

I decorated my altar with a beautiful horn that is (I believe) from a water buffalo, flowers, a chalice of wine to represent the blood of Mielikki and Tapio, my athame at the time—sharpened, a green cloth, and some incense.

We cast a circle, invoked the elements, and then James and Daniela drew down Mielikki and Tapio.

The pledging ceremony followed after circle casting, element invocations and drawing down Mielikki and Tapio.

PST: I stand here as a representative of the Goddess of Earth; Maiden, Mother and Crone, She whose spirit dwells within both Earth and Moon, Lady of the silver magic, Mistress of the Forest, Mielikki, Goddess of all who walk, hunt, sleep and dwell within the Greenwood, now to renew your pledge made to the Great Goddess twelve years ago this night and to make a pledge new.

PT: I stand here as a representative of the Horned God, Oak King, Holly King, Green Man, Young Phallic Lord, Master of the Hunt, Tapio, Master of the Woods, Lord of the Green, now to renew your pledge made to the Horned God twelve years ago this night and to make a pledge new.

PST: Do you come into this rite of your own free will?

Yas: I do.

PST: Under the ancient rite, do you pledge us your life, your love, your soul?

Yas: I do so pledge.

PT: Do you troth to keep alive our work, that should you be the last alive remembering us, you will not fail in your devotion, but keep our worship alive?

Yas: I do so pledge.

PST: Will you pledge to use your magic, talents, and gifts in service to us, to those who seek your help and for your own service, and not turn away when you hear our call to action?

Yas: I do so pledge.

PT: And will you mingle your blood with ours as a sign of joining that you have bound yourself to us by oath?

Yas: I will.

PST: Then take now your blade.

Yas: By earth and air, by fire and water, by crystal and star, I renew now my pledge, Lord of the Greenwood and Lady of the Night, hear me now!

Here I took my athame and sliced my finger. It was funny—I never bleed easily and, as usual, my finger didn't want to bleed where I cut it. Daniela/Mielikki leaned over and looked at my thumb and said, "Give it up!" and the blood suddenly poured out of the cut. I let a few drops of my blood fall into the chalice of wine and stirred it with the athame.

Yas: With this blade I draw my life-force, blood to blood, my soul to Yours, my life in Your hands, and so I bind myself by oath, unto my death I pledge myself to You.

I drank a sip of the wine, then handed it to James/Tapio and Daniela/ Mielikki and they drank.

Yas: As so have I drunk the dark wine, am I Your daughter and Priestess.

PST: As so you have bound your oath to mine own, let nothing dissuade you from my path, for you have pledged your life in my service and I name you my **Priestess and Witch, Maiden, Mother, and Crone.**

PT: As so you have bound your oath to mine own, let nothing dissuade you from my path, for you have pledged your life in my service and I name you my **Priestess and Witch, Consort in human form.**

P/P: So mote it be.

After Mielikki and Tapio withdrew and James and Daniela came out of trance, we celebrated my binding to Mielikki and Tapio with feast and drink. It was a beautiful evening, and though several kinks happened before the ceremony (unexpected people showing up and whatnot), by the time it was over I was floating in a state of grace.

When I look back over the years since I pledged to Mielikki and Tapio, it feels like all the years before then were another world. That night was truly a re-birth, I stepped into a new realm.

I have never regretted it, but now and then I wonder what my life would have been like if the Lord and Lady of Tapiola hadn't taken a fancy to me and called me into Their service. Although I sometimes wonder, I have no desire to find out.

Part 6

rites of death

Death • Rituals of Separation•
Handparting • Einherjar

DEATH

The Ceremony of Cord Cutting

Death to Pagans and Witches doesn't have the same negative connotations that it does to most people—we tend to believe in reincarnation and renewal. Pagans see death as simply another step in the eternal cycle of life.

Without death, there could be no life. Without life, death has no meaning. The two states of existence are inexorably linked, and we cannot experience one without the other. Death is not an evil presence hovering at our shoulder, waiting to snatch us away.

True, everyone must die, some perhaps too soon . . . others not soon enough. The process leading to death can be grisly and painful, but it can also be an easy passing, like simply stepping through a door.

This is not to say we do not grieve; we may rage at nature for stealing our loved ones. We are only human and the loss of a child or spouse is never easy. But underlying that grief is the understanding that death is a part of the cycle; it is the end to our current journey and whether or not it seems fair, people we love will die.

Because of our connection to the realms of spirit and the Gods, sometimes a Pagan or Witch who has lost a loved one is tempted to try and contact their beloved through an Ouija board or a séance. This I can only advise against.

The dead need to let go of this realm—the more tightly we hold them here through our attempts at contact, the more we interfere with their evolution as spirits or souls.

Once in a while, spirits will get lost or confused, they will stay connected to our realm through anger or fear. As Witches, we have a responsibility to help them on their way—to show them through the gate. But except for cases like this, and except for the holiday of Samhain, it is only with great thought and care that we should meddle in the realms of the dead.

It is one thing to keep pictures of our loved ones around, to occasionally talk to them and to wish they were with us, but it's quite another matter to try to lure them back, to go from psychic to psychic desperately seeking contact. If spirits need to contact you, they will—and usually for a specific reason—to clear up a murder mystery, to remind you to go on with your life, to let you know they're okay.

My sister Claudia died in 1986 from cancer. I felt she had let me down—I didn't think she had tried to fight the disease. Her memory haunted me and I fought her death.

On Samhain Eve that year, I had a dream. Claudia took me into a room where my mother and other sisters were talking. I looked around, then at Claudia and said, "But why are you here? You're dead."

She said, "Can't I come back to say hello?"

Then we sat and talked for awhile.

The next night, Samhain night, I dreamt that she came and took me on a journey. She showed me a white house and told me, "This is where I died. This is the house I loved."

I started to cry and told her I missed her. She said, "You have to let go now. I have to go on and you're holding me back. I love you, but I need you to let go."

I agreed, still crying. She hugged me and we got into the car. Halfway across a long bridge over dark water, I looked at the driver's seat and she was gone. I woke up, and I knew that it was time to move on and accept that she was dead.

I know she contacted me on Samhain because that is when the veil between the worlds is thinnest, and Claudia also understood how important the holiday is to me. She needed me to let go so she could move on to the next step in her evolution.

Hard as it was, I did.

The Colors of Death

In Western culture death is symbolized by the color black, but two of the other colors commonly associated with death on a world-scale are white and yellow.

Incenses, Herbs, and Woods

Incenses appropriate to cord cutting ceremonies are myrrh, copal, cypress, and patchouli.

Herbs associated with death are nightshade, mandrake, belladonna, comfrey, pansy, lilies, and rue (be cautious, some of these are poisonous!).

Woods connected with the realm of spirit include yew, elder, cypress, and eucalyptus.

Cord Cutting Ritual for the Dead

One of the simplest and most effective ways to say good-bye is to perform a cord-cutting ceremony.

This can be done as a group ritual (sometimes more effective because it's easier to let go when others are around for emotional support) or as a solitary ritual.

Each person attending will need to bring a three–foot length of cord representing connection to the deceased. Before the ritual each person, while holding the cord, should silently meditate on his or her relationship with the deceased and what that person meant in this or her life.

If the loved one was a Witch and had an athame, so much the better. If you do not have access to their ritual dagger, or if they did not have one, then choose a smooth, straight branch from a yew, elder, or rowan tree, making sure it is at least fifteen inches long.

You will also need a planter filled with compacted dirt and a chalice of burgundy or port wine.

Each person may bring an object that binds them in a special way with his or her friend to set on the altar.

When everyone is assembled, cast a circle and invoke the elements. If the deceased was pledged to a particular God or Goddess, then you should invoke Them, if not then use the following invocation as written.

PST: **I call upon the Goddess Cerridwen, Lady of the Sow, Dark Mother of the Cauldron of Rebirth. Come to us, Lady of Death, and be with us as we cut our cords to the spirit who was** (name).

PT: **I call upon the Dark aspect of Herne, Lord of the Wild Shadow-Wood, Gatekeeper, Challenger. Come to us, Keeper of the Wild, and be with us as we cut our cords to the spirit who was** (name).

PST: *(Picks up the athame or branch as the Priest picks up the pot of soil.)* (Name) **has joined his/her soul with the world of spirit. S/he has returned to the Earth!** *(Plunge the athame or branch into the soil.)*

PT: *(Sets the planter on the altar.)* **The Wheel turns, life into death.**

PST: **So we accept the turning of the seasons, and so we accept the turning of a life.**

One by one, beginning with the Priestess, each person stands in front of the soil and athame, contemplates his or her connection, then ties the cord around the hilt of the dagger or branch. Each person then takes a sip of the wine. When all have done so, the Priestess picks up a long knife with a sharp cutting edge and holds it out at arm's length. The Priest draws a devoking pentacle over it—see Appendix One, page 278.

PT: **I charm thee, blade that severs, in the names of Herne and Cerridwen. As you sever the cords, so shall you sever our links with the soul who was known to us as** (name). **We free him/her to continue his/her evolution and remember him/her with love and fondness, but no longer seek to hold him/her to this realm.**

PST: So mote it be.

The knife is set in front of the planter. Each person, when ready, crosses to the altar and holds their cord taut. If need be, the Priestess should steady the athame. The person then uses the knife to sever the cord, breaking the psychic link with the deceased. Each person then take another sip of the wine. This part of the ritual should be performed in silence. When everyone has finished, the Priestess wraps the cord lengths still tied to the branch/athame with a black cord, binding them tightly against the metal or wood.

PST: (Name) has joined the realm of Spirit. We mourn his/her passing, even as we rejoice in the evolution of his/her soul.

PT: The Wheel turns, death into life.

PST: Lady Cerridwen, we thank you for joining us and attending our rites.

PT: Lord Herne, we thank you for joining us and attending our rites.

Devoke elements and circle. The group now goes out in the woods and buries the athame or the branch, with the cords still tightly wrapped around it. If you are doing this on public land, such as a forest, dig your hole very, very deep so that the dagger won't be found. If it's private land, be sure you have permission. Each person should dispose of his or her half of the cord by tossing it in the ocean, burning it in a fire, or burying it far away from their house.

After your cord-cutting ritual, return to the house and have an old fashioned wake with music and food. Set a special plate of food on the altar for your friend (as you would during Samhain) then feast, share your favorite memories, laugh, cry, and let your loved one go.

The Loss of A Pet

For many of us, the loss of a pet can be as heart-breaking as the loss of a human companion. Unfortunately, our society doesn't recognize the connection between human and animal as binding and important. How many times have you heard someone say, "It's only a dog." or "It's just a cat."?

These are cruel, unfeeling responses to someone who may have just lost the best friend they've ever had. For some of us, our pets act as our children, our confidants, our guardians, and our familiars. To deny the strength of these bonds is to deny the strength of love and loyalty.

A ceremony to say good-bye to your pet can be shared with others or performed alone. I've held mourning circles for some of my four-legged friends and invited my human friends to join me. We go around, each sharing a fond memory of the lost pet and then wish him or her Goddess speed on his or her path.

Then we share a toast to the spirit of the animal and bid farewell.

I have created strong bonds with cats in this life—twice now I've had them return to me—reincarnating into another cat body to come back to me again. I don't force the issue, but when offered the chance to connect with my beloved Circe, (who was killed by a speeding driver, which is why I keep my cats indoors now) I jumped at the opportunity.

When Meerclar grew old and died, she waited a year then chose to return, and I welcomed her home.

Each time I was shown (with Circe in a dream, with Meerclar it was a meditative vision) what each cat would look like when she returned and when I should start watching for her and both times the vision was right on the mark.

Circe left me again—she vanished as if she had never been back, but if she ever wants to come home to me, she knows I'll be waiting with open arms.

Even though other felines share my life now, I've got more than enough love to go around.

Food and Recipes

Persephone's Punch

2 cups pomegranate juice
1 cup cherry juice
1 can orange juice concentrate
2 liters sparkling water
   Juice of 5 lemons

Blend all ingredients and serve in silver or glass punch bowl with lots of ice.
Serves 10.

Remembrance Bread

2 packages dry yeast
2½ cups warm water
¼ cup sugar
2 eggs, separated
1½ teaspoon salt

2 tablespoons chopped rosemary
1 teaspoons sage
7-8 cups all-purpose flour

Preheat oven to 350 degrees. Sprinkle yeast over ½ cup warm water. Add sugar and stir to dissolve. Let stand 5 minutes. Add remaining 2 cups water and stir thoroughly.

Beat egg whites until lightly foamy. Fold into yeast mixture. Stir in salt and herbs.

Add flour, one cup at a time, until dough begins to pull away from bowl. Turn onto lightly floured board and knead for 15 minutes.

Place in buttered bowl, cover, and set in warm place until doubled in bulk. Punch down and divide dough into two loaves. Place in buttered and floured loaf pans and let rise another 30 minutes. Brush with beaten egg yolks and bake 25–35 minutes until toothpick inserted in center comes out clean.

Serves 10.

Wheel of Balance

1 package instant chocolate pudding
3 cups 2% or whole milk
1 cup whipped cream
½ teaspoon mint flavoring

1 package instant vanilla pudding
½ teaspoon rum flavoring
1 graham cracker crumb crust

Whip chocolate pudding, 1½ cups milk, ½ cup whipped cream and mint flavoring together. Let set 5 minutes.

Whip vanilla pudding, 1½ cups milk, ½ cup whipped cream, and rum flavoring together. Let set 5 minutes.

Spoon puddings into crumb crust in a yin-yang pattern.

Chill for 2 hours and garnish with mint before serving.

Serves 6.

Rituals of Separation

Moving and Ending Friendships

There are other forms of separation besides death. Another common period of mourning happens when a friend decides to move far away. This can be painful and often we feel betrayed, even though we usually don't say anything.

It's a natural, though egocentric, point of view to feel that if they cared enough, they'd stay. It's easy to overlook the fact that our friends have their own lives and those lives don't revolve around us.

The point is, it hurts to lose someone we rely on emotionally, and while we can maintain valuable and close friendships through letters, telephone calls, and the Internet, it never seems quite the same as curling up with someone and chatting away the afternoon.

There are also times when we need to take a break from a friendship, when we must put the relationship on hold while we search out new directions for personal growth. This can hurt worse than if someone moves away unless both people realize that sometimes friends grow apart and that it's not either person's fault.

There are so many different opportunities today that it's not uncommon to find our interests diverging, to develop new hobbies, careers, and desires.

If our friendship is grounded in a path with which we're no longer comfortable, then that relationship will suffer unless we take time to reassess whether the connection is still viable. This is common when two people are brought together by a single goal or focus and one person eventually loses interest in that goal.

Letting go is never easy, but sometimes it's necessary for our growth and development. If we become too interconnected we lose our own identity. Then we have to step away and develop the unique style that only we, as individuals, can possess.

Only when two individuals meet as equals can a true and solid friendship be created. Unless inequalities (whether due to class structure, economics, dominance-subordination, etc.) are addressed and cleared, homologous relationships cannot exist.

Going-away parties are fun and helpful in allowing a group of friends to bid farewell to one of their companions, but on a one-to-one basis, ritual can make the separation easier to accept.

Separation Ritual: Moving Away

The following ritual is for use when one friend is moving to another city, state, or country. It is designed to retain the bond between one another while allowing for new growth and friendships to enter the picture. This is not a ritual for casual relationships.

You will need:

> a 4-foot length of pink cord
> a sharp knife
> a chalice of wine or spring water

Each person should bring a lovely, heart-felt gift (one they know their friend will cherish) to the ritual.

I suggest performing this ritual in a warm, cozy spot and spread out a luncheon or dinner of your favorite foods for after the ceremony.

For purposes of clarity, the two friends will be designated as FR1 and FR2, with FR2 being the friend who is moving away.

Cast a circle and invoke the elements.

Perform the following invocation to Isis (if the friends are men, then I suggest invoking Osiris instead—of course, you will adjust gender nouns as well).

FR1: Great Isis, Mother of Egypt, Mother of Mothers, Loyal and Faithful Lady of Life, come to this space and be with us as we pledge our friendship. Watch over (name of FR2) as s/he travels far on his/her journey. Guard and protect him/her through the days to come even as we ask that You guard and protect our friendship.

FR2: Great Isis, Mother of Egypt, Mother of Mothers, Loyal and Faithful Lady of Life, come to this space and be with us as we pledge our friendship. Watch over (name of FR1) as s/he remains here to continue and grow in his/her life. Guard and protect him/her through the days to come even as we ask that You guard and protect our friendship.

FR1 and FR2 should make themselves comfortable. The chalice of wine should rest between them, along with the knife. The gifts, wrapped, should sit next to each person (they will be exchanged later). The two friends should clasp hands.

FR1: You are leaving and I will miss you. You are leaving and I do not want you to go.

FR2: The cycle turns and I must leave. Do not blame yourself. I am not rejecting our friendship.

FR1: I don't want to lose you.

FR2: Nor I, you. When I am gone, you will make new friends. I am leaving my old world behind.

FR1: Your spirit must go with you so you can be whole and centered in your new life. You, too, will make new friends.

FR2: Let us link our friendship, bind it even though the distance divides us.

FR1: Though we go our separate ways, our hearts remain linked by the ties of care and compassion.

Take the pink cord. FR1 ties one end gently around FR2's wrist—not the hand FR2 uses to cut with. Then, FR2 ties the other end gently around FR1's wrist.

FR1: By the powers of love, I bind you to me.

FR2: By the powers of truth, I bind you to me.

FR1: By the powers of honor, I bind you to me.

FR2: By the powers of caring, I bind you to me.

Both: Bound by friendship, bound by love,
Bound by magick, bound by troth,
Bound by heart, our friendship stands,
Bound by the gentle clasp of hands.

*Take each other's hands for a moment and focus on the friendship that
has been.*

FR1: Change comes. Our friendship evolves. The Wheel turns
and we turn with it.

FR2: *(Picks up knife.)* Since I am the one to leave, I claim responsibility for severing the cord. Though separated, we remain
friends. The Wheel is turning, but we are still part of the
same cycle.

*Pull cord taut; FR2 severs cord. Gently untie the knots from one another's
wrists. Coil cords and set aside. Exchange gifts.*

FR1: *(Picks up chalice.)* I drink to your new adventures. May your
journeys be safe and exciting. May you find what your heart
desires. *(Drinks.)*

FR2: *(Accepts chalice.)* I drink to the path that extends before you.
May your journeys be safe and exciting. May you find what
your heart desires. *(Drinks.)*

FR1: Though things will never be the same, may they be wonderful and joyous and full of learning.

FR2: So mote it be.

FR1: Lady Isis, watch over my friend wherever s/he goes. Be the
guiding star in his/her journey.

FR2: Lady Isis, watch over my friend on his/her path. Be the
watchful guardian on his/her journey.

Both: Blesséd be.

Devoke elements and circle. Have a long, leisurely lunch and talk about not only what the friend who is leaving will be doing, but what the friend who is staying has planned. Each person should keep his or her length of cord in a safe place. If the friendship eventually fades away, then quietly and respectfully burn or bury the cords.

Separation Ritual: Severing a Friendship by Mutual Choice

When a friendship ends, the action is often accompanied by hurt feelings and anger. I offer this ritual to ease the division before the friendship sours into animosity.

If both parties agree that it's time to reassess the friendship, then this ritual will help to cushion the break.

It is not meant for use when one person has wronged another—this ritual is designed for two people who feel they've taken their friendship as far as it can go, or who need a break to reassess whether or not the relationship still offers enough mutual interest and growth.

As in the ritual above, the two friends will be designated by FR1 and FR2.

Set up altar as shown below, with two pink candles, two pink roses, one 3-foot pink cord, and the athames of both parties.

Separation Altar

Cast a circle and invoke the elements. Each person lights one pink candle. Both parties should stand together in front of the altar, hands clasped. Stand for a few minutes, contemplating what it is you are doing. Then FR1 begins.

FR1:   **We have been friends for (number) years. So now our friendship has run its course and we are looking in other directions.**

FR2:   **We have shared the joys and sorrows of our lives with one another. Now our paths, like ships, are diverging on the great ocean of life.**

FR1:   **We do not wish to part in anger, so we come before the Gods today to part in mutual agreement, that we might carry no grudge and bear no shame.**

FR2:   **Where once we shared much, now we share little.**

FR1:   **Where once our interests converged, now they take different directions.**

FR2:   **Where once we shared the joy of connection, now we chafe at the yoke we created.**

FR1:   **I will not bind you to a relationship that makes you uncomfortable.**

FR2:   **I will not bind you to a relationship that might impede your personal growth.**

FR1:   **It is better to part ways amicably than to part in anger.**

Take up cord. Each should tie one end of the cord to a chair. Then take up both athames and stand together in front of the center of the cord.

FR2:   **Then you agree to go your way?**

FR1:   **Even as you go yours.**

Bth: **Then let us sever our friendship while still retaining respect for one another.**

Together, simultaneously cut the cord in the center with both knives. When the cord is severed, move the chairs apart and replace the athames on the altar. Exchange roses as the following is said:

FR2:   **A token of respect for the friendship we've shared.**

FR1:   **A token of compassion and caring for the bonds we've just severed.**

FR2:   *(Blows out one candle.)* **So I extinguish the fires of my friendship, even as I accept my place as your acquaintance.**

FR1:   *(Blows out other candle.)* **So I extinguish the fires of my friendship, even as I accept my place as your acquaintance.**

FR2:   **The path is clear and open, should there come a day when we decide to rekindle our close ties. We part not in anger, but in sadness . . . not in fury but in quiet acceptance that life changes.**

FR1:   **So the Wheel turns and our paths diverge.**

Burn the two pieces of cord or bury them under an oak tree, and take the roses home. Dry the petals and keep in a special place as a memory of all the good times you shared as friends. If and when the time is right, you will come together again. Speak no ill of the other, or your acceptance of the situation will sour and you will never be able to remember your connection with joy.

Separation Ritual: When a Friend has Wronged You

Sadly, friends do hurt us. Sometimes they don't mean to, and those actions can usually be repaired; but other times we discover that someone we thought was a friend has chosen to betray us. Perhaps our best friend had an affair with our spouse, or perhaps they are spreading vicious rumors about us (as opposed to the common gossip that runs through all circles), maligning our character.

When this happens, we often find that we can't get satisfaction by confronting our attacker—either they try to justify their actions because they know they've done wrong, or they do their best to avoid us.

You have several options. You can take revenge. While this may be appropriate at times, you must have a clear head in order to assess what needs to be done.

You can ignore the situation, but I guarantee that unless you address the pain that your ex-friend caused, you won't be able to shake that feeling of betrayal that has a way of nestling in your heart. It tends to rear its head at the most inopportune times. I have experienced this and know how deep anger can root itself in our lives.

This ritual is designed to reclaim your sense of personal power when it feels like it's been stripped away. The ceremony is meant to give you a sense of disconnection so that you can see clearly.

You will need the following:

> a black candle
> a white candle
> a red rose
> a bowl of salt water
> a few drops of rose geranium oil
> a glass of cold peppermint tea
> a smudge stick

If possible, perform this ritual next to a stream of running water or next to the ocean. This will keep the leftover energy from building up in your home.

Cast a circle. Turn to the north and say:

> **Spirits of the Earth, come to me in my need. Help me ground myself in the reality of the situation and the strength of my personal truth. Guard me and give me the strength with which to face this betrayal.**

Turn to the east and say:

> **Spirits of the Air, come to me in my need. Help me clear my mind so that I might see the truth of the situation. Catch my pain up on your breezes and carry it away so that I can let go of the anger and constructively focus on my own path.**

Turn to the south and say:

> **Spirits of the Fire, come to me in my need. Help me burn away the shadows of lingering anger and transform my fury into creative power so that I can build new, positive paths in my life.**

Turn to the west and say:

> **Spirits of the Water, come to me in my need. Help me wash away the betrayal with my tears, let me purify my sense of self and renew my inner vision so that I may once again experience the joys of life.**

Light the white candle and say:

> **Great Isis, Mother of Egypt, Mother of Mothers, Loyal and Faithful Lady of Life, I call on Your compassionate heart to help me in my sorrow! I have been betrayed by** (name). **Now I must let go of** (name) **as my friend and accept him/her for what s/he has shown himself/herself to be.**

Light the black candle and say:

> (Name) **I once called you friend, now I see you for what you truly are. I withdraw my energy, I reclaim my power, I take back all that I gave you, I no longer support you in any emotional or physical manner. I provide no foundation for your energy.**

Anoint your forehead with the rosemary oil and say:

> **I am complete, unto myself, and set my boundaries so that** (name) **is excluded from my heart.** (Name) **will not hurt me again. I protect and shield myself against all attacks that** (name) **might aim towards me. My actions and my words will shine through** (name)**'s betrayal so that everyone will know the truth.**

Take up the red rose and say:

> **This rose represents the friendship we once had. I dismantle that friendship.** *(Tear petals off rose.)* **If** (name) **has true remorse and sorrow, perhaps we shall one day mend the break, but** (name) **must prove himself/herself by word and action if s/he desires to win my trust again.**

Dip fingers in salt water and anoint your heart. Then pick up bowl and vent all your anger and pain into the water. Yell, scream, cry . . . say all the painful, angry, and bitter things you need to.

When you have exhausted yourself and your heart feels numb, pour the water into the stream or ocean and toss the petals in after it. Watch as the current washes them away.

After a few minutes, wash your face with cool water (from the stream, if possible, or from a bottle of spring water) and drink the tea. Light the smudge stick and let the smoke drift over you, breathe deeply and hold the purifying sage in your lungs. Turn to the west and say:

> **Spirits of the Water, wash away my pain and clear my heart. Transform my sorrow into joy.**

Turn to the south and say:

> **Spirits of the Fire, kindle in me the will to persevere and grow. Transform my anger into creativity.**

Turn to the east and say:

> **Spirits of the Air, blow through my aura and remove any lingering remnants of humiliation. Transform my confusion into clarity.**

Turn to the north and say:

> **Spirits of the Earth, ground me in the reality of life and remove any obstacles to my growth. Transform my loss into abundance.**

Focus on the black candle and say:

> **(Name), I name thee pariah, no longer a part of my life. Go meet your karma even as I reclaim any energy I ever gave to you.** *(Snuff out candle and break in half.)*

Focus on the white candle and say:

> **Lady Isis, be with me in the days to come, let me weep on Your shoulder, instill new joys in my heart. Be my solace and my comfort. Blessed be.** *(Snuff out candle.)*

Gather your things, throw the black candle (with the flame thoroughly snuffed) into the garbage before you return home. Put the white candle on your nightstand and burn a little each night for the next seven days, knowing that Isis will watch over you and that She's there to hear you when you call. Have as little to do with the friend who betrayed you, do not speak his or her name unless necessary, do not give them any attention or energy during this time.

Focus on your own growth and your own needs.

HANDPARTING

Dissolving a Marriage

When two people are in a relationship and consider themselves married (opposite or same sex) they form a bond that is stronger than friendship. When those same two people decide they can no longer live together and that they're headed in different directions, they separate, get a divorce, or sometimes one just disappears.

If both agree that separation is the best thing, the parting becomes easier. If one doesn't want to see the relationship dissolve, then the situation grows more difficult. If children are involved, the complexities multiply exponentially.

I offer two rituals—one for someone who is being left, for a person who doesn't want the relationship to end or was unprepared for the sudden collapse of a marriage. It is designed to help the person cope with the feelings of rejection and disbelief that go hand-in-hand with shock.

The other ritual is designed for two people who know they are no longer meant to be with one another and so have agreed amicably that it's time to part.

Remember, however, that while both parties at first might agree that they want to remain friends, it's very easy for viewpoints and emotions to shift—so don't be overly surprised if your ex-partner suddenly turns on you and begins accusing you of ruining the relationship.

It happens, it's common, and it can be a natural reaction to the fear that sets in once a person realizes he or she is alone again.

When You Don't Want to Let Go

Your lover/husband/wife comes home one day and announces he or she has found another love and they want their freedom to marry. Or you come home early and find your partner in bed with someone else and blaming you for the need to roam and says he wants a divorce. Maybe your spouse of fifteen years suddenly proclaims that she's off to find herself and she'll be leaving in the morning.

Whatever the circumstances, you've suddenly been thrust into a dizzying world of pain and confusion and you don't quite understand what happened. It was all so quick and, try as you might, you don't know what went wrong. All you know is that you still love the person, but they're leaving and they say they won't be back.

If you want them to stay, you can try to persuade them to go to counseling. If that fails, you've got no choice—you have to accept that you're going to be on your own, no matter how much that frightens you.

Letting go of a partner, even an abusive partner, is difficult. Counseling is a great help; talking to friends who have been in the same position can also provide support. This ritual is meant to be performed when you've gone as far as you can on the practical level, and now you need a boost to push you over the last vestiges of shock, into acceptance of your new state of affairs.

Ritual to Strengthen Self-Image

This ritual works best when performed between the Waning and the New Moon. You will need:

>   frankincense incense
>   a bottle of rose water and your magic mirror
>   (see chapter on Samhain—a hand mirror will do if you
>   do not have a magic mirror)
>   white candle
>   a pot of peppermint tea—hot or iced

a small muslin pouch filled with:
rose petals
lavender
rosemary
3 cups boiling water
rose or lavender bubble bath

Make sure that your bathroom and bedroom are clean. Strip your bed and put on clean sheets, new if possible, and air out the room before the ritual.

Pour the three cups of boiling water over the pouch of herbs in a bowl. Let it steep for thirty minutes. During this time, prepare your teapot (have the kettle on the stove, ready to heat when you finish your bath). Put the mirror and the rose water on the nightstand next to the teapot. If you like, add a saucer of your favorite cookies to the table, and a vase of your favorite flowers.

Light the incense in the bathroom and let burn for a few minutes, then place on nightstand along with tea, and other accouterments.

Fill the tub with water (temperature suited to your taste), bubble bath, and the herb-water.

Light the candle and close the door. Cast a circle, then turn to the north and say:

> **Spirits of Earth, come to my circle and ground me in the strength of myself. Let me feel joy in solitude, grounding in my home, and peace with my life.**

Turn to the east and say:

> **Spirits of Air, come to my circle and cleanse me of my sorrows. Let me feel joy in my thoughts, clarity in my vision, and peace with my life.**

Turn to the south and say:

> **Spirits of Fire, come to my circle and regenerate my spirit. Let me feel joy in my situation, radiance in my soul, and peace with my life.**

Turn to the west and say:

> **Spirits of Water, come to my circle and wash clean my heart.
> Let me feel joy even through sorrow, beauty in my face and
> form, and peace with my life.**

Step into the tub and stand, saying:

> **Lord and Lady of the Greenwood, Gracious Goddess and
> Gentle Hunter, be with me. Strengthen my will, lift my spirits
> that I might find the courage to continue. Bring joy to my
> heart and soul. Let me heal from this wound, this ache.**

Soak in the water, letting the scent of the herbs soothe your tired
thoughts. When you are ready, dry yourself and slip into a clean
(preferably new) bathrobe, pajamas, or nightgown and heat the
water for your tea. Carry the candle into your room and place it
next to the mirror.

While the tea is steeping, wash your face with the rose water and
say:

> **Water of roses from brilliant red flowers,**
> **Strengthen my beauty and increase my power**
> **To laugh and take joy in things great and small**
> **To walk with pride, head and shoulders held tall**

Look in the mirror and say:

> **Mirror of magic and fortune, show my beauty to me**
> **Let me rejoice in the image I see**
> **For faces so fair can hold hearts that are dark**
> **And a woman/man thought ugly might sing like a lark**

Focus on the candle and say:

> **Flame rise and fall, your passion be mine**
> **My heart—it knows love, no more shall I pine**
> **If (name of ex) does not love me then so mote it be**
> **As new love approaches, I'll forget about thee.**

Drink a few sips of the tea and say:

**Peppermint, peppermint, clear now my mind
So that it be clear when new love I do find
Cleanse out my anger and blow it away
And help me rejoice as life races my way!**

Now let the candle burn out while you finish your tea and climb under the new sheets with a favorite magazine or book. Leave the rose water and the mirror on your nightstand for a few nights to remind you that beauty begins in the heart and that no one can negate your esteem if you refuse to allow it.

Handparting Ritual

A handparting ritual sets asunder the ritual/magickal energy of a marriage. It divides the couple in the eyes of the Gods. If you are legally married, you should take care of the divorce before the handparting—the ritual should be your last act together.

When you've agreed to a handparting, it should take place on the bed you've shared as partners. Make the bed with the usual bedding that you used as a couple, and in the center place a wedding picture of you that you won't mind destroying. If possible, after the ritual sell the bed and buy a new one. Give the bedding (unless it's a family quilt or something) to charity.

This ritual should be performed with few onlookers. It is a private affair, after all, and not one that most of your friends will feel comfortable attending.

Ask close friends to act as Priest and Priestess—if they performed your handfasting, so much the better.

While I'm using the man and woman combination here, this ritual can easily adapt to same-sex marriages.

If you have a handfasting cord from your wedding, so much the better. If you don't have a special cord, then the couple should braid one before the ceremony to represent the bond they've shared.

A bouquet of white roses should be on the nightstand.

The couple sits in bed together, the picture near them and the cord wrapped around their hands, which are clasped.

The Priest should have a pair of scissors, the Priestess a sharp athame. Cast the circle and invoke the directions as usual.

PST: We gather today to witness the parting of ways between (name) and (name). They have shared their lives with one another, but now feel it is time to part.

PT: (Man), are you willing to undergo this ceremony of separation? Do you willingly forfeit your right to claim (woman) as your wife and partner?

M: I will forfeit that right.

PST: (Woman), are you willing to undergo this ceremony of separation? Do you willingly forfeit your right to claim (man) as your husband and partner?

W: I will forfeit that right.

PT: You were joined in love. Do you declare your love changed and transformed so it no longer binds your hearts? Are you willing to sever those ties?

M: I loved you and accepted you as my wife. Now my love has transformed. My needs are no longer the same. I claim the right to follow my own path wherever it may lead me, though it means an end to our pairing.

W: I loved you and accepted you as my husband. Now my love has transformed. My needs are no longer the same. I claim the right to follow my own path wherever it may lead me, though it means an end to our pairing.

PST: Will you agree to respect one another and speak no ill against the one you once loved?

M: I agree.

W: I agree.

PT: So be it. Under the sight of the God I do declare you separate and divided, beholden no more. *(He picks up the picture and cuts it half, then in half again.)*

PST: So be it. Under the sight of the Goddess I do declare you separate and divided, beholden no more. *(She uses the athame to sever the cord binding their hands.)*

PT: This marriage is dissolved.

PST: This union has ended.

M: I let you go, I release you and wish you well.

W: I let you go, I release you and wish you well.

PST: So mote it be, in the eyes of the Gods you are no longer husband and wife.

If the couple has a handfasting broom they jumped over, now is the time to break the broom. Later you can toss it into the fire or the ocean. Devoke elements and circle.

EINHERJAR

The Feast of the Fallen Warriors

Modern Veteran's Day, a day on which we commemorate the soldiers of our armies and wars, has an ancient history. Whether or not deliberately planned, the fact is that in Norse tradition, November 11 is known as the Einherjar—the Feast of the Fallen Warriors, when all warriors slain in honorable battle are remembered and honored.

Today, when war is seldom desired and we consider all the carnage done in the name of differing religions and beliefs, we can find other ways in which to celebrate this holiday. No doubt some followers of Norse tradition will disagree with me, but I think that we can celebrate Einherjar by remembering those who have lived and died honorably, who have been true to their Gods, and matched their actions to their words.

There are many types of warriors—just the act of carrying a sword or gun doesn't automatically insure that one deserves the title. Some of the strongest warriors I can think of carried no weapons save their tongues . . . others died fighting to make their world a better place.

Gandhi immediately comes to mind, and the students who died in Tiananmen Square. A woman who dies protecting her child, a nun who is tortured because she won't recant her beliefs, a black

man shot for refusing to move from his land when white suprema-
cists try to burn him out—these are all warriors in my opinion, and
they all deserve respect for dying true to their beliefs.

Einherjar Ritual

Since Einherjar is a Norse festival, I designed this ritual to have
more of a Norse flavor than typically Celtic or Wiccan, invoking the
four dwarfs who hold up the sky instead of invoking the elements,
using a hammer (a small sledgehammer that can stand upright)
instead of an athame, and a drinking horn instead of a chalice.

You will also need mead or wine. If you cannot drink alcohol,
you might want to substitute a honey-lemon tea or sparkling grape
juice; but if you have no problem with alcohol, use it for this ceremony. Decorate your altar with pictures and symbols of those you
wish to remember. The Priest and Priestess lead the ceremony.

PT: *(Using hammer, casts circle.)* **I cast a ring of power protection,
let it encircle this sacred space, allowing nothing unwelcome
to enter in.**

PST: *(Facing east.)* **Austri, mighty dwarf who holds up the eastern
quarter of the sky, I call to you—come to this place and join
us, you who bring clarity and illumination to the world.**

PT: *(Facing south.)* **Sudhri, mighty dwarf who holds up the southern quarter of the sky, I call to you—come to this place and
join us, you who bring creation and transformation to the
world.**

PST: *(Facing west.)* **Vestri, mighty dwarf who holds up the western
quarter of the sky, I call to you—come to this place and join
us, you who bring emotion and purification to the world.**

PT: *(Facing north.)* **Nordhri, mighty dwarf who holds up the northern quarter of the sky, I call to you—come to this place and
join us, you who bring stability and manifestation to the world.**

Priest and Priestess come to the center of the circle.

PT: Odhinn, All-Father, we ask that you join our rites as we remember those honorably slain in battle. Be with us, Wise One, Rune-Bringer, and guide us in our rites tonight.

PST: Freyja, Queen of Valkyries, we ask that you join our rites as we remember those honorably slain in battle. Be with us, Great Dis, Lady of Magick, and help to guide us in our rites tonight.

PT: Tyr the One-Handed, we ask that you join our rites as we remember those honorably slain in battle. Be with us, Bravest of Gods, and help to guide us in our rites tonight.

PST: We come together to remember the fallen, to honor those who died in service to just causes. We drink to their memory and toast them with the golden nectar of the Gods.

As the Priestess holds up the drinking horn, the Priest first pours a little mead outside in honor of Odhinn, then fills the horn and offers it to the Priestess.

PST: I drink, remembering *(Lists those she specifically wants to remember.)*, **all of whom died in battle and all who died for their beliefs.** *(Drinks.)*

The horn is passed to the Priest, then around the circle, being refilled as necessary, until everyone has toasted the dead. The remaining mead in the horn should be poured outside and then the Gods should be thanked and the circle opened. Feasting should follow—this is not a time for sparsity— good, solid food and drink are called for.

Part 7

rites of love

Kitty Birthday •
Lupercalia • Weddings

KITTY BIRTHDAY

The Blessings of Bast

People love their pets. Pagans love their pets. Jews love their pets. Buddhists respect and revere all animals. Even staunch Christians love their pets. Religion can play into a person's interaction with animals, but the love and devotion for the cats, dogs, snakes, pigs, birds, and the other varied species who share our daily lives transcends the boundaries of personal belief systems.

Having said that, the Pagan can combine devotion to deity with devotion to their furry friend and help out homeless animals at the same time.

My husband and I have four cats. Someday when we're able to build our dream-house, we will have room for a couple more. These are our children, and we worry about them as any parent worries about a child. Because of the rampant abuse, traffic, disease, and general mayhem out there, our personal opinion is that our cats are better off indoors. They are bouncy, happy, fluffy balls of fur and razor blades who enrich our lives, and I wouldn't be without them.

Because we think so highly of our cats, because these are other living beings who share our lives, we promote and encourage responsible pet care and ownership at every available opportunity. Keep your pets' vaccinations up-to-date, spay or neuter them if you aren't a pedigreed breeder, keep them safe from traffic and nasty neighbors, love them, and don't ignore them.

Because most of our friends have pets (mainly cats) instead of children, we tend to talk about them and bring treats for them when we visit. So a number of years back I developed our Kitty Birthday Party, and it has evolved into an annual holiday that our friends look forward to almost as much as we do. It doesn't matter if you prefer dogs to cats, or whatever . . . just adapt the ritual as you need to.

Kitty Birthday

When we started Kitty Birthday it was mainly just a potluck for the humans and lots of treats and adoration for the cats. One year, as Kitty Birthday rolled near, it struck me that although our cats are fat and healthy, there are thousands of starving, unwanted animals out there. So many small groups are doing their best to help out, but the demand for donations far exceeds the supply.

Since we invoke Bast (Egyptian Cat Goddess) as the protector of our animals, it occurred to me we could invoke Her help on this day—Kitty Birthday.

It also crossed my mind that magickal help alone just isn't enough, so I asked all our friends who attended Kitty Birthday to bring a bag or box of cat food for Concern For Animals (a nonprofit, volunteer organization that attempts to find homes for all the strays they take in). We found one of our girls through C.F.A., and I don't know what we'd do without her.

The idea worked so well and felt so good that I made it an annual tradition—if you want to come to Kitty Birthday, you've got to bring a donation! We collected forty-two pounds of cat food at a recent party.

I encourage all pet owners, Pagan or not, to adopt this practice—you don't have to invoke a Goddess, but throw a party and collect the donations.

Bast Blessing Ritual

Everyone who attends the ritual brings at least a one pound (preferably more) bag of cat food and sets the food near the altar.

Cast your circle and invoke the elements as usual.

PST: I call upon the Lady Bast, You who are Goddess of all Catkind, Lady of Dance and Song, of Joy and Protection, come to this space and be with us. Bless our beloved feline friends with long life, good health, and happy hearts.

Bring out your special treats for your cats. This can include treat food, catnip, and new toys. Let the cats fully enjoy themselves, pet them, play with them. When the cats are sated with attention, then everyone gathers around the altar and joins hands.

PST: Lady Bast, bless this food, that it might multiply ten times and ten times again. Let it reach those in hunger and pain and bring joy and relief to our friends in the feline world. We ask that you bless your children, those without homes and those unloved, and aid us in comforting them. Please, open the hearts of irresponsible owners even as we encourage them to prevent the unnecessary death and cruelty that their lack of foresight can bring. Together, Lady Bast, we may make a difference. Bless¨d be.

All: Bless¨d be.

Open the circle and enjoy your own potluck. Then donate the gathered food to animal welfare organizations around your area and decide what you can do on a personal level to make a difference.

Two fun movies to watch while feasting are *The Three Lives of Thomasina* and *Homeward Bound*.

If everyone who owns a pet would have a similar birthday party, the amount of donations would dramatically rise. It's a fun reason to get together, you get to spoil your own pets and help out animals in need at the same time.

As far as dates—I have always assigned the first Sunday in April to be our Kitty Birthday—between Spring Equinox and Beltane, the time of growth and life.

LUPERCALIA

Festival of Lovers

Hearts, lace and chocolate . . . love and promises of honor and fidelity . . . she-wolves and children . . . it is February 15 and it is Lupercalia, a Roman festival of fertility and love. In honor of the God Lupercus, a pastoral deity, the festival honors fertility, sex, and love.

Lupercalia is also thought to have connections to the story of Romulus and Remus, the original founders of Rome. Their mother, Rhea Silvia, a Vestal Virgin, was raped by the God Mars while she slept. If her vows of chastity were found broken, she would be killed. When her twins were born, she tucked them in a basket and set it adrift.

When the river overflowed, the waters deposited the basket in the grotto of Lupercal, where a wolf found the children. She nursed and raised the boys until they were discovered by a shepherd and his wife. So the festival of Lupercalia also has connections to the mother/child bond. Though Romulus and Remus weren't even her species, the wolf cared for them as if they were her own.

The festival was Christianized (and moved to February 14) into St. Valentine's Day.

Images surrounding Valentine's Day are definitely Pagan in origin. The cherubs represent Cupid, the son of Venus (Goddess of Love). Cupid is said to strike with the arrows of love when you least expect it. The symbol of the heart on the valentine was originally a Norse sex rune, and flowers and sweet foods certainly enhance magick for love and fertility.

Valentine's Day or Lupercalia?

This is one of the few holidays that I don't object to celebrating the Christianized form. To begin with, most of the symbology is Pagan in origin, and secondly, I'm not going to object to a festival devoted to love and pleasure.

I do think that all Pagans should at least know the origin of the celebration, however, and then decide which they feel more comfortable with.

One nice thing about Lupercalia is that the love and caring shared isn't focused just towards romance and passion. If a man or woman has no significant partner or perhaps has just lost someone, they aren't going to feel good about a holiday focusing on that aspect of love.

Lupercalia encourages that you show honor and love for your partners, your children, your parents, and your friends.

The Colors of Lupercalia

Colors associated with love and joy are red, pink, green, sea green, aquamarine, and lavender.

Incenses, Herbs, and Woods

Vanilla, rose, tangerine, honeysuckle, jasmine, and ylang ylang all make wonderful incenses for love spells and Lupercalia.

Herbs associated with love and fertility include basil, coriander, ginger, rose petals, jasmine flowers, orange blossoms, acorns, pine cones, and nuts.

Woods appropriate to love and fertility rituals include oak, apple, willow, and peach.

A Lupercalia Love Spell

What better day to cast a love spell than Lupercalia?

Spend a month or two before February 15 looking for a heart-shaped rock. There are rocks out there that are naturally heart-shaped and if you look long enough, you should find one. If, after all your searching, you still can't find a heart-shaped piece of stone then you can buy one (if you choose to buy, go for rose quartz—the stone of love and peace).

You will need:

> vanilla incense
> a new red pillar candle
> a sheet of pink paper
> a pen with red ink (you can use dragon's blood ink)
> your heart-shaped stone
> Lupercalia Love Oil (page 221)
> the dried petals of a dark red rose
> a piece of red lace
> a pink ribbon
> a red silk rose

On the night of February 14, near midnight, cast a circle and invoke the elements in your usual manner. Light the incense and candle.

On the paper, with red ink, write down the qualities you are looking for in a lover or partner. Think about this carefully—if, for example, you don't like camping, but you ask for an outdoorsman, you might find conflict in the relationship.

When you have finished your list, then let the ink dry.

Anoint the heart-shaped stone with the Lupercalia Love Oil, then hold up to the north and say:

> **Spirits of Earth, ground this stone; aid me as I seek to manifest and materialize love into my life. Let my new love be stable and secure in himself/herself and let him/her encourage me to be grounded and confident in myself.**

Turn to the east and say:

> **Spirits of Air, blow over this stone; aid me to see clearly the person best suited to be my match. Let my heart be perceptive, let my intuition be strong and protective as I meet new people.**

Turn to the south and say:

> **Spirits of Fire, spark through this stone; aid me in bringing passion into my life and myself. Let my inner beauty glow through my body and radiate outwards to magnetize the one I seek.**

Turn to the west and say:

> **Spirits of Water, flow over this stone; aid me in filling my life with the joy I desire and deserve. Let me understand the nature of both sorrow and joy, and let me heal from past wounds so I might try again with a light heart.**

Fold the paper and place it on the stone. Sprinkle with rose petals over the paper and cover stone, paper, and flower petals with the lace. Tie with the ribbon. Affix the silk rose. Hold the stone and say:

> **Cupid, Cupid shoot your arrows**
> **Aim them towards my love-to-be**
> **Venus bring me heart and joy**
> **Hasten now my love to me.**

Peak the power through the chant and release it. Keep the stone on your nightstand, along with the candle and each night, light the candle for a brief minute and repeat the chant, knowing that the Universe is searching for your new partner and that he or she will appear when the time is right.

Lupercalia Love Oil

¼ ounce light olive oil   3 drops peach oil
3 drops rose petal oil   2 drops jasmine oil
3 drops vanilla oil   1 drop tonka oil

Blend all oils while focusing on drawing love and joy into your life, then add a garnet or ruby chip and a few rose petals or jasmine flowers to the bottle. Charge in circle to empower.

Food and Recipes

Lupercalia Cake

1 boxed chocolate fudge   ½ cup strawberry juice
  cake mix   1 cup raspberry jam
¼ cup vegetable oil   3 cups chocolate frosting
3 eggs   2 cups whipped topping
1¼ cups cold water

Note: When you make this cake, stir the batter deosil (when using an electric mixture, turn the bowl in a deosil direction). Focus on creating a scrumptious, sweet, and rich dessert for a night of pleasure.

Preheat oven to 350 degrees. Beat cake mix, oil, eggs, and water for 3 minutes on medium speed until thoroughly mixed.

Pour into two greased and floured pans (8-inch rounds) and bake for 20–25 minutes until top springs back at touch. Remove and cool on cake racks.

Blend juice and jam.

Whip frosting and topping together.

Carefully slice each cake layer in half to make four layers. Place bottom layer on plate and brush with jam-juice mixture. Spread with a thin layer of frosting-topping. Cover with second layer and repeat, then third and repeat, then fourth.

Spread rest of frosting-topping over top and sides of cake and decorate with fresh raspberries and mint leaves. Chill. Serve with Framboise or cream sherry.

Serves 10.

Fruit and Cheesecake

½ cup sliced strawberries
½ cup sliced kiwi
½ cup blueberries
3 tablespoons sugar
¾ cup water
4 eggs
3 teaspoon vanilla
14 ounces sweetened
   condensed milk

¼ cup butter
3 (8-ounce) packages
   cream cheese
1 tablespoon flour
1 graham cracker
   crumb crust
¼ cup chocolate sauce

Preheat oven to 325 degrees. Separate fruit into three bowls. Mix sugar and water and toss ¼ cup with each of the three fruits. Chill.

Blend eggs, vanilla, and condensed milk. Beat in butter and softened cream cheese. Beat in flour.

Pour into crust and bake for 45–50 minutes until set. Remove from oven and cool thoroughly.

Layer the fruits over the cheesecake and chill another hour. Drizzle with chocolate sauce and serve.

Serves 8.

WEDDINGS

The Rite of Handfasting

A warm June afternoon, bees droning in the background, trees decorated with origami cranes and ribbons . . . the bride is dressed in vivid red and her husband-to-be wears white . . . roses decorate the altar . . . it's time for a wedding, time for the handfasting to begin!

Marriage: Legal and Otherwise

In many countries, marriage is an economic union, in others a religious rite, and still others pursue it for emotional reasons. No matter the original intent, marriage is a serious affair, not to be entered into lightly.

Blending two lives is precarious at best, and while marriage can be wonderful and exciting, it can also be a horrible mistake if you end up with the wrong person.

A good partnership, legally bound or not, takes hard work and a willingness to compromise certain aspects of the self. Couples who rush into marriage often fail to realize how disparate their personalities are and they end up hurting everyone concerned.

In some cultures, marriage is a lifelong decision, no reprieves allowed. In other cultures, divorce is an option if the union doesn't work. In any case, children make matters more complicated—creating a bond between parents that can never be fully broken.

By definition, marriage is a legal institution recognized by the government and therefore receiving certain rights denied to other domestic partnerships.

In America, same-sex marriages are proscribed, all gay and lesbian relationships are denied the right to exist as a legal entity. These strictures are brought about through bigotry, fear, and misguided religious precepts. While we are working to change the laws, the fact remains that gay and lesbian couples cannot legally marry. (At the time of this writing, Hawai'i is closer than any other state to approving same-sex marriages and this makes many state governments nervous.)

Other couples have chosen to voluntarily forego the legal connection of marriage due to prior bad experiences, the desire to leave their options open, and numerous other reasons.

There are so many opinions on the subject of marriage that I can't help but believe that someone, somewhere will get offended by what I or any other author writes about the subject. Marriage is a very personal, highly volatile subject.

Handfasting

In the Pagan community, our marriage rituals are called handfastings. The term handfasting has been around for hundreds of years and refers to the clasping hands to seal a pledge, in this case—marriage.

In Pagan terms, handfasting doesn't necessarily imply legal commitment. Some people choose to limit their partnership to a year-and-a-day (a common Pagan time unit), at which time they can renew their vows if they wish. Others bind themselves "as long as love shall last." Still others, "unto the Summerlands," which in effect says, "until death do us part."

If you choose to legally marry, you can, by searching out Pagan clergy recognized by your state, make the handfasting your single ceremony.

If you cannot find a Pagan clergy in your area who has the approved state backing, you may have to opt for one ceremony with a Justice of the Peace, then hold your actual wedding separately. Unfortunately, this is symptomatic of our society's narrow recognition of religious rights and offices. The Catholic Priest and the Wiccan Priestess are not going to be treated with the same respect in most areas of our nation.

If you've decided on a ceremony bound by oath but not by the legal system, then you don't have to worry about it.

Making Sure You're Ready

Latest statistic: 60 percent of all marriages fail.

Over the years, I've seen so many Pagan handfastings form and dissolve within weeks or months of the ceremonies that it seems as if the oaths taken during the ceremony meant nothing.

As a Priestess, when asked to perform a handfasting for two individuals, I insist on at least one or two meetings before the ceremony so I can ascertain how serious the couple is about the ritual.

If I feel they aren't serious about their commitment, or if they approach the handfasting in a lackadaisical manner, then I ask them to find another Priestess to perform the ceremony, because I won't accept an oath from someone who appears to have no intention of keeping it.

This may seem judgmental, but as a Priestess pledged to the Gods, I understand the nature of oaths. Better to withdraw than to put my blessing on a union that I don't think is going to make it. It's a matter of respect for myself, as much as for the couple's future.

With any marriage, Pagan or not, I would say: take your time and think about it. Don't rush into anything. My husband and I got engaged shortly after we met, but our engagement lasted over five months. During that time we were able to discuss the sensitive issues that have a way of breaking up relationships and even now, we both feel that we rushed things.

Talk to your partner, hash things out before you get married, and don't assume that problems will take care of themselves—they won't.

Also, as every psychologist will tell you, don't expect marriage to change a person's basic nature. If they cheat on you before you're married, it will continue afterward. If they're a slob when you're dating them, they won't miraculously turn into the fastidious Felix Unger of the *Odd Couple* after marriage! It just doesn't happen. While marriage can have a stabilizing effect on some, it doesn't work that way for everyone.

If you're under twenty—what are you doing getting married? Wait for a while, meet lots of people, go to school, travel, and experience life . . . if you love someone, they'll wait for a year or so. If they aren't willing to wait, then it wasn't meant to be.

And lastly, don't get married just because you get pregnant. You have options and a baby is the wrong reason to say "I do"— you've made one mistake (birth control does exist); don't make another mistake.

When you know that you have to be with this other person— when you know that you can live just fine without him or her, but you don't want to—then you're ready to get married.

The Colors of Handfastings

Anything goes! A Pagan bride does not have to wear white because she has nothing to prove, since the original meaning of the word "virgin" meant a woman who owns herself, not a woman who has never had sex. The old "white equals pure" myth doesn't hold out.

My wedding dress was a royal blue/purple. A friend got married in red. Coordinate your wedding around your favorite colors and create your own tradition.

Incenses, Herbs, and Woods

Incenses should reflect the love that binds two people—rose, peach, honeysuckle, vanilla, jasmine, ylang ylang are all good choices. Orange blossom has long been magickally associated with love and marriage.

Herbs include yarrow, apple blossom, plumeria, violet, marjoram, orchid, lotus, vervain, and vetivert.

Among the woods associated with marriage and love are the banyan tree, apple, and peach. Orange tree branches would also work well.

One Thousand Cranes for Good Fortune

A beautiful Japanese tradition is the practice of origami—folding cranes for peace, harmony, and good fortune. My husband, who lived for many years on the Big Island of Hawai'i where many diverse traditions co-exist, can fold cranes in his sleep. When we were planning our wedding he left most of the planning to me but asked that we include one thousand gold foil cranes.

I love craft-work and although origami does not come easily to me, we folded cranes for months. Friends helped us. Occasionally, we'd dump the whole box and count them.

We left them unopened (in the final step, you pull them open from their folded state) until the night before the wedding. When the wedding party and a few other friends gathered on our friends' property, we had a massive crane-opening-and-stringing bash.

Our wedding took place in an apple orchard, and we hung strings of cranes from the trees, nestled them in the grass, had them peeking out of every spare corner.

It was a lesson in patience and perseverance, and it must have worked because our marriage has been blessed with much happiness and contentment.

Crane-folding is a beautiful art, and there are several good origami books on the market. I encourage you to add at least a few of these ephemeral decorations to your handfasting, if not the full thousand. It's traditional to burn them afterward, and since we had a huge bonfire that night, everyone gathered the cranes and tossing them in the fire.

Braiding the Handfasting Cord

Braiding the cord for your handfasting is a magickal act in itself. You will need three cords, each nine feet in length. The colors can either match your color scheme for your wedding or they can be red, black, and white to represent the Triple Goddess.

Cast a circle and invoke the elements as usual.

Tie the cords together at the top. One partner holds the knot taut while the other begins braiding. While you braid the cords, both partners should chant one of the following chants (or make up your own based on your personal needs), bringing the power to a peak as you finish the braid and tie off the end.

1.   **Love—Joy—Harmony—Health**
      Peace—Growth—Home—Wealth!

2.   **A braid for love, A braid for life**
      A braid to bind a joyful wife
      A braid for health, A braid for land
      A braid that weaves our wedding band
      A braid for joy, A braid for the broom
      A braid to bind a loving groom!

3.   **Weave now the marriage braid**
      Of our separate lives it's made
      Weave now the cord that binds
      Joyful hearts and willing minds
      Weave now from the Lady's loom
      A happy bride, a loving groom!

The Broom

The origins of jumping the broom aren't clear, however it has long been a custom in Pagan circles.

The broom represents, among other things, cleansing and clearing away the past. When you jump the broom into your marriage, you are essentially jumping into a new existence.

If you can't hand-make your broom, at least buy a new one for your wedding. Don't use it for anything else—many people suggest using your coven's broom or your personal magickal broom for the ceremony, but I don't agree.

I think your wedding broom should be used for this one act only. The broom serves as a tangible reminder of your wedding and your vows. If the marriage should ever fail, breaking the broom signifies the end of the relationship.

You can decorate the room with whatever you like, though I don't recommend fresh flowers—they mold easily. We used silk flowers, metallic ribbon, a huge plum colored silk rose, beads, tassels—a little bit of everything—and it's just as pretty now (if a little dusty) as it was on the day of our wedding. Follow your color scheme, match the ribbons and flowers to your broom, and you can't go wrong.

Toasting Glasses

Not a necessity, but fun to have. Choose these with your personal tastes in mind, and keep them for use on your anniversaries. Ours were inexpensive, delicate little goblets and we bring them out every anniversary. It's a nice touch that doesn't have to cost more than a few dollars.

Where to Hold the Handfasting

Where do you want to hold it?

A cave out in the desert? A black sand beach in Hawai'i? The middle of the Olympic Mountains? The top of Mount Rushmore?

While the handfasting is a sacred, religious rite, it doesn't matter where you hold it. As long as you, as a couple, are happy with your choice, and the site you choose can be consecrated for the ceremony, there shouldn't be a problem.

Your concerns should be with accessibility for your guests (if you're having a small wedding and everyone is able-bodied, then it's less of a concern); expected weather, if you're holding it outside, and the ease with which you can set up everything. Also, you should give a thought to privacy—the middle of the public campground might be pretty, but do you really want a dozen boy scouts watching?

We got married in an apple orchard. It poured in the morning, but the showers stopped during the ceremony, then started up again right afterwards. Talk about the Gods doing what They could to help out!

Choosing the Priest and Priestess

Choosing your clergy is an important decision.

For the sake of clarity, let's say you're getting married by the Justice of the Peace and planning a separate wedding. Who will you ask to officiate at your handfasting?

Think carefully before asking.

We made the wrong choice at first with the man we chose to be our Priest. Aside from having severe health problems that he refused to get medical care for, as time went by it became obvious that he had emotional blocks to the fact that we were getting married.

We had all been roommates to start with and I think he felt my husband and I pushed him away when we fell in love and got engaged. We ended up having to replace him in the ceremony and it cracked the friendship. Sadly, his health deteriorated further and he died the day after our wedding.

If we had thought a little more, we might have foreseen the potential problems, thus avoiding the stress and headaches our choice caused.

You want to choose someone with whom you both feel comfortable. The Priest or Priestess who officiates should have your best interests at heart and should truly bless your union.

Don't automatically assume that anyone who leads a coven is going to be your best choice. Perhaps you know a solitary Witch who would be perfect as your Priestess, or maybe you and your partner want to pledge yourselves together without an intermediary—so you might choose to be your own Priest and Priestess (I've seen this work).

Whatever your decision, make certain that you're both comfortable with the choices involved.

Creating the Handfasting Ritual

A handfasting ritual, like a dedication ritual, is very personal and I believe that every couple should write their own. Don't rely on stock ceremonies unless you have absolutely no ability to string words together.

Every relationship is unique; every relationship has individual needs. You need to tailor the ritual to suit your own purposes. If you have trouble doing this, the Priest or Priestess should be able to help you figure out what you do and don't want to include.

Your meetings with the Priest or Priestess should cover such issues as:

- length of pledged commitment;

- fidelity;

- the involvement or expectation of children in this union; and decisions about what religion or tradition they will be raised in.

You can also ask for help in developing your personal vows to your partner, but never agree to anything that feels uncomfortable or wrong.

Sam and I chose to become blood-bound as well as handfasted—an oath that cannot be broken unless one of us dishonors our vows. It is an oath I've taken with only two other people—both blood-sisters now—and not one to take lightly. Sam is my blood-brother and as such, I owe him honor, faithful support, and trust, in addition to the vows of love we made. If we ever do separate (by mutual choice) then we will still owe each other support and friendship due to our being blood-bound.

The Handfasting Ritual

Since every ritual should be tailored to the individual couple, I present an abbreviated version of our handfasting from which you can take your model. I wrote the vows with Sam's approval and input as I went along.

I've excluded some of our personal choices and oaths (i.e., the blood binding), and you can adapt as you need to.

Since I am pledged to Mielikki and Tapio, we married under Their sight. Pele was also a silent witness—in the leis sent over from Hawai'i by friends and family, and Pan made Himself known in the necklace that my husband chose for his wedding necklace (he can't wear rings). I have altered the specific God and Goddess names for general usage, you will have to decide which God and Goddess you want to invoke if you want a specific deity.

We videotaped our ceremony and, although at first I had reservations, now I'm glad we did. It was a beautiful wedding and when I look at the tape, I still wonder how we managed it on such a tight budget. Magick, good friends, and artistic talent work wonders!

The area for the ritual should be prepared in advance. Five tall saplings are to be cut and decorated with ribbons, their colors designating the directions. Two of these mark the north (Earth), and are spaced about four feet apart to form a gate through which everyone enters.

The altar is set slightly off-center, toward the north, and the broom is placed on the grass near the west edge of the circle.

When the announcement is made to enter circle, one member of the wedding party will lead all the guests in a line through the north gates, deosil until everyone is spaced evenly around the circle. During the procession, the following chant will be sung until everyone is in place.

All: **Come children come**
        To the radiant sun!
        Oh-oh-oh-oh (*Repeat.*)

The Priest and Priestess should enter the circle from the north and take their places at the altar. The wedding party enters the circle next, single file, each person stopping for a moment at each directional marker to bid welcome to the elements—enter in this order: Best Man, Groom, Matron of Honor, Bride. During this time, someone can be playing the music chosen by the couple as their wedding theme. Come to rest in front of the altar. The Matron of Honor takes the Bride's bouquet and moves a step or two back, as does the Best Man.

Priest and Priestess should cast a silent circle, three times around the entire area.

PT: (*Face the north gate.*) **Spirits of the North, Spirits of the Earth, Spirit of the Wolf, I call you forth to this sacred rite. Be with us, you who are the green body of the Goddess under our feet. Let your strength and stability infuse these rites and**

this union. **Bring your fertility and growth to this couple that they might know continuing love and peace.**

PST: *(Face east marker.)* **Spirits of the East, Spirits of the Air, Spirit of the Hawk, I call you forth to this sacred rite. Be with us, you who are the winds of change and purification. Let your flexibility and illumination infuse these rites and this union. Bring your clarity and honesty to this couple that they might know each other's true hearts.**

PT: *(Face south marker.)* **Spirits of the South, Spirits of Fire, Spirit of the Salamander, I call you forth to this sacred rite. Be with us, you who are the Phoenix incarnate. Let your ability to rise unscarred from the ashes infuse these rites and this union. Bring your passion and creativity to this couple that they might always burn brightly for each other.**

PST: *(Face west marker.)* **Spirits of the West, Spirits of Water, Spirit of the Shark, I call you forth to this sacred rite. Be with us, you who are the waters of love. Let your ability to flow through the heart leaving joy in your wake infuse these rites and this union. Bring your love and understanding to this couple that they might always find deepest happiness with one another.** *(Draw invoking pentagram over the broom.)* **I ask that a protected gateway be left open, with nothing unwelcome entering within.**

Priest and Priestess return to altar.

PST: *(Light Goddess candle.)* **Lady of the Moon, Lady of the Greenwood, Queen of Faerie, Enchantress and Mother of All, come to us. Look down upon these rites and bring Your bright blessings and crystalline sight to this gathering.** (name of bride) **comes before You to be wed to her love** (name of groom), **as You are wed to the Horned Lord of the Greenwood. Bestow upon them the strength of Your love and wisdom. Welcome and Blessèd be.**

PT: *(Light God candle.)* **Lord of the Forest, Pack Master, Gentle Lover and Laughing God, Wild Hunter, come to us. Look down upon these rites and bring Your bright blessings and**

gentle strength to this gathering. (name of groom) **comes before You to be wed to his love** (name of bride)**, as You are wed to the Lady of the Greenwood. Bestow upon them the strength of Your love and perseverance. Welcome and Blessèd be.**

PST: Before stone and tree, sea and river—

PT: Before cloud and breeze, sun and flame, we gather to witness the joining of two who wish to pledge their loves and lives together.

PST: (Name) and (name) step forward to the altar.

Bride and Groom step forward.

PST: Do you (Bride) truly desire to wed this man?

Brd: I do.

PT: Do you (Groom) truly desire to wed this woman?

Grm: I do.

PST: Join hands. *(She binds their hands loosely with the handfasting cord.)* **As so your hands are bound, so are your oaths binding before the Gods, before each other, and before this company. Look into each other's eyes.**

PT: Listen now to the words of the Troth of Nine to which you have agreed to bind your lives together.

PST: (Name) and (name), this is the pledge of truth. Listen well, for in your listening so do you make oath. The first pledge: To love deeply, on a basis beyond superficiality; to commit yourself to each other, to any children that may result from this union, and to those with whom you hold faith.

PT: Second: to have courage, to speak for what you know you must and to stand up for one another when the occasion arises.

PST: Third: to be honest to yourselves, to each other, and to forsake hypocrisy.

PT: Fourth: to be faithful to one another, to your pledged Gods and beliefs, and to those you call family.

PST: Fifth: to have patience, to master your talents, and to support each other in your will to create and learn.

PT: Sixth: to be independent and yet ask for help when you need it, to give support to one another when asked.

PST: Seventh: to continue against all odds when you know what needs to be done, to persevere in the face of adversity, to unite to overcome problems rather than letting them divide you.

PT: Eighth: to let passion fill your lives, to embrace the intensity of your relationship, to celebrate the joys of your bodies together without shame or exploitation.

PST: Ninth: to embrace knowledge and the will to learn and to use wisdom in applying that knowledge. These are the nine pledges to life. Will you abide by them and apply them in your life together?

Bth: I will.

PST: Then now, before gathered friends and loved ones, make your personal vows and pledges that all may hear and remember. Your vows are as binding as this cord that joins your hands.

PT: (Name of groom), **what do you pledge to** (name of bride) **as her husband, lover, companion and friend?**

Grm: *(State personal pledges.)*

PST: (Name of bride), **what do you pledge to** (name of groom) **as his wife, lover, companion and friend?**

Brd: *(State personal pledges.)*

PT: Then know that you have pledged before the Gods, your friends, and each other the most solemn vows of love and loyalty. Even though this cord be unwound, your oaths are not, they are woven into the very braid of this ribbon and it

shall stand as a reminder of this day. *(Remove handfasting cord and place on altar.)*

PST: *(Holds bride's ring on tray.)* **I ask that the Lord and Lady of the Greenwood bless this ring as a symbol of union between** (name) **and** (name), **may it ever remind** (name of bride) **of her vows to her beloved. Take this ring and place it on her finger.**

Groom take ring and place on Bride's finger.

PT: *(Holds groom's ring on tray.)* **I ask that the Lord and Lady of the Greenwood bless this ring as a symbol of union between** (name) **and** (name), **may it ever remind** (name of groom) **of his vows to his beloved. Take this ring and place it on his finger.**

Bride take ring and place on Groom's finger.

PST: **In the sight of the Lady and Her beloved Lord, you are now joined as husband and wife. So mote it be!**

PT: **Circle 'round from west to west and jump the broom into your new life together!**

Bride and Groom circle deosil from west to west, then jump over the broom. They return to the altar. Matron of Honor and Best Man fade back into circle.

PT: *(Speaks to crowd.)* **Please join hands as** (name) **and** (name) **celebrate their union with the first dance of the day!**

Bride and Groom dance to their choice of songs—it's really nice if the Priest/ess and/or Matron of Honor/Best Man can sing for them.

PT: *(As song fades out.)* **Great Lord of the Greenwood, thank you for joining us in this rite. Be with us during feasting if You will, and bestow Your laughter and joy on our celebration!**

PST: **Lady of the Greenwood, thank you for joining us in this rite. Be with us during feasting if You will, and bestow Your laughter and joy on our celebration!**

PST: *(Face west marker.)* **Spirits of the West, Spirits of Water, Spirit of the Shark, thank you for attending our rites. Go if you must, stay if you will. Hail, farewell and Blesséd be!**

PT: *(Face south marker.)* **Spirits of the South, Spirits of the Fire, Spirit of the Salamander, thank you for attending our rites. Go if you must, stay if you will. Hail, farewell and Blesséd be!**

PST: *(Face east marker.)* **Spirits of the East, Spirits of the Air, Spirit of the Hawk, thank you for attending our rites. Go if you must, stay if you will. Hail, farewell and Blesséd be!**

PT: *(Face north gate.)* **Spirits of the North, Spirits of the Earth, Spirit of the Wolf, thank you for attending our rites. Go if you must, stay if you will. Hail, farewell and Blesséd be!**

Priest and Priestess devoke circle.

PST: Please join us for the cutting of the wedding cake and the celebration that follows!

Priest and Priestess, Bride and Groom, Best Man and Matron of Honor lead the way out and everyone else follows in a single line through the north gates.

Food and Recipes

I suggest a wedding potluck if your budget is limited—spend the money on the wedding cake (buy *The Cake Bible* if you want to make your own—this is the most incredible cookbook I've seen) and a main course (like turkey or salmon) and ask everyone else to bring side dishes, appetizers, fruits, salads, or other dishes.

One word to the Matron of Honor and the Best Man: fix plates for the Bride and Groom, they'll be so busy accepting congratulations that they won't have time to get in line at the buffet and they will need the food. Claim your right as a member of the wedding party to go first and make sure they get a bite of everything—don't forget yourselves, either. Weddings are hard work, and when a magickal ritual is involved, the ceremony takes even more energy.

Hawaiian Meatballs for a Crowd

Meatballs:

2	pounds lean ground beef	3	tablespoons cider vinegar
1½	pounds ground pork	3	tablespoons soy sauce
5	eggs	½	finely minced onion
3	cups bread crumbs	1½	teaspoons parsley
2	(6-ounce) cans tomato paste	1½	teaspoons tarragon
		1½	teaspoons basil
1	cup crushed pineapple	½	teaspoon nutmeg
3	tablespoons brown sugar		Olive oil

Sauce:

3	quarts spaghetti sauce	½	cup cider vinegar
2	cups crushed pineapple	1	tablespoon parsley
½	cup soy sauce	1	tablespoon tarragon
½	cup brown sugar	1	tablespoon basil

Preheat oven to 350 degrees. In large bowl blend all ingredients for meatballs. Shape into one-inch balls and brown lightly in a thin layer of olive oil, turning as needed. Place in a single layer in large baking dishes. Bake for ten minutes in pre-heated oven.

Blend all sauce ingredients and heat in stainless steel pot until just below boiling. Pour over meatballs and cover with aluminum foil. Return to oven for another 15 minutes.

Makes 60–70 meatballs.

Part 8

celebrations and traditions

New Year's Celebration • *Kalevala Day* •
Festival of Bacchus • *Kamehameha Day*

NEW YEAR'S CELEBRATION

The Festival of New Beginnings

Clear white snow blankets the earth, stars sparkle through the crisp night, and though the days are beginning to grow longer, spring still hides her face from us. Yule has come and gone, and the merry-making gives way to planning for the year to come.

One last celebration remains in the calendar year, one last party before we turn our attention to the cold days ahead that mark the beginning of another cycle.

The calendar we align our days with is based on the Gregorian system of time-keeping. Throughout the eons, humans have measured time with a number of different systems, but the one we are familiar with divides the solar year into twelve months, each containing between twenty eight and thirty one days to make a total of 365 days (366 on Leap Year).

While the Wheel of the Year begins with Samhain, no Pagan can avoid the psychological effects that New Year's brings. Just writing down a different year on your check makes you stop to think about how quickly time passes.

So we celebrate the New Year, not as a particularly religious holiday, but as a magickal marker in our lives. Knowing how many people worldwide are celebrating at the same time can bring an incredible rush of energy to our rituals.

New Year's Resolutions?

I don't make New Year's resolutions. All too often they are the same year after year, producing no results except guilt when we break them.

Instead, I have what I call my Wish Box and my Wish List Ritual.

More goal-oriented than resolutions, they focus on accomplishments rather than traits likely never to change. I find this ritual produces better results, and it is a nice way in which to end the old year. It's fun to open up my Wish List from last year and see what I've accomplished (I always manage to accomplish at least two or three things I set out to do), as well as what I've let go of. Sometimes I surprise myself.

New Year's Eve

In our home, the Yule decorations are still up, though we are getting tired of them by now. Tomorrow we will take everything down to start the year with a clean house.

Tonight we celebrate with our Wish List Ritual.

Wish List Ritual

Cast a circle and invoke the elements as usual.

Open last year's Wish List (if you have one) and note what has happened, what is in the process of happening and what has yet to begin. Decide if there are ideas you want to carry over to the current year. Are there things you thought you wanted but actually don't?

Put aside the list and examine those things from this past year that you want to release. Once you are certain you want to let them go, carve runes or words to symbolize them on a black or purple votive candle.

Charge and light the candle.

Now think about what you want for the coming year and write out a new Wish List—events you'd like to happen, material success you want, goals you're making—things that are at least feasible.

Light a plain, uncarved white votive candle for the coming, as-yet-untouched New Year.

Fold your wish list tightly and tape.

Drip some of the white wax on it to form a seal and put it away in your Wish Box until next year.

Burn your old list after noting in your journal what wishes you actually manifested, then devoke the elements and the circle.

The Wish Box

Procure a white box, either stone or wood, on which you can burn or etch the following runes:

Good Fortune   Serendipity   Happiness

Love   Peace   Protection

After you have carved or burned the runes into the box, cast a circle, invoke the elements and charge the box for use only for your New Year's Wishes. Smudge with sage or cedar incense, saying:

> **Box of white, as white as snow**
> **In your belly my wishes go**
> **Charm their power by three times three**
> **My will be done, so mote it be!**

Sprinkle with salt water and say:

Lady of the Silver Moon
Lady of the Golden Sun
Lady of the Crystal Stars
Let my will and wish be done!

Set out under the full moon (protected from the elements). Say:

Moon that turns around the Earth
To my wishes give form and birth
To my desire give strength and will
My hopes and dreams, please fulfill!

Let the box sit under the moon all night and then keep in a safe place and use only for your family's New Year's Wish Lists.

New Year's Day

According to tradition, all holiday greenery should be down and out of the house by January 6. We schedule New Year's Day for "stripping" the house.

We take the Yule Tree, Yule ornaments, and decorations down as we reflect on the season that has just passed. After everything is carefully put away, we exchange the Yule altar for an austere one to match the rest of winter. We thank the Spirit of Yule and bid it farewell until the next season, change the altar cloth to one of white lace and add red candles and a rose quartz sphere. On Imbolc, we will add Brighid's Bed and red carnations (see Imbolc).

We pour the last of the winter cordial at the offering shrine and clean house so that all remnants of Yule are tucked away. The Winter pictures of Mielikki and Tapio stay up until the end of Imbolc, but I change the Yule collage for one showing stark scenes of snow-covered mountains and barren plains.

Journal Work

I find that New Year's Day is a good day to reflect in my journal about the year just ended. At the beginning of each year, I list my accomplishments, note progress made and where I slipped up, and I also re-read my journal from the last New Year's Day. It's a time of introspection for me, a day of quiet insight into my life.

Since my birthday is in January, I also begin mentally preparing for the change in age—a process that I require a few weeks to build up to. I do not fear aging—only stagnation—and I use the coming fortnight to take stock of my life-goals, something that everyone can do on New Year's Day.

Visiting Friends

Unfortunately, the proliferation of hangovers on New Year's Day has curtailed the long-standing custom of visiting friends on that day. Perhaps the decline of household servants has contributed to this, since a majority of people also have to clean up after their New Year's Eve parties (a ritual I personally don't enjoy).

I'd much rather revive the custom of dropping in on friends for "just a minute" with a little gift—perhaps a jar of jelly or a small bouquet of flowers to wish them a happy New Year, as long as the visiting hours are limited to the afternoon.

For those of you who wonder, I also like the custom of calling cards and always carry a supply wherever I go. Poverty, busy schedules, and the modern era are no excuse for lacking those little touches that give grace to a situation.

New Year's White Dinner

In contrast to Yule's Golden Dinner, I like to serve an all white dinner on New Year's Day, to mirror the severity and iciness of the season.

The menu varies from year-to-year, but one I particularly like consists of:

Chicken Breasts Poached in White Wine
Potatoes and Leeks in Cream Sauce
Rolls and Sweet Butter
Rice Pudding
Milk

Food and Recipes

Chicken Breasts Poached in White Wine

2	boneless skinless chicken breasts	2	cups chicken stock
1½	cups white wine	½	teaspoon crushed black pepper
¼	cup white vinegar		salt to taste
1	tablespoon dill		

Pound chicken breasts until very thin. Mix wine, vinegar, dill, chicken stock, and pepper in heavy skillet. Add chicken breasts and bring to a boil. Lower heat to medium-low, cover, and simmer for 15–20 minutes. Remove chicken breasts from broth and cover to keep warm.

Reserve one cup of the broth to make cream sauce for Potatoes and Leeks in Cream Sauce.

Before serving chicken breasts, sprinkle with dill, pepper and salt.

Potatoes and Leeks in Cream Sauce

5	medium Yellow Finn potatoes	1	cup broth (from above)
½	cup chopped leeks	1½	cups half-and-half
¼	cup butter	½	teaspoon crushed black pepper
¼	cup flour	½	teaspoon parsley

Wash potatoes but do not peel. Chop into one-inch cubes. Add leeks, cover with water, and bring to a boil. Cook until fork pierces potato easily. Remove from heat and drain.

In heavy skillet, melt butter and whisk in flour. Cook, whisking constantly, for 5 minutes. Slowly whisk in broth, then half-and-half. Add pepper and parsley.

Cook (do not boil) until thickened, whisking constantly. Pour over potatoes and leeks, toss lightly to coat and serve with chicken breasts.

KALEVALA DAY

A Finnish Celebration

The Finnish tradition was chiefly an oral one with legend and myth recorded through long songs and poems. Finnish bards (often known as Rune-Masters) were notorious for their abilities to chant for hours on end, and the Finns used the ancient songs with their magickal content for everything from kitchen work to healing to hunting. The Finnish culture was intrinsically shamanistic, everything within the natural world was seen as charmed or imbued with a power of one kind or another.

Finland (also known as Suomi) remained one of the last Scandinavian countries to be Christianized. Its terrain, climate, and reputation kept all but a few brave hearts safely outside the borders. With the notorious power of its sorcerers and witches, and the cunning, quick intellect that pervaded the culture, Suomi was given a wide berth by those fearing its people.

No written language existed in Finland until the missionaries began their efforts to convert the isolated country that for so long remained intact.

While the missionaries quickly developed a written language for the Finns, they also managed to destroy most of the ancient traditions and beliefs. Today, Suomi is largely Lutheran, with few vestiges of what was once an intricate, shamanistic culture.

In 1820, Reinhold von Becker published what was to become an historic essay, *On Väinämöinen,* in which he compiled and organized a small selection of songs from Finnish legend, and the *runos,* or verses, contained many common links that weave through all the ancient tales.

Elias Lönnrot, a student of von Becker's, was inspired by his mentor's work and went on to gather enough material to publish what was titled the Old Kalevala in 1835. He continued his work and, in 1849, published the collection we commonly know as the Kalevala. Various translations exist, with differing degrees of agreement over certain names and meanings.

The word Kalevala refers to a legendary region mentioned in some of the Finnish mythos and songs, and as a whole, is not the most appropriate term to use (as you would refer to the ancient Norse sagas by the term Eddas, for example) but it is the only word we have for the collection of runos at this time.

The inroads on Finland were beginning as early as the sixteenth century, when the Christian church went to battle with the runo singers (bards) maintaining that the ancient songs were Pagan and, therefore, Satanic. A schism occurred between the common folk (who remembered the old ways and still practiced them) and the upper classes who embraced the newer beliefs.

When the Enlightenment began to influence belief, the study of folklore became more acceptable, at least from a scholarly point of view, and interest in the runos grew.

Then, during the war of 1808–1809, Russia annexed Finland. Once the Finns fell to Russia, a strong grassroots nationalism began to take hold. Apparently a common saying went, "We aren't Swedish; we can never be Russian, let us therefore be Finns."

Finland was granted status as an autonomous territory of Russia and began to reclaim its identity. This coincided with the collections and printings of the Kalevala, and the Finns' pride in their nation and ethnicity began to strengthen.

February 28 was established as Kalevala Day to further rekindle Finnish pride, but the celebrations, as nationalistic as they might be, still carry with them the remnants of the old Finnish religion and culture, and can be celebrated in a way the creators perhaps never imagined.

The Gods of the Finns

While the subject contains far too much material for an in-depth study here, the primary Gods of the Finnish religion include the following.

Ukko: The Ancient Father who rules the highest heavens; He who makes all things possible; sky god and leader of the Finnish pantheon.

Rauni: Ukko's wife; divine Mother; goddess of lightning and grain.

Tapio: Dark Bearded One; forest/vegetation god, rules over the realm of Tapiola; protector of family and forest.

Mielikki: Tapio's wife; Queen of Tapiola, protects all who walk, hunt, sleep, or dwell within the forest, Lady of Animals and the Hunt; Queen of the Metsanhaltija (the forest spirits/faeries); created the bear.

Ahto: Lord of oceans and waters.

Ahti: Wife of Ahto; Lady of rivers, lakes and streams.

The heroes of the Finns are as important in the ancient tales as the Gods. Väinämöinen, Lemminkäinen, and Ilmarinen are considered the three primary heroes of the runos, and their exploits are filled with foolhardiness, bravado, cunning wit, and endurance. Their mothers often had to come to their rescue, however, and the concept of motherhood was held in high esteem by all the Finns.

Celebrating Kalevala Day

Since the Finns adored a good evening of song and drink, what better way to celebrate the day by reading poetry (including selections from the Kalevala, of course), feasting, and drinking?

Mead and beer are good drinks with which to celebrate the day (Mielikki's forests are said to drip with golden honey, so what better drink than mead to celebrate the heritage from which Her tradition springs?), and vodka and schnapps are all too popular among the Finns today.

There is a terrible problem in Finland with alcoholism and so, if you prefer, you might substitute fruit shakes and honey-teas for the alcohol.

For a holiday dinner, the traditional Finn would serve a *voileipäpöytä,* or a "bread and butter" table (commonly known by the Swedish term s*mörgäsbord*).

Seven categories of food make up the most elaborate of voileipäpöytä. These include:

1. Various breads and butter
2. Salted and smoked fishes
3. Warm fish dishes and/or deli meats, pâtés, etc.
4. Hot appetizers
5. Main course meat dishes and potatoes
6. Salads, eggs, cheeses, pastries
7. Fruits

Served as a buffet, proper etiquette indicates that each diner should take a clean plate for each course, and the courses should be eaten in the order given. For a small group of people, some of the courses may be eliminated (but seldom, if ever, eliminate numbers 1, 2, and 6).

Creating a Runo Staff

Under a full moon, cut a straight birch sapling and strip it of bark. Wood-burn or etch the following runes on it:

Ukko (Ancient Father)   *Rauni (Divine Mother)*

Shaman (Finnish Shaman/Rune-Master)

When you have finished etching the runes, let the staff dry until the next full moon.

On the second full moon, stain the wood with a light oak color and paint the runes with black paint. Decorate with bones, feathers, beads, and bits of fur and crystals. Set it aside until the next full moon.

On the third full moon, consecrate your staff. Wait until the wind is blowing, then light a smudge stick and take the staff outside and smudge with sage. Hold the staff up in the wind and say:

> **Wind of change, wind of thought**
> **Wind blowing wild, catch me not**
> **Wind of stories and songs of old**
> **Wind, free my tongue and make it bold**
> **Charge this staff with all your might**
> **With ancient runos sung on darkest nights**
> **Wind, empower this staff and me**
> **With your keenest sight and clear memory!**

Keep the staff in a safe place and use during spells for creativity, knowledge, studying, when working with the Finnish Gods, or during Kalevala day.

The Kalevala Day Ritual

Each person should come prepared with three or four poems or a short story or several songs. Give each person a selection from the Kalevala, as well.

Designate one person to be the Rune-Master, and that person should lead the story-circle and pass the Runo Staff to whoever has the next turn.

Everyone form a circle. The Priest and Priestess begin by casting the circle. The following invocations are written to be similar in form and style to the runos of the Kalevala.

PT: I cast this circle now around us,
      Cast it in the name of Ukko
      Ancient Father Who Rules The Heavens
      Ancient One Who Rules the Skies
      That nothing evil touch this space
      As we make sacred now this circle.

PST: I cast this circle now around us,
      Cast it in the name of Rauni
      Mother of the Land and Lightning
      Wife of Ukko, Lady of Rowan
      That nothing evil touch this space
      As we make sacred now this circle.

RM: I cast this circle now around us,
      Cast in honor of the Bards
      The Rune-Masters of ancient lore
      Who sing the legends that we now sing
      Who keep the lore safe in memory
      That we might learn, also our children
      I ask that nothing evil enter
      As we make sacred now this circle.

PST: *(Face north.)* Spirits of North, come before us
      Spirits of Earth, hearken to us
      You who ancient mountains embody
      You of greenest grass and tree

Come to our circle, join us now
Spirits of Earth, join our rites.

PT: *(Face east.)* Spirits of East, come before us
Spirits of Air, hearken to us
You who wind and sky embody
You of mist and swirling fog
Come to our circle, join us now
Spirits of Air, join our rites.

PST *(Face south.)* Spirits of South, come before us
Spirits of Fire, hearken to us
You who flame and spark embody
You of sun and flowing lava
Come to our circle, join us now
Spirits of Fire, join our rites.

PT: *(Face west.)* Spirits of West, come before us
Spirits of Water, hearken to us
You who ocean and stream embody
You of swirling pools and eddies
Come to our circle, join us now
Spirits of Water, join our rites.

PT: *(Light a blue candle.)* Ukko, Father of Ancient Heavens
Ukko, come now to our circle
Greatest God of Suomi-Land
Be here now, come before us
As we celebrate now Your country,
As we sing the ancient runos
And recite the ancient rhymes.

PST: *(Light a red candle.)* Rauni, Mother of Mothers we call you,
Rauni, come now to our circle
Lighting Mistress, Mother of Rowan,
Be here now, come before us
As we celebrate now Your country,
As we sing the ancient runos
And recite the ancient rhymes.

RM: *(Light a yellow candle.)* **Tonight we gather in our hall,**
We gather to sing the ancient tales
Who will be the first to sing
The tales of heroes and of Gods
The songs of cunning and of magick
The stories of love and of courage?

One by one, each person accepts the Runo Staff from the Rune-Master and recites their piece. After each poem, story or song, everyone should drink a toast to the reader. The Runo Staff is to be given back each time to the Rune-Master, who will pass it to the next person. When each person has read two or three pieces and the circle is winding down, the Priest and Priestess again take the floor. The Rune-Master recites the following and then makes way for the Priest and Priestess.

RM: *(Extinguishes yellow candle.)* **We have sung the ancient songs**
And have told the ancient stories
And have recited the ancient tales
Now we bid farewell and blessings
To the Masters of the Runos
Whose spirits have come to listen
To remember their ancient exploits
The Runo Staff once more is hidden
Until the year rolls 'round again
Let us not forget the Gods
But bid Them farewell and many thanks
For joining us in our rites tonight.

PST: *(Extinguishes red candle.)* **Ancient Rauni of Lighting and Rowan**
I bid You farewell now this evening
With many thanks we say good-bye
With many smiles we bid You return
To Your realm with Ancient Ukko
Sacred Lady, Blesséd be.

PT: *(Extinguishes blue candle.)* **Ancient Ukko of Highest Heavens**
I bid You farewell now this evening
With many thanks we say good-bye
With many smiles we bid You return
To Your realm with Mother Rauni
Sacred Lord, Blessèd be.

PT: *(Faces west.)* **Spirits of Water, now we bid you**
Hail, farewell and Blessèd be
Go in peace and in peace stay
Within our hearts, so mote it be!

PST: *(Faces south.)* **Spirits of Fire, now we bid you**
Hail, farewell and Blessèd be
Go in peace and in peace stay
Within our hearts, so mote it be!

PT: *(Faces east.)* **Spirits of Air, now we bid you**
Hail, farewell and Blessèd be
Go in peace and in peace stay
Within our hearts, so mote it be!

PST: *(Faces north.)* **Spirits of Earth, now we bid you**
Hail, farewell and Blessèd be
Go in peace and in peace stay
Within our hearts, so mote it be!

PST: *(Sweeps circle open.)* **Circle of power, ancient line**
Protecting all within
Be open now but still unbroken
Until we meet again!

After the ritual, everyone should help set up the buffet and feast for the rest of the evening. You might want to rent documentaries on Finland for your VCR or check out picture books from the library for people to look at.

Food and Recipes

As mentioned above, the deli platter is probably closest to the Finnish traditional dinner as we can get. Baked goods and potato dishes are also very popular.

Lihapyöryköitä (Finnish Meat Balls)

¾	cup cracker crumbs	1	teaspoon cloves
1	cup heavy cream	¼	teaspoon allspice, ground
½	cup minced onion	¼	cup vegetable oil
1½	pounds lean ground beef	¼	cup flour
1	egg	2	cups milk
1	teaspoon salt		

Soak crumbs in ½ cup cream. Mix onion, meat, and cracker crumbs. Add the egg, salt, cloves, allspice, and mix. Roll into balls, (tablespoon sized).

Heat oil in skillet and brown meatballs on all sides. Remove from pan. Whisk flour into remaining oil and drippings until smooth and slowly whisk in milk and ½ cup cream. Heat but do not boil. Return meat balls to pan, cover, and simmer for 20 minutes.

Serves 6.

Pitko (Yeast Coffee Bread)

1	package active dry yeast	½	teaspoon ground cardamom
½	cup warm water	½	cup rose water
1½	cups milk, scalded and cooled	¾	cup melted butter
		4	eggs
1¼	cups sugar	9-10	cups flour
1	teaspoon salt	2	beaten egg yolks

Preheat oven to 375 degrees. Sprinkle yeast onto warm water and let dissolve. Beat in cooled milk, sugar, salt, cardamom, rose water, melted butter, and 4 eggs. Add 3 cups flour and beat until smooth.

Slowly add flour, 1 cup at a time, until dough begins to pull away from side of bowl.

Turn onto floured board and knead for 15 minutes. Place in buttered bowl, cover, and set in warm area until dough doubles in bulk.

Punch down and divide into six equal balls. Shape each ball of dough into long rolls. Braid the dough, using three coils of dough per loaf. Brush with water and beaten egg yolks. Bake 25–30 minutes, until golden brown. Remove braided loaves from oven and brush with melted butter.

Serves 4.

FESTIVAL OF BACCHUS
Or, Why All Good Pagans Should Avoid Celebrating St. Patrick's Day

Why not celebrate St. Patrick's Day? Every March 17, millions of people worldwide fancy themselves a bit Irish, even if not a drop of the blood runs in their veins.

So what's wrong with that?

Nothing, inherently.

The problem lays with the fact that St. Patrick's Day celebrates one of the Druids' worst enemies. St. Patrick was responsible for encouraging the extermination of Druids, their families, the Pagan folk who followed the old ways, and the razing of the sacred groves.

Based on my own research and conclusions, I've found that the old tales about St. Patrick driving the snakes from Ireland are metaphorical for the genocide of the druidical orders and the people who followed those beliefs. Many of the druids, and some of the Pagans, at that time wore tattoos of snakes around their wrists and arms. These are the snakes to which the old tales refer—to brag about St. Patrick driving the snakes away is to brag about the extermination of a religion and hundreds, if not thousands, of lives.

Do we really want to celebrate that?

It's one thing to be proud of your heritage. I'm three-quarters Irish and I'm proud enough of it. But it's quite another matter to celebrate a holiday based on a man who destroyed an entire way of life through religious hatred and intolerance.

The day I found out about the truth of St. Patrick's deeds was the last day I ever considered celebrating my heritage on March 17. I can find other ways to celebrate being Irish, if so inclined, and it won't involve my spiritual karma.

The Festival of Bacchus

One day a friend and I were trying to decide how to rebel against St. Patrick's Day, and how to encourage other Pagans we knew not to celebrate it—even though we told them the history of the day, some were still trying to rationalize their celebrations.

So we did some research and came up with the bit of trivia that March 17 was also celebrated as a festival for Bacchus, the god of wine, (the Roman equivalent to Dionysus) and that was enough for us!

If Pagans want to party on March 17, if they want to imbibe and indulge, that's fine—sometimes I like to let loose, too. But we decided that if we were going to celebrate on that day, we'd do it in the name of the God from whom the vine springs!

So, I implore you—don't celebrate St. Patrick's Day! If you feel you must celebrate, say a few prayers and words of remembrance for all those destroyed by the murdering zealot and, if you still want to party, hold a wake for them in true Dionysian/Bacchanalian style.

The Colors of Bacchus

Colors for your Bacchanalia should be centered around green (for the vine) and purple or burgundy (for the wine). I think accents of gold, for the sun which encourages the fruit to ripeness, are a nice touch.

Incenses, Herbs, and Woods

Musk, patchouli, and sandalwood are all good choices for your incense. You also might consider incenses devoted to Pan or the Horned God as well, since His energy is very much akin to that of Bacchus.

If you are planning magick on this day and want to use specific herbs, my suggestions would be lilac, rose, jasmine, narcissus, patchouli, vetiver, or valerian—all intoxicating herbs.

As far as woods go, what better wood than grape vine? It makes wonderful wreaths and when properly soaked for pliability, can be woven into baskets and pentacles.

Decorating the Altar

Start with a beautiful cloth of green, perhaps with gold sparkles running through it. Set a green pillar candle in the center— although this is one festival for which I don't encourage the use of candles. If people do imbibe more than is manageable, you don't want them knocking over the candles and lighting the place on fire. You might want to use low lighting in the background or colored lights (Yule lights) in green or purple instead of candles.

Drape the altar in real or silk ivy, depending on whether or not your animals or children have access to it. Add flowers—big bunches of spring daffodils and tulips, narcissus and jonquils, hothouse roses.

If you live in tropical climes, then gather orchids and plumeria—intoxicating scents that add to the ambiance.

Next, arrange trays and platters of fruits, cheese, crackers, and chocolates on the altar. Drape grapes over a silver tray, fill a crystal bowl with strawberries, arrange truffles on a tiny china saucer.

Unlike the brawling stereotypes of the St. Patrick's Day parties, give your festival a luxurious, sensual atmosphere.

Have plenty of music on hand, and choose wine and champagne that you enjoy—go for quality rather than quantity. If you want to have a Bacchanalian festival without alcohol I'm not going to fault you for it. There are many wonderful non-alcoholic wines and sparkling ciders on the market and just as much fun can be had at a party that's alcohol-free as any other.

Unlike the Roman debacles, we're trying to create a new synthesis of sensuality, luxury, indolence, and creativity!

Crystals make pretty additions to the altar, though I don't recommend amethyst—it's supposed to prevent drunkenness and that defeats the purpose if you are aiming at an intoxicated state.

Clothing and No Clothing

Encourage people to wear comfortable clothing that is floral, flow-ing, and pretty (another reason for watching the candle flames—flowing robes and fire don't mix). You should decide in advance what to do if couples or groups decide they want to take the sensu-ality any further—will you have a room to which they can discreetly retire? Or is anything beyond feeding each other grapes taboo? Plan for this before you start the party and let everyone know the boundaries in advance.

A Sobering Note on Drinking and Safety

When your guests arrive, take their car keys—be smart, be safe, and be happy. Make sure everyone contributes cab fare for those too intoxicated to drive—and if someone insists on driving while drunk, tell them no.

We have to face facts.

There are far too many drunk drivers on the roads and the tragedy caused by their lack of concern is unimaginable. I live with the knowledge that a member of my family killed someone while driving drunk. She drank a few beers and ran her pick-up truck into the back of an eighteen-wheeler while trying to pass it. There were several people in the truck with her and one of them died.

She insisted she wasn't drunk, but her blood alcohol level was above the legal limit and she never would face the truth. Her stu-pidity and her unwillingness to accept responsibility are two things I could never forgive. As much as I loved my sister, it was difficult to show her respect after that.

She spent seven months in jail—not long enough for a crime of utter stupidity.

I suppose her misdeed could have died with her (she died of an unrelated disease). I'd just as soon not remember what happened but since her stupidity caused a death, I feel that it is my responsi-bility, as a member of her family, to use her as an example. If one life can be saved by what I say here, then it's worth it.

If you are hosting the party and there is alcohol involved, you are liable for your guests. Think about who you invite to your festival.

The Festival of Bacchus

When everyone has arrived, cast your circle and invoke the elements as usual.

PST: **We gather here to remember those murdered in the name of religious intolerance by St. Patrick and his followers. We protest the celebration of his life, for he lacked respect for others' lives and beliefs.**

PT: **We gather here to celebrate the lives of those who died for no other crime than living by their beliefs. We celebrate them on this, the festival of Bacchus, with song and dance and drink and food.**

PST: **We invoke thee, God of the Vine, that you might join us in circle tonight and lead our revelries. Be with us, oh Golden One of Grapes and Ivy, watch over our rites and set free our hearts on this day of mourning.**

PT: *(Holds up chalice of wine, pours some of it on the ground or into a planter of earth, to be put outside later.)* **To the God of the Vine!**

All: **To the God of the Vine!**

PST: **To the God of the Wine!**

All: **To the God of the Wine!**

PT: **To the Goddess Divine!**

All: **To the Goddess Divine!**

PST: **Let the celebration begin!**

For the rest of the evening eat, drink, listen to music, talk, dance, move as the mood strikes, taking care to respect other's choices and boundaries. When the evening is over, thank the God and Goddess and devoke the elements and circle.

KAMEHAMEHA DAY

A Hawaiian Celebration

On December 22, 1871, King Kamehameha V of the Kingdom of Hawai'i proclaimed that June 11 would thereafter be a holiday in recognition of King Kamehameha I, who unified the Hawaiian Islands into a nation.

Even after the Kingdom of Hawai'i was overthrown and annexed by the United States in 1893, the holiday remained. Today, some thirty-eight years after Hawai'i was granted statehood, King Kamehameha Day is an official state holiday and the people of Hawai'i celebrate and remember how Kamehameha, aided by the Goddess Pele, took control of the islands.

King Kamehameha, whose name means The Lonely One, rose to power as he followed the war God Ku and led his armies from island to island. The deciding factor granting him sovereignty came when Pele destroyed an entire army as they passed under Her mountain. With one gush of ash, lava, and cinders, She rained down Her fury on Kamehameha's rival and his army succumbed. Their footsteps can still be seen on the borders of Her crater.

The unification of the islands came just in time—the Europeans, namely Captain James Cook, landed in Hawai'i's harbors in 1779 (some records say 1778), and from that day on Hawai'i would never be the same. Shortly after their discovery, the Europeans swiftly eyed the beautiful paradise for exploitation, the missionaries saw a chance to assimilate another religion in the name of Christianity, and the land that once housed almost a million native Hawaiians soon watched as her population (decimated through venereal disease, leprosy, and intolerance) fell to barely 40,000.

King Kamehameha was able to hold off the inevitable for a while, but his people and the land were no match for the insatiable appetites of colonial countries desiring to enlarge their borders.

The United States finally won out, annexing the land in 1893, as it overthrew the Hawaiian government and bound Queen Liliuokalani (the ruling monarch by then) to house arrest for the rest of her life. But the people would not forget their kingdom, and the gods and ghosts of Hawai'i would not be stilled.

Pele Remembered

As Hawai'i became a major tourist attraction, visitors began to steal the rocks from Pele's craters and bring them back to the mainland as souvenirs. This seemed to stir the Goddess to life again, for the rocks are sacred, the *aina* (land) belongs to Pele and is considered part of Her body. To steal a rock is to steal from Her essence, and the Goddess makes Herself known to those who have the audacity to pilfer stray pebbles, visiting them with nasty turns of fortune, broken bones, cars that catch on fire, appliances that won't work, money slipping away . . . Pele has no compunction about reminding those who steal from Her that She doesn't appreciate it.

So tourists began mailing back the rocks and the park service now returns thousands of pounds of rocks to the craters in which they were born each year.

Throughout the twentieth century, Pele, whose fires were relatively silent throughout much of the takeover, re-emerged to claim the land again and, in 1983, She once more began to spew molten fire after an attempt was made to force geothermal wells into Her mountain.

The town of Kalapana found itself entirely engulfed by the lava flows . . . not surprising since the Kahunas warned the developers that the land was sacred and if they built there, Pele would come and destroy the houses.

The developers, eager in their greed, ignored both spiritual and geological warnings and built over one hundred houses in a subdivision called the Royal Gardens. Pele sent Her lava down the mountain and the subdivision now stands in a field of dark, hardened pahoehoe—useless and empty. The houses burned.

The one thing saved from destruction was an ancient *heiau*, or temple. The lava rose up its walls and stopped, parting to flow around the temple rather than through it. The heiau was spared Pele's wrath until this past year, when it too succumbed and returned to the Goddess of the Volcano.

The Gods of Hawai'i

The Hawaiians worshiped an astounding pantheon of gods besides Pele. Indeed, their chants speak of 4,000 Gods, 40,000 Gods and 400,000 Gods. These include the:

Akua (ah-koo'-a): the Gods

'Aumakua (ow-ma'-koo-a): the deified ancestor spirits

Kupua (Koo-poo'-a): the spirits and elementals

Only one deity in Hawai'i required human sacrifice, and that was the war God Ku (or Kuka'ilimoku). No one was ever thrown into a volcano, be they virgin or otherwise. Since Pele was seen as a giver of life, it was considered inappropriate to sacrifice life to Her. Perhaps in other cultures this may have been the case, but not in Hawai'i-nae.

Hawaiian Magic

To understand Hawaiian magic, you must first know a little about the spirituality of the Hawaiian people. Originating from Polynesia, the Hawaiians are animists, seeing life and spirit within all things—whether it be plant, animal, mineral, or cloud.

The energy we call magic, as well as the energy we label as an aura is known as *mana* (mah'nah) in Hawai'i. It can be transferred from person to person, or person to object through breath or saliva. (Kahunas pass their own mana to their students at the time of their death through these means).

Women have a different type of mana than men, but it is seen as powerful and strong in its own right.

Mana can be lost or taken away through misuse, neglect of use, disrespect to akua and 'aumakua, et cetera.

The magical use of one's own mana, or the mana belonging to natural objects such as stones and plants is known as Ho'okalaka-pua (ho'-o-kah'lah-kah'-poo-ah). This would be the equivalent of casting a spell.

Not all magic was reserved for the kahunas, quite a bit was actually performed by commoners. Usually, a mixture of natural objects (plants, shells, stones) were chosen for their particular mana, then empowered through breath (transferring personal mana into object) and chants. After that, the object was used—it might be thrown into the sea, buried, kept near the recipient of the spell, or often it was offered up to the akua.

Magic was seen as intrinsic to life, the people of Hawai'i couldn't imagine life without mana. As with most shamanistic cultures, their lives were intimately entwined with the land and therefore the land was seen as a living entity. This is especially true when it comes to the Big Island—Hawai'i Island—where the land still steams and lava flows to the ocean, where the Goddess Pele makes Her home.

People still take offerings to the shrines up to Kilauea for Her.

Much of the magical work in Hawaiian tradition is performed in the dream-state. It is then that the spirit, or 'uhane (u-ha'-nay) can leave the body via the spirit hole (the inner corner of the eye) and go do its spiritual work. The 'uhane can meet with the aumakua during this time and receive valuable information. If a person died before their time, the kahuna can see the spirit fluttering around the body and force it to re-enter, resuscitating the person as they do so.

After death, the 'uhane travels to the leina (lay-ee-na) or "leaping off place" (each island has one). There it will jump into Po (Poh), the underworld which is a place of water and trees and forests. Po is seen as being West, past the sunset, and it is ruled by Milu, a shadowy akua about whom not much is known.

If the 'uhane was disrespectful of the aumakua during life, or of the akua, then they are not shown to the leina and they will wander the island in *lapu* (lah-poo) form, as a ghost.

The Kahuna

The kahuna are the sorcerers of Hawai'i's people. But they are much more than that. The term *kahuna* means expert, and there are many different branches. There are women kahuna, known as *kahuna wahine* (kah-hoo'-nah wah-hee'-nee). Prayer and oral tradition were two of the most important facets of the kahuna class.

Just as we have teachers, doctors, witches, navigators, executioners, and astronomers today, so all of these fields would be classified as a kahuna of one sort or another. Many of the kahuna were of the ali'i class (the royal class), especially the *kahuna nui* who were considered experts in all things. They served as counselors to the chiefs. The kahuna helped enforce the kapus and were greatly feared and respected.

Ka Huaka'i O Ka Po

Occasionally people will see or hear the Night Marchers, a ghostly procession of dead warriors, chiefs, kahuna, akua and 'aumakua (much like the Wild Hunt of Western Europe). The sight is said to kill those who do not lay in the dirt and hide their faces, or, at the very least, do not hide from the Marchers. Sightings are still reported today.

Heiau

The temples of Hawai'i were known as *heiau* (hay-ow). They were most commonly built of stone, though a few were made of wood. These shrines were found everywhere, from family shrines, to fishing shrines, to shrines guarding pathways and trails, to occupational shrines, fertility shrines . . . as well as heiaus devoted to the different deities.

During the first thirty years of this century, more than eight hundred heiaus were discovered in Hawai'i nae. Unfortunately, many of these have been destroyed by development, though the ones that were preserved are generally under protection and still considered kapu to visitors.

Hula

The hula is a sacred ritual dance. It combines oral history with spirituality. Sometimes the hula was performed for pure joy, but seldom for entertainment. Today it has become sanitized and watered down in the hotels and tourist luaus, but traditional hula is making a strong comeback.

There are many Goddesses of hula, including Pele, Laka, Kapo, and Hi'iaka. The schools teaching hula are known as hula halau (hae-low) and the teacher or master is the kumu (koo-moo) hula.

While in training during the pre-colonization days, the hula student was under a strict regimen. Sex was kapu and personal cleanliness was of highest importance. Breaking kapu resulted in the wrath of the Goddess and could only be assuaged by offering 'awa (a sacred plant) and a young pig to the Goddess in question.

In 1830, after Ka'ahumanu (wife of Kamehameha I) was baptized Christian, she bowed to pressure and public display of the hula was forbidden, considered obscene and lascivious by the missionaries.

In 1874, King Kalakaua, also known as the Merrie Monarch, reinstated the hula and called it a vital symbol of Hawai'i's past and present. It was changed, but not lost and the ancient traditional dances have been revived. At many hula contests, one of the components for gauging the winner is by how much mana they portray in their dances.

Kapu

Kapu (kah-poo) . . . taboo . . . many of the taboos in ancient Hawai'i seem strict, even tyrannical, but there were strong ecological reasons for a number of those kapus. It was kapu to eat certain fish at certain times of the year, it was kapu to gather certain plants, it was kapu for women to eat bananas, pork, and coconuts.

It is highly probable that many of these kapus directly related to supply and demand. When the fish were spawning, the Hawaiians knew better than to hunt them . . . when the population began to grow, the only form of birth control was to feed the women a less than nutritious diet.

Other kapus were related to class and royalty. It was kapu to touch the shadow of one of the *ali'i* (ah-lee'-ee), the royalty. Kapu breakers were treated harshly, usually condemned to death unless they could reach Pu'uhonua, one of the places of refuge where their "sin" would be cleansed and forgiven. These places were difficult to reach and many failed, but those who made it were taken in by the kahuna and when they returned to society, it was as if nothing had happened.

Menehunes

The Hawaiians have a rich history of faerie folk, they are known there as the Menehunes (Mehn-eh'-hoo-nays). Much like the gnomes and dwarfs of Europe, the Menehunes are a builder race and often create elaborate walls and structures during the night. They do not work by daylight, and examples of work credited to them still exist.

The Menehunes often live in the Banyan trees. Interestingly enough, when I was in Hawai'i, there was a banyan tree that I was absolutely fascinated by. I tried to take a picture of the area that pulled me, but the camera wouldn't work . . . that is, until I moved a few inches away from that particular area. Only then was I able to snap a photograph.

The Colors of Kamehameha Day

Colors appropriate for a Hawaiian celebration include bright yellow, red, blue, and floral prints (known as aloha prints). Green makes a nice addition, considering how green the Islands are.

Incenses, Herbs, and Woods

For incense, choose white ginger, frangipani, hibiscus, lotus, orchid, plumeria, or one of the other tropical scents.

If you want to work with herbs, I would suggest using fern, ti leaf, dragon's blood resin, and banana leaf.

Woods appropriate to the celebration include acacia, sandalwood, macadamia, bamboo, and koa.

Celebrating King Kamehameha Day

I suggest that you have a big party to celebrate the day. Decorate your altar with an appropriate cloth, fern fronds, ivy, and big bunches of flowers (if you can buy orchids or tiger lilies, these seem to fit the mood). Add a fresh pineapple and platters of bananas, mangos, papaya, macadamia nuts, chocolates (beloved everywhere), strings of seashells, and pearls.

When everyone has arrived in festive dress, stand in a circle and join hands. The Priest and Priestess should stand in the center.

PST: Aloha! We gather today to celebrate and remember the Hawaiian culture, to honor King Kamehameha I, who led his land to unification, and to pay homage to the Gods of Hawai'i-nae.

PT: There are 4,000 Gods, there are 40,000 Gods, there are 400,000 Gods. We honor Their memory.

PST: We honor the Goddess Pele, Mistress of the Volcano, that She might continue Her watch over Her lands and Her children. May Your fires burn ever bright and ever strong, Madame Pele!

PT: Diversity is strength, tolerance and acceptance are the two paths to respect. We honor other cultures as we respect our own—we seek to understand, not to ridicule, to celebrate their joys even though we may not follow their paths. We come as open-minded and willing students, with honor in our hearts and joy in our voices.

PST: Once Hawai'i nae stood as a nation, once it stood free and sovereign in its own right. Even though it now sits under the shadow of a new country, let the culture not be lost and the Gods not be forgotten. Blesséd be.

All: Blesséd be.

Spend the afternoon or evening feasting, listening to Slack-Key Guitar (a truly unique Hawaiian form of music), watching documentaries about Hawai'i and the volcanoes (see Bibliography, page 295) and looking at pictures and books to better understand the culture and to lose the average American's narrow view of the islands, which are, in my opinion, still paradise if one only looks beyond the trappings of the tourist-mindset.

If you live near a beach, spend time out on the shore, in the water if it's warm enough. If you happen to live near Mount St. Helens in Washington State, plan a field trip to the volcano. St. Helens is vastly different from the volcanoes of Hawai'i, but they are both still conduits for the Earth's fire to rise up and be known, and both places are awe-inspiring.

Food and Recipes

When planning the menu for your party, try to serve pork, pineapple, bananas, mangos, and papaya—all common foods in Hawai'i. Since the Islands are so racially diverse, you can find everything from Chinese to Japanese to Portuguese to Hawaiian to traditional American cuisine over there, but for your celebration, try to choose foods that are tropical in flavor or origin.

Sausage Mango Stir Fry

¼ cup soy sauce
1 cup orange juice
   concentrate
1 teaspoon parsley
1 teaspoon tarragon
1 teaspoon basil
1 teaspoon crushed
   black pepper
½ cup olive oil
1 pound pork sausage links

1 green bell pepper, diced
⅛ teaspoon red pepper
   (not cayenne)
1 bunch green onions, diced
2 cloves garlic, minced
1 cup broccoli, chopped
2 mangos, cored,
   peeled and chopped
Cooked rice

Blend soy sauce, orange juice concentrate, herbs, and ¼ cup olive oil. Chop sausage links into ½-inch slices and marinate in sauce overnight.

The next day: heat ¼ cup olive oil until hot. Using a slotted spoon, drain the sausage and add it to the oil. Fry, turning as needed, until done. Remove from pan.

To remaining oil, add pepper, onions, garlic, and broccoli. Stirring constantly, cook for 5 minutes. Add mango and cook another 2 minutes. Add sausage links and sauce. Cook over medium-high heat another 5-10 minutes until sauce is reduced, stir every minute or so to prevent sticking.

Serve over cooked rice.

Serves 4.

Part 9

resources

Appendix One • Appendix Two

APPENDIX ONE

Waters, Pentagrams, and Correspondences

Moon and Sun Water

Moon water is water that has been charged under the moon's energy. Sun water is water charged by the light of the sun.

Full Moon Water

Fill a glass jar with water. Add a moonstone to the jar and cap. Three days before the full moon, set the jar outside at night where it can capture the moon's rays (it doesn't matter if it is overcast). Bring it in the following morning. Repeat this for the next two nights. After this, every month add water each month to the jar if needed and set the jar outside the night before the full moon to capture the moonlight.

New Moon Water

Fill a glass jar with water. Add a piece of black onyx to the jar and cap. Follow directions as above, except set the jar outside during the new moon (and three days before it), instead of the full moon.

Sun Water

Fill a glass jar with water. Add a piece of citrine or carnelian to the jar and cap. Set outside on three consecutive sunny days, taking inside at dusk. For added strength, set outside at dawn on the morning of the Summer Solstice. Use for solar rituals and spells.

Invoking and Devoking Pentacles

The pentacle is a symbol of power used in many spells and rituals. It is the sign of the Witch, one I feel we must reclaim from its supposed connection to Satanism portrayed by the media and Christianity.

It is a symbol of honor and power and it belongs in our religion/Craft.

I get irritated when I see someone wearing a pentacle who does not follow the Old Religion—I don't wear a crucifix because I am not Christian. I wouldn't even think of it. I expect the same respect from people of other religions or those who practice no religion.

When used as a symbol during ritual and magick, it either attracts or repels energy.

There are a number of ways in which to draw this symbol, and so I present the most common for invoking.

I use a different devoking pentacle than that of many Pagans, but I do so because I believe that when you devoke, or remove, a symbol or energy or force, you should begin the devocation in the opposite fashion from which you invoked.

Invoking, Devoking, and Traditional Devoking Pentagrams

Elemental Correspondence Tables

The Element of Air

Sabbats: Imbolc, Ostara
Direction: East
Rules: The mind, all mental, intellectual and some psychic work; knowledge; abstract thought; theory; mountain tops; prairie open to the wind; wind; breath; clouds; vapor and mist; storms; purification; removal of stagnation; new beginnings; change
Time: Dawn
Season: Spring
Colors: White, yellow, lavender, pale blue, gray
Zodiac: Gemini, Libra, Aquarius
Tools: Censer, incense, athame, sword
Oils: Frankincense, violet, lavender, lemon, rosemary
Faeries: Sylphs
Animals: All birds
Goddesses: Aradia, Arianrhod, Nuit, Urania, Athena
Gods: Mercury, Hermes, Shu, Thoth, Khephera

The Element Of Fire

Sabbats: Beltane, Litha
Direction: South
Rules: Creativity; passion; energy; blood; healing; destruction; temper; faerie fire, phosphorescence, and Will o'the Wisps volcanoes; flame; lava; bonfires; deserts; sun
Time: Noon
Season: Summer
Colors: Red, orange, gold, crimson, white, peridot
Zodiac: Sagittarius, Aries, Leo
Tools: Wand, Candle

Oils:	Lime, orange, neroli, citronella
Faeries:	Flame Dancers, Phoenix
Animals:	Salamander, Lizard, Snake
Goddesses:	Pele, Freya, Vesta, Hestia, Brid
Gods:	Vulcan, Horus, Ra, Agni, Hephaestus

The Element of Water

Sabbats:	Lughnasadh, Mabon
Direction:	West
Rules:	Emotions; feelings; love; sorrow; intuition; the subconscious and unconscious minds; the womb; fertility; menstruation; cleansing; purification; oceans; lakes; tide pools; rain; springs and wells
Time:	Twilight
Season:	Autumn
Colors:	Blue, blue-green, gray, aquamarine, indigo, white
Zodiac:	Cancer, Pisces, Scorpio
Tools:	Chalice
Oils:	Lemon, lily-of-the-valley, camphor
Faeries:	Undines, Sirens, Naiads
Animals:	All fish and marine life
Goddesses:	Aphrodite, Isis, Mari, Tiamat, Vellamo, Ran, Kupala
Gods:	Ahto, Osiris, Manannan, Neptune, Poscidon, Varuna

The Element of Earth

Sabbats: Samhain, Yule
Direction: North
Rules: The body; growth; nature; sustenance; material gain; prosperity; money; death; caverns; fields; meadows; plants; trees; animals; rocks; crystals; manifestation; materialization
Time: Midnight
Season: Winter
Colors: Black, brown, green, gold, mustard
Zodiac: Capricorn, Taurus, Virgo
Tools: Pentacle, salt
Oils: Pine, cypress, cedar, sage, vetiver
Faeries: Gnomes, dwarfs
Animals: All four-footed animals
Goddesses: Ceres, Demeter, Gaia, Persephone, Kore, Rhea, Epona, Cerridwen
Gods: Cernunnos, Herne, Dionysus, Marduk, Pan, Tammuz, Attis, Thor

APPENDIX TWO

Supplies, Periodicals, and Organizations

Most, if not all of the shops listed here offer mail-order service and catalogs. Be aware, however, that retail shops go in and out of business with alarming frequency, so some of those listed may not be in service when you write to them. Others will spring up after the writing of this book.

As far as local supplies go: look for candles in drug stores, stationery stores, grocery stores, and gift shops. Grocery stores and florists carry flowers, as do your friends' gardens. You can sometimes find essential oils in gift shops or perfume shops, and crystals can be located in gift shops and rock shops. Gather your herbs wild or purchase them through grocery stores or food co-ops, herb shops, and local plant nurseries where you can buy the plant itself.

Unusual altar pieces can often be found at local import supply stores and second-hand stores. Altar cloths are easy: go to your favorite fabric shop and buy a piece of cloth large enough to cover your altar table.

Lastly, don't overlook the Yellow Pages. Look under the headings: Metaphysical; Herbs; Books (bookstores often carry far more than books); Lapidary Supplies and Jewelry.

Magical Supplies

1. Abyss
   48-NWL Chester Road
   Chester, MA 01011-9735

2. White Light Pentacles
   P. O. Box 8163
   Salem, MA 01971-8163

3. Serpentine Music Productions
   P. O. Box 2564-L1
   Sebastopol, CA 95473
   (Carries a wide variety of hard-to-find pagan music.)

4. Eden Within
   P. O. Box 667
   Jamestown, NY 14702

5. Gypsy Heaven
   115 S. Main St.
   New Hope, PA 18938
   (catalog costs $3.00; they say it's refundable through purchase. Money Orders only.)

6. MoonScents and Magickal Blends
   P. O. Box 3811588-LL
   Cambridge, MA 02238

Pagan/Magical Journals and Magazines

1. New Moon Rising
   12345 SE Fuller Rd. #119
   Milwaukee, OR 97222

2. Green Egg
   P. O. Box 488
   Laytonville, CA 95454

3. SageWoman
   P. O. Box 641LL
   Point Arena, CA 95648

4. Shaman's Drum
   P. O. Box 430
   Willits, CA 95490-0430

5. Open Ways
   P. O. Box 14415
   Portland, OR 97293-0415

6. The Beltane Papers
   P. O. Box 29694
   Bellingham, WA 98228-1694

7. The Sacred Horn
   Unickorn Press
   P. O. Box 143262
   Anchorage, AK 99514-3262

Videos

Look for the video tapes I mentioned at your local video rental shops—most are easy enough to find, though some, like *The Wicker Man,* are usually found in the "Cult Classics" section.

Other Resources Mentioned

1. Aquarian Tabernacle Church (ATC)
   P. O. Box 409
   Index, WA 98256

2. Crossroads Learning Center
   P. O. Box 12184
   Seattle, WA 98102

3. Childfree Network (CFN)
   7777 Sunrise Blvd. Ste. 1800
   Citrus Heights, CA 95610

GLOSSARY

A'a: rough, chunky slow-moving lava.

Aina: Hawaiian for land.

Akua: Hawaiian for Gods.

Ali'i: the Hawaiian nobility class.

Altar: the ritual layout of magickal/ritual tools and symbols.

Asperge: to sprinkle with water during or preceding ritual; to purify with sprinkled water.

Athame: a double-edged dagger for ritual use.

'Aumakua: Hawaiian deified ancestor spirits.

Aura: the energy field existing around all living things.

Austri: the Norse dwarf holding up the eastern corner of the sky.

Balefire: a fire lit for magickal purposes, usually outdoors. Traditional fires were lit on hills during Beltane and Samhain.

Beltane: May 1 Sabbat celebration of life and sexuality.

Book of Shadows: a book of magickal spells, rituals, and lore.

Book of Mirrors: a journal of magickal workings.

Bower: an outdoor boudoir specifically set aside in which couples may retreat to make love.

Burryman: a scape-goat; often represented by a man who carries the village troubles away from the town and disposes of them; he then is welcomed with honor for his deeds.

Caer Arianrhod: the castle of Arianrhod, Goddess of the Silver Wheel.

Censer: an incense burner.

Centering, to Center: to find an internal point of balance.

Chalice: a ritual goblet.

Charge: to infuse an object or person with energy; also an oath or instruction.

Childfree: the state of having no children by choice.

Circle: a sphere constructed of energy, created by a Witch; sacred space.

Cleansing, to Cleanse: to remove negative energy, to purify.

Corn Dolly: a doll made of corn stalks/husks representing the spirit of the corn and/or an aspect of the Goddess.

Coven: a group of Witches who come together to practice magick and celebrate the Sabbats.

Craft, the: Witchcraft, natural magic.

Crone: the aged aspect of the Goddess, representing wisdom, experience and the Underworld.

Deosil: clockwise (sun-wise).

Deva: a powerful Faerie land or mineral spirit; a collective oversoul.

Devoke; Devocation: to dismiss; a formal farewell in ritual, usually to the Gods and/or elements.

Divination: magickal arts of discovering the unknown through use of such tools as cards, runes, stones, or crystals balls.

Divine Marriage: (see Hieros Gamos).

Dumbfeast: the silent supper commemorating the dead on Samhain.

Eddas: the Norse sagas.

Einherjar: the Norse festival of the Fallen Warriors, celebrated on November 11.

Elements: the four building blocks of the universe—Earth, Air, Fire, Water. Major forces used in natural magic.

Equinox, Autumnal: The point during autumn when the Sun crosses the celestial equator; day and night are of equal length, (see Mabon).

Equinox, Spring: (see Vernal Equinox) (see Ostara).

Equinox, Vernal: The point during spring when the Sun crosses the celestial equator; day and night are of equal length (see Ostara).

Faerie: one of many nature spirits that inhabit a realm or dimension next to our own.

Faerie Kingdom: the realm of Faerie.

Fey: to be like or of the Faerie.

First Harvest: the harvest of grain. (see Lughnasadh)

Flower Bride: a female faerie/fertility aspect of divinity, encountered during Spring.

Green Man: a male aspect of divinity, symbolized by the vegetation and forests. (see Jack Frost and Jack-in-the-Green)

Greenwood: the sacred grove of the Goddess; a term for the divine aspect of the forests.

Grounding, to Ground: to root self firmly in the physical world in preparation for magickal/metaphysical work.

Halau: Hawaiian for a group or school, as in hula halau.

Handfasting: a Witch, Wiccan, Pagan wedding.

Handparting: a Pagan ceremony marking the end of a marriage.

Hawai'i nae: an inclusive term for all the Hawaiian Islands.

Heiau: an Hawaiian temple.

Herbalist: one who works with herbs.

Hieros Gamos: the sacred mating of the God and Goddess.

Holly King: the aspect of the God that rules over the Waning Half of the year (from Litha to Yule).

Ho'okalakapua: the use of mana to create change; i.e., magick and spellwork.

Hula: sacred Hawaiian ritual dance.

Hunt: the Wild Hunt led by (various) Gods and/or Goddesses.

Hunter: the Horned God of the Witches.

Imbolc: festival of the Goddess Brid; Sabbat celebrated on February 2 each year.

Immolg: literally means, "in milk." Name for Imbolc.

Initiation: a process of formally introducing and/or admitting the self or someone else into a Coven, group, religion, etc.

Invoke, Invocation: an appeal or petition to a God/dess, element or energy.

Jack Frost: the winter aspect of the Green Man, personified in human terms (see Green Man and Jack-in-the-Green).

Jack-in-the-Green: the summer aspect of the Green Man, personified in human terms. (see Green Man and Jack Frost)

John Barleycorn: the spirit of the corn personified in human terms.

Ka Huaka'i O Ka Po: Hawaiian Night Marchers (ghosts)

Kahuna: Hawaiian magick worker; sorcerer.

Kalevala: the compendium of Finnish songs and tales compiled by Elias Lönnrot.

Kapu: Hawaiian taboo.

Kapua: Hawaiian elemental/nature spirits.

Kitska: a tool used in Pysanky. (see Pysanky)

Kumu: Hawaiian for teacher; i.e., kumu hula (hula teacher).

Lapu: Hawaiian for ghost.

Leina: the "leaping off" place on the Hawaiian Islands for the spirit to enter the realm of the dead.

Litha: (see Solstice, Summer). Sabbat festival honoring the Oak King and the Goddess in Their prime.

Lughnasadh: festival of the God Lugh; Sabbat celebrated on August 1 each year.

Lupercalia: Roman festival of love, sexuality, and fertility celebrated on February 15.

Mabon: (see Equinox, Autumnal). Sabbat festival honoring the harvest. A Pagan Thanksgiving.

Magic/Magick: the manipulation of natural forces and psychic energy to bring about desired changes.

Magic Mirror: a mirror charged with energy, used only for magickal scrying and spells.

Maiden: the youthful aspect of the Goddess, representing freedom, adventure, and playfulness.

Mana: the natural energy field that permeates everything.

Maser: mead with fruit (juices) added. (see Mead)

Maypole: a tree or long pole used for dances during Beltane, representing the phallus of the God. (see Beltane)

Mead: an alcoholic drink made of honey, yeast, and water.

Meditation: a state of reflection, contemplation.

Metheglin: mead with spices added. (see Mead)

Menehunes: Hawaiian faerie spirits.

Metsanhaltija: the Finnish wood nymphs and dryads under the rule of Mielikki, Goddess of the Hunt and of Faerie.

Midsummer's Eve: the night preceding the Summer Solstice. Often celebrated for its connections with the Faerie Kingdom.

Mother: the fertile, full-grown aspect of the Goddess, representing the prime of life, creativity, and adult sexuality.

Nordhri: the Norse dwarf that holds up the northern corner of the sky.

Oak King: the aspect of the God that rules over the Waxing Half of the year (from Yule to Litha).

Old Religion: Paganism, in all its myriad forms. A religion pre-dating the Judeo-Christian religions.

Origami: the Japanese art of folding paper into ephemeral shapes and sculptures.

Ostara: (see Equinox, Vernal). Sabbat festival celebrating the Goddess Eostre and the advent of Spring.

Pahoehoe: smooth, rapidly flowing lava.

Pagan, Paganism: (a follower of) one of many ancient (and/or modern revivals) Earth-centric/eco-centric religions.

Pentacle: a ritual object or piece of jewelry with a pentagram inscribed or woven into it.

Pentagram: five-pointed star.

Perseids: an annual meteor shower through which the Earth passes every August.

Phoenix: Egyptian bird that was consumed by fire every 500 years and rose, renewed from the ashes.

Po: the Hawaiian underworld.

Polarity: the concept of equal, opposite energies.

Pomander: a charm or decoration made from fruit and spices.

Pysanky: the art of Ukrainian egg decoration. (see Kitska)

Reincarnation: the doctrine of rebirth. Most Pagans and Witches accept this as a fact and see it as a part of the Wheel of Life.

Ritual: ceremony.

Ritualist: one who takes part in ritual.

Rumtopf: a mixture of rum and fruit.

Runes: symbols carved onto rocks, crystals, clay, etc., which embody powerful energies to be used during magic.
Also: symbols used in early alphabets.

Runo: a stanza from the ancient Finnish songs comprising the epic Kalevala. (see Kalevala)

Sabbat: one of the eight Pagan holidays which comprise the Wheel of the Year.

Samhain: Sabbat festival celebrated every November 1, to honor and remember our ancestors and the dead.

Scry: to gaze into or at an object while in trance, to open oneself to visions from the future; to discern hidden motives and energies behind an event or situation.

Second Harvest: the harvest of fruits. (see Mabon)

Shaman: a man or woman who has attained a high degree of knowledge concerning altered states of consciousness. Usually an honored title associated with a structured form of study in what are generally regarded as primitive or aboriginal religions.

Shamanism: the practice of Shamans.

Sidhe (Daoine Sidhe): children of the goddess Danu. The Celtic Faerie-Folk.

Skyclad: to practice magick and ritual in the nude; naked.

Smörgäsbord: Swedish term for buffet dinner.

Smudge, Smudging: to purify or cleanse the air through the use of smoke. (see Smudge Stick).

Smudge Stick: a bundle of herbs used for smudging. (see Smudging)

Solstice, Summer: when the sun is at its zenith over the Tropic of Cancer, during the month of June. The longest day of the year, (see Litha).

Solstice, Winter: when the Sun is at its zenith over the Tropic of Capricorn, during the month of December. The shortest day of the year (see Yule).

Spell: a magickal ritual used to produce certain results in the physical world.

Sudhri: the Norse dwarf that holds up the southern quarter of the sky.

Sun King: another name for the Oak King. (see Oak King)

Suomi: another name for Finland.

Sylphs: Faerie spirits of the air.

Talisman: a magickally charged object used to attract a specific force or energy to its bearer.

Third Harvest: the harvest of meats. (see Samhain)

Totem: an animal spirit to which a human soul is linked.

Tradition: a specific subgroup of Pagans, Witches, Wiccans or magick-workers.

Troth: an oath or binding pledge.

Turning of the Wheel: movement from one Sabbat/Season to another—the cycle of life.

'Uhane: Hawaiian for *spirit* or *soul.*

Underworld: the realm of the spirit; realm of the dead.

Undines: Faerie spirits of the water.

Unicorn: a magickal horned horse.

Virgin: a woman who is not controlled by a man.

Visualization: the process of forming mental images.

Voileipäpöytä: Finnish term for buffet dinner (means "bread and butter table").

Walpurgis Night: April 30, known as the Night of the Witches.

Wheel of the Year: the cyclic turn of the seasons.

Wicca, Wiccan: (a participant of) a modern revival of ancient Earth-centric religions focusing on the God and Goddess of Nature.

Wiccaning: dedicating a child/baby to the God and Goddess.

Widdershins: counterclockwise.

Will o'the Wisp: Faerie lights/energy beings that can and will lead humans astray in swamps, marshes, moors, and the forest.

Witch, Witchcraft: (a practitioner of) the craft of magick, (usually also a member of a Pagan religion).

Yule: (see Solstice, Winter) Midwinter Sabbat festival celebrating the rebirth of the Oak/Sun King.

BIBLIOGRAPHY

Andrews, Ted. *Enchantment of The Faerie Realm.* St. Paul, MN: Llewellyn Publishing, 1993.

Beranbaum, Rose Levy. *The Cake Bible.* New York: William Morrow and Co, 1988.

Cabot, Laurie. *Love Magic.* New York: Dell Publishing, 1992.

———. *Celebrate The Earth.* New York: Dell Publishing, 1994.

Campanelli, Pauline. *Ancient Ways.* St. Paul, MN: Llewellyn Publishing, 1991.

Conway, D.J. *The Ancient and Shining Ones.* St. Paul, MN: Llewellyn Publishing, 1993.

———. *Celtic Magic.* St. Paul, MN: Llewellyn Publishing, 1991.

Cunningham, Scott. *The Complete Book of Incenses, Oils and Brews.* St. Paul, MN: Llewellyn Publishing, 1989.

———. *Hawaiian Magic.* St. Paul, MN: Llewellyn Publishing, 1994.

———. *Encyclopedia of Magical Herbs.* St. Paul, MN: Llewellyn Publishing, 1985.

———. *Wicca.* St. Paul, MN: Llewellyn Publishing, 1988.

Farrar, Janet and Stewart Farrar. *The Witches' Goddess.* Custer, WA: Phoenix Publishing, 1987.

———. *The Witches' God*. Custer, WA: Phoenix Publishing, 1989.

———. *Eight Sabbats For Witches*. Custer, WA: Phoenix Publishing, 1981.

Frazier, Sir James George. *The Golden Bough*. New York: Criterion Books, Inc., 1959.

Freeman, John. *Victorian Entertaining*. Philadelphia: Running Press, 1989.

Frierson, Pamela. *The Burning Island*. San Francisco: Sierra Club Books, 1991.

Galenorn, Yasmine. *Trancing The Witch's Wheel*. St. Paul, MN: Llewellyn Publishing, 1997.

———. *Embracing The Moon*. St. Paul, MN: Llewellyn Publishing, 1998.

Kane, Herb Kawainui. *Pele, Goddess of Hawai'i's Volcanoes*. Captain Cook, HI: Kawainui Press, 1987.

Lönnrot, Elias. *Kalevala*. Translated by: Francis Peabody Magoun, Jr. Cambridge, MA: Harvard University Press, 1963.

———. *Kalevala*. Translated by: Eino Friberg. Helsinki, Finland: Otava Publishing Company, LTD, 1988.

Murray, Liz and Colin Murray. *The Celtic Tree Oracle*. New York: St. Martin's Press, 1988.

Ojakangas, Beatrice. *Finnish Cookbook*. New York: Crown Publishers, 1964.

Pennick, Nigel. *Practical Magic In The Northern Tradition*; London: Aquarian Press, 1989.

Peschel, Lisa. *A Practical Guide To The Runes*. St. Paul, MN: Llewellyn Publishing, 1991.

Ross, Anne and Don Robins. *The Life and Times of a Druid Prince*. New York: Simon and Schuster, 1989.

Sargent, Denny. *Global Ritualism*. St. Paul, MN: Llewellyn Publishing, 1994.

Stone, Margaret. *Supernatural Hawaii*. Honolulu, HI: Tongg Publishing, 1979.

Thorsson, Edred. *The Book of Ogham*. St. Paul, MN: Llewellyn Publishing, 1992.

Recommended Videotapes

A Christmas Carol

A Christmas Story

Darby O'Gill and The Little People

Dead Poets Society

The Four Seasons

Halloween Tree, The

Holiday Inn

Homeward Bound

Little Women

Rudolph the Red Nosed Reindeer

Secret Garden, The

Secret of Roan Inish, The

Something Wicked This Way Comes

Three Lives of Thomasina, The

Wicker Man, The

Volcano Scapes I, II, III, IV, V

INDEX

M

☾ REACH FOR THE MOON

Llewellyn publishes hundreds of books on your favorite subjects! To get these exciting books, including the ones on the following pages, check your local bookstore or order them directly from Llewellyn.

ORDER BY PHONE

- Call toll-free within the U.S. and Canada, 1-800-THE MOON
- In Minnesota, call (651) 291-1970
- We accept VISA, MasterCard, and American Express

ORDER BY MAIL

- Send the full price of your order (MN residents add 7% sales tax) in U.S. funds, plus postage & handling to:

  Llewellyn Worldwide
  P.O. Box 64383, Dept. K300-X
  St. Paul, MN 55164–0383, U.S.A.

POSTAGE & HANDLING

(For the U.S., Canada, and Mexico)

- $4.00 for orders $15.00 and under
- $5.00 for orders over $15.00
- No charge for orders over $100.00

We ship UPS in the continental United States. We ship standard mail to P.O. boxes. Orders shipped to Alaska, Hawaii, The Virgin Islands, and Puerto Rico are sent first-class mail. Orders shipped to Canada and Mexico are sent surface mail.

International orders: Airmail—add freight equal to price of each book to the total price of order, plus $5.00 for each non-book item (audio tapes, etc.).

Surface mail—Add $1.00 per item.

Allow 2 weeks for delivery on all orders.
Postage and handling rates subject to change.

DISCOUNTS

We offer a 20% discount to group leaders or agents. You must order a minimum of 5 copies of the same book to get our special quantity price.

FREE CATALOG

Get a free copy of our color catalog, *New Worlds of Mind and Spirit*. Subscribe for just $10.00 in the United States and Canada ($30.00 overseas, airmail). Many bookstores carry *New Worlds*— ask for it!

Visit our web site at www.llewellyn.com for more information.

Embracing the Moon
A Witch's Guide to Rituals, Spellcraft & Shadow Work

Yasmine Galenorn

Do you feel like toasting the Gods with a glass of mead as you revel in the joys of life? Ever wish you could creep through the mists at night, hunting the Wild Lord? *Embracing the Moon* takes you into the core of Witchcraft, helping you weave magic into your daily routine. The spells and rituals are designed to give you the flexibility to experiment so that you are not locked into dogmatic, rigid degree-systems. Written to encompass both beginning and advanced practitioners, *Embracing the Moon* explores the mystical side of natural magic while keeping a common-sense attitude.

Packed not only with spells and rituals, but recipes for oils, spell powders and charms, this book is based on personal experience; the author dots the pages with her own stories and anecdotes to give you fascinating, and sometimes humorous, examples of what you might expect out of working with her system of magic.

1-56718-304-2, 6 x 9, 312 pp., illus.   **$14.95**

To order, call 1–800–THE MOON
prices subject to change without notice

Trancing the Witch's Wheel
A Guide to Magickal Meditation
Yasmine Galenorn

Meet the Wind and the Queen of Air; stand watch as the Sun King is reborn on Yuletide day; cross the barren lava fields with Pele, and learn to shapeshift like Gwion in his flight from Cerridwen.

In *Trancing the Witch's Wheel,* you will find twenty intricate and beautiful guided meditations, written to lead you into the very heart of the seasons, the elements and the nature of the Divine. This book offers beginning and advanced students a guide as they journey through the cycles of the Pagan year.

Discover how to hone your sense of focus and clearly envision what you want to create in your life. The meditations in *Trancing the Witch's Wheel* are designed for both solitary and group work, and each chapter includes an overview of the subject and suggested exercises to help you in your explorations.

1-56718-303-4, 6 x 9, 224 pp., softcover   **$12.95**

To order, call 1–800–THE MOON
prices subject to change without notice

Green Witchcraft

Folk Magic, Fairy Lore & Herb Craft

Aoumiel Moura

Very little has been written about traditional family practices of the Old Religion simply because such information has not been offered for popular consumption. If you have no contacts with these traditions, *Green Witchcraft* will meet your need for a practice based in family and natural Witchcraft traditions.

Green Witchcraft describes the worship of nature and the use of herbs that have been part of human culture from the earliest times. It relates to the Lord and Lady of Greenwood, the Primal Father and Mother, and to the Earth Spirits called Faeries.

Green Witchcraft traces the historic and folk background of this path and teaches its practical techniques. Learn the basics of Witchcraft from a third-generation, traditional family Green Witch who openly shares from her own experiences. Through a how-to format you'll learn rites of passage, activities for Sabbats and Esbats, Fairy lore, self-dedication, self-initiation, spellwork, herbcraft and divination.

This practical handbook is an invitation to explore, identify and adapt the Green elements of Witchcraft that work for you, today.

1-56718-690-4, 6 x 9, 288 pp., illus.   **$14.95**